ARZIVAL

A Forerunner of the Modern Human Being

Sonia A.L. Setzer

*Published with the support of the
Waldorf Educational Foundation*

Waldorf Publications at the
Research Institute of Waldorf Education
351 Fairview Avenue Unit 625
Hudson, NY 12534

Title: *Parzival: A Forerunner of the Modern Human Being*
Author: Sonia A.L. Setzer
Translator: Christina Thornton
Copy editor: Melissa Merkling
American researcher: Eric G. Müller
Proofreader: Ruth Riegel
Layout: Ann Erwin
Cover design: Roberto Strauss 1st edition, 2008; with permission
Cover illustration: Luzius Zaeslin; with permission *(in memoriam)*
© 2024 Waldorf Publications
ISBN: 978-1-943582-29-7

Brazilian edition:
Title: *Parsifal: Um precursor do ser humano moderno*
Author: Sonia Setzer
2nd revised and expanded edition. São Paulo: Antroposófica, 2012
Copyright © 2008 by Sonia A. Lanz Setzer
Rights reserved to this issuer.
Anthroposophical Publisher Ltd.–R. da Fraternidade
180 04738-020 São Paulo–SP–Tel / Fax (11) 5687-9714
www.antroposofica.com.br–editora@antroposofica.com.br

Contents

Introduction	7
Prologue	12
CHAPTER 1: The Middle Ages	14
CHAPTER 2: Works Relating to the Grail	28
CHAPTER 3: Wolfram von Eschenbach's *Parzival*	40
About the Author	40
Summary of the Work	42
CHAPTER 4: The Structure of *Parzival*	97
CHAPTER 5: Important Encounters and Events in the Life of Parzival	103
Summary of the Encounters	103
Sigune	116
Cundrie	123
Trevrizent: The Meeting on Good Friday	128
CHAPTER 6: General Considerations about *Parzival*	134
CHAPTER 7: The Symbol of the Sword	148
CHAPTER 8: Differences in the Communities of Arthur and the Grail	157
CHAPTER 9: Differences between Gawain and Parzival	165
CHAPTER 10: The Journey of Gawain	176
CHAPTER 11: The Symbol of the Lance	187
CHAPTER 12: The Symbol of the Grail	194

CHAPTER 13: Historical Currents Related to the Grail 223
    The Essenes. 224
    The Manichaeans. 227
    The Catholic Church. 232
    The Bogomils 238
    The Cathars 239
    The Order of the Knights Templar and
        the Order of Christ 245
    Freemasonry. 254
    The Grail Temple 262
    Esoteric Christianity after the 13th Century 266

CHAPTER 14: The Trajectory of *Parzival*. 271

Appendices
    The Meanings of Some of the Names 322
    The Crown of Lucifer 328
        The Dispute of the Troubadours in Wartburg
    General Bibliography. 330
    Works by Rudolf Steiner 334
    Bibliography for Selected Topics. 336

Index of Key Words. 338

Introduction

udolf Steiner (1861–1925) was an important Austrian thinker who was active in Europe, mainly in Germany and Switzerland. Besides teaching courses and giving lectures (all of them published) in many European countries, he also wrote about thirty books on various subjects. At the beginning of the 20th century, after serving for some years as Secretary General of the German section of the Theosophical Society, he gave up his position and founded the Anthroposophical Society. Based on objective research conducted in the spiritual world, he formulated the initial concepts of what he called "anthroposophical spiritual science." Later he introduced several innovations in the arts (painting, sculpture, architecture) and created Eurythmy and the Art of Speech, both new artistic expressions in movement and recitation drama, respectively. In his later years and upon request from members of these professions, he revitalized the areas of pedagogy, medicine, pharmacology, therapeutic education, and agriculture, among others.

In 1919 the first Waldorf School was founded in Stuttgart in response to a request by the workers of the Waldorf-Astoria cigarette factory, who desired for their children a broader and more humane education. The curriculum and structure of the Waldorf pedagogy developed by Steiner represented (and still represents) a revolution in the educational system. As Steiner described it, the foundation of Waldorf education is the development of children and adolescents based on spiritual research. For 11th grade students, around the age of seventeen, he introduced the study of *Parzival* by Wolfram von Eschenbach, in the context of Medieval German literature.

Today there are schools all over the world that implement the Waldorf educational system. In Brazil, the first Waldorf school, the present Rudolf Steiner Waldorf School of São Paulo, was founded in 1956. When a high school was added, my father, Rudolf Lanz (1915–1998), one of its founders who was responsible for parts of the curriculum, suggested that the Parzival theme be taken up as a one-week class outing. It would include lectures complemented by painting classes. His suggestion was accepted, and since 1974 this course has been offered at this school and some other Brazilian Waldorf schools. Lanz taught the course himself in an entirely new way, compared with the way it had been taught in Europe until then.

In several lectures Rudolf Steiner revealed the importance of Wolfram's *Parzival*, not only as literature of the age of chivalry, but as the bearer of a profound esoteric message beneath all the adventures. He even stated that Wolfram was an initiate, able to impart important spiritual truths in the language of a minstrel. Thus any of his listeners familiar with spiritual contexts would know what he meant; those who did not possess this esoteric knowledge could nevertheless enjoy the adventures as they subconsciously absorbed the profound hidden messages, as can also happen with the fairy tales of the Brothers Grimm.

In 1990, Lanz fell ill and could not teach the course as expected. I worked as school doctor at the same institution, and one day a group of teachers asked me if I would be willing to teach the course in his place. Like Gawain (whom we will meet in this book), I accepted the challenge. I prepared myself with the help of my father, who instructed me on the course structure and bibliography. At the time, I had the opportunity to talk to some foreign Waldorf teachers who were in Brazil and also to several friends, so I received a lot of help. The first course was more or less a copy of my father's approach, though I introduced some minor changes. The following year, although fully recovered, my father decided not to resume teaching the course. Since then, therefore, for many years I dedicated myself to this task, but with a more devoted attitude toward *Parzival*, meaning that I delved deeper into the subject, studying and reading everything I could get my hands on in various languages. Little by little I added new aspects, modifying the "inherited" material.

There came a time when, for personal reasons, I could not teach the course, but there was no one to replace me; so I ended up teaching most of the classes anyway, at great personal cost. I knew then that I needed to prepare somebody else to share this task with me. There was almost no literature on the subject available in Portuguese; besides, to teach this course with the right inner attitude, the teacher would need to have some familiarity with anthroposophy. I found a wonderful partner in the teacher Ilka Roth, and for several years we shared this task. However, I felt the need to make available to other teachers the materials I had studied, the new ideas I had developed, and our cumulative experiences. Maybe someone would wish to teach this course but would not have easy access to the rich existing literature in other languages.

Thus, the idea of writing this book was born. Initially it was in the embryonic state, as there was still much reading material to cover, mainly regarding the hidden esoteric aspects behind the obvious content, which one would not pass on to students. In the beginning I wrote down only the material to be shared with students, allowing myself more time to develop the deeper aspects, despite considerable pressure (albeit very positive) from my husband, Valdemar Setzer, to finish this book as fast as possible. I also started teaching courses for adults on *Parzival*, increasingly exposing its more spiritual content.

Meanwhile, the embryo developed into the fetal stage, grew, gained weight, and was about to be born. In fact, from my early research to the moment of "birth," the moon would have completed approximately one cycle around the zodiac: The so-called lunar node occurs every 18 years and 7 months.

As with all my courses, I begin this book with a brief description of the Middle Ages, so as to evoke the mood of the times and provide important background information for what is covered later. An overview of several works on the theme of the Grail, Parzival, and other related subjects follows. Then comes a summary of Wolfram's *Parzival*, with the description of the characters and scenes. My analysis of *Parzival* begins with its (absolutely amazing) structure; how happy I was to find the solutions to this puzzle! Next, I approach the important events in the life of the hero. It is fascinating that after so many years and dozens of courses, I am still having new insights about several of the meanings.

I then identify the three cultural streams represented in *Parzival*: the Celtic culture, Christianity and Arabism, followed by the three symbols of the Grail: the sword, the spear, and the Grail itself. In order to compare King Arthur's court with the Grail Community, the mystery surrounding the Grail sword must be addressed first.

After examining the situations and attitudes that distinguish the figures of Parzival and Gawain, I introduce a chapter addressing Gawain's spiritual development (which is not part of the course for students). Next, I analyze the meaning of the Grail and the spear. This part is not presented to students in such depth; when teaching them I omit much of its esoteric character and prefer to let the images speak for themselves. The following chapter deals with various historical currents. It begins with a description of the pre-Christian Jewish sect of the Essenes, whose members prepared themselves intensely, and in a very peculiar manner, for the coming of the Messiah. Next, heretical and mystical streams of esoteric Christianity are discussed. There is also mention of the Catholic Church, highlighting its mission and examining what differentiates it from the other streams.

In the final chapter, I attempt to show the process of Parzival's initiation; here, too, I omit many aspects in the course for students. For their particular age group, it is more important to impart strong images that impress them. Once they become adults and wish to acquire deeper knowledge, they may do their own research. Perhaps this book will also help them in that regard.

There are numerous quotations from Wolfram's *Parzival*. They are marked as follows: B stands for "book"; the book's number follows in Roman numerals, followed by a comma and the stanza number in Arabic numerals. A stanza always consists of thirty verses. Thus, "B. V, 231" means Book V, stanza 231, as found in the margin. The footnotes refer to the works mentioned in each chapter. At the end of this book is a bibliography with all the researched and referenced works.

For all these years I have received help from many people, and it would be impossible to name them all. However, I must express my immense gratitude to my closest collaborators: Ilka Roth (deceased) and painting teachers Luzius Zaeslin (deceased) and Eleonora Oiticica Canaes. I would like to point out that Luzius Zaeslin donated the paintings that illustrate this book [the original Portuguese edition and the cover for this English translation], which were inspired by our joint work on *Parsival*. Many years of dedication, combined with great sensitivity and depth, have resulted in the creation of paintings whose colors and content reveal so well the enigmatic, profound, and ever-so-colorful character of this narrative.

I also wish to thank the teachers responsible for the classes I had the privilege to work with at the Waldorf Rudolf Steiner School of São Paulo, the Colégio Waldorf Micael de São Paulo, and the Free School of Porto Cuiabá, Mato Grosso; and the hundreds of students in my courses—young people and adults, from Waldorf schools and Waldorf teacher training courses, as well as Waldorf teachers, people from other professions and the general public, who inspired me with countless new ideas that emerged during the classes, and who made many direct contributions. Without all these people it would not have been possible to mature this theme and develop this wonderful path in my life.

– Sonia Annette Lanz Setzer
2nd edition, March 2012

Prologue

MEDIEVAL GERMAN

Ist zwîfel herzen nâchgebûr,
daz muoz der sêle werden sûr.
Gesmaehet unde gezieret ist,
swâ sich parrieret unverzaget mannes muot,
als agelstern varwe tuot.
Der mac dennoch wesen geil:
wande an im sint beidiu teil, des himels und der helle.
Der unstaete Geselle hât die swarzen varwe gar,
und wirt ouch nâch der vinster var:
sô habet sich an die blanken der mi staeten gedanken.

MODERN GERMAN

Ist Unentschiedenheit dem Herzen nah,
so muss der Seele daraus Bitternis erwachsen.
Verbindet sich—wie in den zwei Farben der Elster—
unverzagter Mannesmut mit seinem Gegenteil,
so ist alles und rühmlich und schmachvoll zugleich.
Wer schwankt, kann immer noch froh sein;
denn Himmel und Hölle haben an ihm Anteil.
Wer allerdings den inneren Halt völlig verliert,
der ist ganz schwarzfarben und endet
schliesslich in der Finsternis der Hölle.
Wer dagegen innere Festigkeit bewahrt,
der hält sich an die lichte Farbe des Himmels.
– Translation by Wolfgang Spiewok

ENGLISH
If vacillation dwell with the heart
The soul will rue it.
Shame and honour clash where the
Courage of a steadfast man
Is motley like the magpie.
But such a man may yet make merry,
For Heaven and Hell
Have equal part in him.
Infidelity's friend is black all over
And takes on a murkey hue,
While the man of loyal temper
Holds on to the white.
– Wolfram von Eschenbach, *Parzival* (B. I, 15)

CHAPTER 1
The Middle Ages

"If knightly deeds with shield and lance
Can win fame for one's earthly self,
Yet also Paradise for one's soul,
Then the chivalric life has been my one desire. [...]
I fought wherever fighting was to be had,
So that my warlike hand has glory within its grasp."
– Wolfram von Eschenbach, *Parzival* (B. IX, 240–241)

efore addressing the subject of *Parzival*, let us contextualize it in space and time. Historians usually divide the Middle Ages, during which chivalry played such an important role both in Europe and the East, into two major periods: the Early Middle Ages, from the 5th century with the fall of the Roman Empire, to the 10th century; and the Late Middle Ages, between the 11th and 15th century, 1453 to be exact, when Constantinople was conquered by the Turks. As will be seen later, the story of the knight Parzival takes place in the 11th century, therefore in the Early Middle Ages, although several authors place the story between the end of the 12th and the beginning of the 13th century, the second half of the Middle Ages. However, the work describes situations from the first period; therefore, I will consider this period in greater detail.

During the expansion of the Roman Empire important cities sprang up in the conquered regions, but with the invasions of Germanic tribes from the north of Europe the empire began to crumble, the population migrated to the countryside, and imposing cities were reduced to a few thousand inhabitants. For example, experts estimate that in the 4th century, Rome, the center of the empire, had around three hundred thousand inhabitants, which were reduced to twenty thousand in the 6th century.[1]

During medieval times, Europe was covered by dense forests; communication between cities was quite difficult and complicated, and most people lived in small fortified villages or fortresses, built strategically on the tops of mountains, along canyons, or along important rivers. The biggest problems were war and hunger, for life in the country depended on agriculture and livestock, and often crops were poor.

Medieval society consisted of three main groups: the clergy, holders of knowledge and providers of spiritual and cultural orientation; the knights or warriors, who defended society and took care of justice; and the peasants, responsible for society's upkeep. In other words, one can say that the Church, representative of divine power, held the big picture; the king or emperor, representative of temporal power, and the feudal masters, ruled over legal and military matters; and the common people served both. To administer these vast and often impenetrable lands, the so-called feudal system was created and worked as follows. The sovereign divided the land between the Church and the feudal lords who were subservient to the sovereign; these, in turn, subdivided their properties among other nobles of lower rank, who became subservient to the feudal lords. Each of these lords had at their service peasants, serfs, and artisans. This subdivision would repeat itself several times, thus constituting the "feudal pyramid" in which each vassal owed obedience and loyalty to his superior, from whom he received protection. It was an honor to serve an important lord. Among the noblemen there were the knights and the administrators. The latter tended to be managers; they were not knights and never got involved in disputes or wars. Knights thought themselves superior and looked down on those who were not on horseback.

---

1 J.R. Macedo, *Viver nas cidades medievais*.

As in the late Middle Ages, only the clergy could read and write; arrangements and contracts between the feudal lords were sealed with a handshake, which was considered a commitment. It was part of the knight's code of honor to commit himself to a given word. At that time, a knight was considered a distinguished warrior, a "superior man," noble, dignified, and disciplined, keen on adventure, and expected to display virtues such as optimism, courage, boldness, and a fighting spirit. A knight also had to be skilled in handling weapons and, most of all, had to show loyalty to friends and vassals, and enemies. Furthermore, knights had to fight and be adventurous in search of fame and praise; they had to maintain law and order in the country, deter violence and injustice, support women and maidens in difficulty, be generous, protect the weak and needy, and obey the church.

Medieval fortresses were built in strategic locations that were easy to defend from enemy attack. Some were situated on mountains, surrounded by steep cliffs; some were along river canyons that separated them from the surrounding land; or deep moats were dug to isolate them even more. In the latter two cases, access was by means of a drawbridge leading to a single castle gate. In the former situation, there was always a road that led to this gate. The fortified cities were completely surrounded by ramparts with surveillance towers. There were several doors in the surrounding walls that were always watched and closed at night and, in wartime, also during the day.

Often, besides this outer wall, there were also one or more internal walls. Each wall enclosed a patio and other areas. For example, the shacks of peasants and artisans, workshops, barns, stables, the mill, the well, and the washing facilities would be in the lower courtyard, located between the first (external) wall and the second. In times of peace, the peasants and artisans lived in shacks outside the castle walls, but in times of war all were housed and protected within the walls. Between the second and third walls was the upper patio with the barracks, chapel, kennels, dovecotes, falconry, warehouses, deposits, and kitchens.

Though not always located at the geographic center, the center of the castle was the turret. It had several floors and, besides being the abode of the feudal lord, was also the legal and military headquarters. It housed a great room that was the communal center, serving as dining room, living room, courtroom for prosecutions and trials, space for receptions and festivities, and so on. There were many bedrooms, too, since more often than not there were visitors. Castles were usually built of heavy stones, unlike the houses of the common people, which were made of wood and could burn to the ground with terrifying speed.

As glass was very expensive, the windows were high and narrow, closed by wooden shutters and trusses. There was little decoration; ornaments were displayed only when visitors arrived, and consisted of tapestries with hunting scenes, shields, spears, and hunting trophies. The furniture was simple and rustic, made of wood and serving multiple purposes. Long, narrow chests stored crockery, silverware, and documents, and when equipped with arms and backrests, also served as benches. Banquet tables were boards on wooden trestles. One can imagine the darkness in these rooms with their thick, gray stone walls and small windows.

Daylight hardly entered such premises, and artificial light was meager: torches, lamps, and tallow candles. Candles were very expensive and therefore denoted luxury and the wealth of the feudal lord. Fireplaces provided heat, meaning that during the long harsh winter months there was little light and much smoke inside the castle. Over the centuries, with the increase in power and wealth of the sovereigns, the castles became more comfortable and luxurious; however, the castles featured in fairy tales—full of light, mirrors, polished floorboards, and expensive ornaments—are of a much later time. Most garments were rough and coarse, made of wool, flax, and hemp that was spun, woven, and sewn mostly in the castle itself. Everyone wore wool socks or breeches and long linen shirts.

The male costume consisted of breeches, tunic, hood, and cloak; women wore blouses, long skirts, aprons, head scarves, and robes.

Gradually fashion started to differentiate the richer people from the poorer. Only wealthy noblemen could afford to buy colorful clothes of silk and velvet from merchants who came from the East.

There was a great difference between the foods eaten by the nobles and the common people. The latter ate grains, mainly in the form of bread and porridge, and fruit and vegetables, often cooked into a thick soup; meat, eggs, and cheese were consumed only on special occasions. The nobleman's diet, although apparently richer, was less healthy, as it consisted mainly of game, spicy fish sauce, and fruit, but little grain, bread, or vegetables. During banquets offered in the castle, guests sat at one side of the table and were served by meat carvers and servants who stood ready on the opposite side. In the early Middle Ages there were still no forks; meat chunks served by carvers were held in the hand and dipped in sauce before being eaten. Sometimes two or more people shared a knife, wine glass, or soup bowl. Many paintings from the period illustrate this way of eating, and also show dogs under the table: It is said that they were there so guests could clean their greasy hands on their fur.

During the winters, life at court was rather monotonous, because, in addition to short days and long nights, the cold was intense. Women performed domestic chores in the castle, supervised the many tasks of their numerous servants, knitted, did embroidery, or sewed. Men cleaned and repaired their weapons. Chess and some dice games were already known and helped to fill the days. In fact, chess was the only intellectual occupation exercised in the castle, for thinking was not an essential activity for knights; the clergy did the thinking. The occasional arrival of minstrels and pilgrims broke up the monotony; they animated the long nights with their stories and reports of foreign lands.

In spring and summer the castles were livelier places. The inhabitants went hunting, went to war, or held tournaments. These usually lasted three days and featured jousting between two knights or groups of knights on horseback, armed with lances. The winners received an award announced in advance. At night the wounded were cared for, while the others amused themselves banqueting and dancing. There were other festivities with musicians, actors, and jugglers, promoted by the nobles or the Church.

Nativity and Easter plays and others were performed in front of churches during Christian festivals.

Until the age of seven, children of both sexes were educated by their mothers, acquiring the basic rules of social conduct. After age seven, the girls continued with their mothers and learned all that was necessary to run a home: good manners, singing, dancing, entertaining guests, sewing, and managing servants, including checking their work to make sure it was done satisfactorily. In some cases, girls were sent to the house of a noble friend to learn these skills from the lady of the manor. The daughters of peasants and artisans not only learned housework from their mothers, but also accompanied them during work in the fields. Boys from poor families helped their parents in their duties as peasants or craftsmen from a very early age, acquiring skills and continuing the work of their parents. Boys from noble families were sent at the age of seven to the house of another nobleman, where they eventually became young esquires. They learned good manners, horsemanship, the use and handling of weapons, hunting, falconry, and more. Alternatively, they were sent to a monastery and educated into a religious life. Childhood ended at the age of fourteen. Many were already married at that age, therefore effectively adults, yet many boys still remained in the service of the liege lord as squires. They learned how to fight and took part in tournaments, and when their lord considered them sufficiently well prepared, they became knights.

Initially, any youth could become a knight, but later on only noblemen were allowed to do so. The knights were socially aware: They followed a code of honor and practiced good manners. The French knights were considered the most refined, and to speak French was a sign of good upbringing, elegance, and precision. Even today we consider French words to be a sign of refinement: After all, it is more elegant to eat dainty morsels of bread with *pâté* instead of meat spread or *consommé* instead of soup, and beef (*boeuf*) instead of cow. We also find French words for clothing, like *berets*, *cravats*, and *culottes*, to be chic, just as the knights and their ladies did.

Knighthood was a ritual in its own right, preceded by a vigil. The youth knelt before the king or feudal lord and swore an oath of obedience and allegiance. Then the king or lord touched his shoulders with the sword and invited him to rise, pronouncing him a knight. Only then did he receive a sword and spurs. Under exceptional circumstances, a young squire could be knighted on the battlefield in recognition of his courage and nobility, and as a sign of being considered trustworthy. The equipment of a knight was elaborate and quite expensive, which is why in later times only wealthy noblemen could afford it for their offspring.

The following description of a knight's basic equipment is taken from a book by Michel Pastoureau.[2] Over a robe made of coarse material, the knight wore a coat of mail made of small intertwined metal rings to protect especially the parts not covered by armor, such as the neck, armpits, elbows and groin. About 30,000 rings made up a good coat of mail, which could weigh twenty to twenty-six pounds. The armor was worn over it. Initially armor was made of leather, but soon it became metallic. Sometimes it was richly crafted. There were light, heavier and very heavy armors, their weight averaging between thirteen and forty-four pounds. The helmet covered the head and had a pivoting visor, with one opening to enable vision during a fight, and another for ventilation. When he was not fighting, the knight raised the visor of his helmet. The shield was made of thick wood or metal, often with some ornamentation. The average shield was five feet high by fifty to seventy inches wide, and almond-shaped. It totally covered the warrior. The spear was a two- to three-yard-long shaft, made of solid wood and ending in a metal tip. It weighed four to eleven pounds and was used in combat mainly to overthrow the opponent, pierce his shield, and try

---

[2] M. Pastoureau, *No tempo dos cavaleiros da Távola Redonda*.

to tear his mail. The sword was made entirely of metal, and the handle, blade and sheath were often highly ornate. The sword's shape varied according to the season and also the region. The most common swords were about a yard long with a seven- to nine-inch-wide blade, and were forged of steel.

The sword weighed approximately four pounds. It was used as a cutting weapon, in addition to piercing shields and tearing mail, and was considered the noblest of weapons. One can imagine what it meant to carry between thirty-three and sixty-six pounds of equipment, besides the weight of the attack and defense weapons; and the poor horse also often wore chain mail and armor and had to bear the knight's weight as well.

Coats of arms were developed to identify certain individuals, families, or communities. Although at first they were used mainly by the head warriors, their use was not limited to the nobility; later they were used by all nobility as well as the up-and-coming classes and peasants. The coats of arms became necessary as it was impossible to recognize combatants under their armor. Initially, shields were decorated with colors and perhaps figurative elements; the repetition of the same pattern became the identity of the knight. Later on the pattern would identify not only a single knight, but his family or community. The pattern of colors and shapes remained the same but became part of a representative figure on the shield. Sometimes sons took on the crest of their fathers; sometimes they chose a new and exclusive one.

As mentioned above, during the Middle Ages culture was basically in the hands of the clergy. The priests could read and write, and most available texts were religious in character, written in Latin, the language of the Church. The first libraries were in the monasteries. The famous Frankish king, Charlemagne (747–814), who ruled at the beginning of the 9th century, was illiterate; he tried to learn to read and write but had great difficulty. Nevertheless he determined that, in addition to works of a religious nature, some secular literature should also be made available, written in the language of the common people so that everyone could understand it. The first schools emerged in the 12th century, and the teaching was done by the clergy; the first universities also date back to that time. More and more the sons and daughters of nobles who valued education were sent to these schools. As a consequence, many noblewomen knew how to read, unlike the knights, who were only prepared for war.

Particularly significant in the culture of the knights were the minstrels, who performed poetry and music, especially in praise of chivalrous love. These troubadours may or may not have been knights, but they definitely did not belong to the clergy. W.F. Veltman points out that the minstrels' importance derives from the fact that their music helped inspire people to master the soul's instinctive impulses.[3] Therefore, the troubadour addressed a person's "true human aspect" and dignified human beings by extolling the overcoming of the more instinctive part of their nature.

These traits of the troubadour were also typical of the Arthurian knights, since they also sought to dominate their basic instincts. Meanwhile, the clergy took care of legal matters and also sought power, a key attribute of life in Rome, where bureaucratization and public service originated. By the time of Charlemagne the decay of chivalry can already be observed; the chivalrous spirit began to be replaced by bureaucracy. The bureaucrat is the counter-image of the true knight.

The monks and priests adorned their carefully transcribed texts with illuminations—illustrations and ornaments in vivid colors, interspersed with gold and silver, which decorated the initial letters and borders of the parchment pages. The priests of Reichenau[4] in Germany were among the most renowned artists.

---

3 W.F. Veltman, *Tempel und Gral*.
4 Island located on Lake Constance, near the town of the same name. Three countries border this large lake crossed by the River Rhine: Germany, Switzerland, and Austria.

As the faithful were mostly illiterate, internal church walls were covered with biblical scenes. The early ones were painted by clerics such as Fra Angelico (1395–1455) and Fra Filippo Lippi (c. 1406–1469). But not only painting and calligraphy were solely in the monks' hands: Monks were also musicians, and we can still listen today to Gregorian Chant, Latin texts sung in a single melodic line, performed by Benedictine monks. Only much later, especially during the Renaissance, were polyphony and secular (or profane) music introduced, accepted, and performed by people not belonging to the clergy. The Church was also dominant in the realm of architecture, in the building of churches and monasteries, especially the development of the Romanesque (1000–1100) and Gothic (c. 1100–1500) styles.

The clergy established the date and time, although an exact date, for example July 28, 849, would be of interest only to scholars. The common people measured time in a different way. Years were measured according to the sovereign on the throne: For example, it was said that a particular event had occurred in the third year of the reign of a certain king.

The months were linked to the farming calendar. In January, due to the cold, the livestock was kept in the stables; January was also the month of food and feasting. February was cold and rainy, and people would turn in and rest by the fireplace. In March, fieldwork began again, with the pruning of the vines. In April, in full spring, flowers and medicinal herbs were picked. In May, weeds had to be cleared from the beds, and it was also time for hunting and jousting. June was the month of haying and preparing the hay for winter. In July wheat was harvested, then threshed in August. September was the month of harvesting and pressing grapes to make wine, which extended until October, when the earth was prepared for sowing. November was the month to gather wood for the winter and acorns to fatten the pigs to be slaughtered in December. The meat was made into sausages to be enjoyed during the January holidays. On sunny days, the hour could be read on the sundial, while on cloudy days and at night hourglasses were consulted, mostly by the clergy. A priest rang the church bell to announce the hour to the population, always in relation to the religious services performed at three-hour intervals.

To tell time at night, in addition to the hourglass, the priests lit candles that would take three hours to burn down. Thus the priest knew how many pages he had read in his breviary in three hours. If he fell asleep and lost count, he would resume when he woke up and catch up over the course of the next day. Church services were well distributed during the twenty-four hour day:

HOUR	SERVICE
0:00	*Matins*
3:00	*Lauds* or Dawn Prayer
6:00	*Prime* or Early Morning Prayer
9:00	*Terce* or Midmorning Prayer
12:00	*Sext* or Midday Prayer
15:00	*Nones* or Midafternoon Prayer
18:00	*Vespers* or Evening Prayer
21:00	*Compline* or Night Prayer

It should be noted that several of these designations appear in the New Testament.

It is important to mention the role women played in this period. The lady occupied a very particular position, as she was the one who inspired the knights. So-called courtly or romantic love, directed toward an idealized, delicate woman who was admired and revered by the knight, had nothing sensual or carnal about it. According to Pastoureau, courtly love seems to have originated as a reaction against religious morality, since the Church frowned on carnal love: It led to adultery and threatened marriage stability. However, for the minstrels of the 12th century love was not madness, but wisdom. Instead of degrading the lover, love strengthened his moral and spiritual capacities.

It animated the knight and made him gentle, generous, humble, sincere, cheerful, and a conqueror.

This kind of love required a perfect understanding of desire and was therefore of an exalted nature. The knight was submissive to his lady without expecting any reward. On the other hand, when the woman discovered the power she exerted over the man, she used this power to ennoble him. It is a fact that many knights found in courtly love a kind of religious contemplation.

Thus, according to Rudolf Meyer, "true courtly love is a mystical fact" because it allows the soul to be permeated "by the primeval image of another (soul)."[5] In a situation of conflict or struggle, one appeals to the spiritual forces of another soul. Many beautiful songs and poems have been dedicated to the ideal and sublime woman. One can also calculate the importance given to the ideal woman in the second half of the Middle Ages by the sheer number of churches dedicated to the Virgin Mary.

An important feature of this time was the nature of human encounters. The degree of conscious awareness usually found in people of the Middle Ages differed from humanity's state of consciousness today. In a lecture on February 26, 1922,[6] Rudolf Steiner mentioned that before the 15th century, human souls still had much more of a direct reciprocal awareness, meaning that people knew what others were experiencing and thought.

With the advent of modern intellectualism, a greater separation between people has manifested. Nowadays it is evident that everybody wishes to show him/herself to others in the best way possible. This means that we all wear a mask, from approximately the age of three. Only a child before that age, or people with developmental disorders, show themselves as they really are. This is perceived by others as pure innocence or naïveté: Nothing is hidden, and such people open their

---

5 R. Meyer, *Der Gral und seine Hüter.*
6 Rudolf Steiner, *Old and New Methods of Initiation*, GA 210.

souls to one another. Something similar was the case, in general, with people in the Middle Ages.

From the middle of the 12th century onward, cities recovered their importance. Many people from the countryside became urbanites and there were major changes in society. Rural servants became craftsmen in the cities, where life was easier in some ways than in the country. Trade increased, more money circulated, customs offices were created, taxes and fees proliferated. To manage defense and wars, noblemen began hiring soldiers for pay, thus eliminating the ancient bond of fidelity and loyalty to the nobleman they served: They were now loyal only to their new contractor. Chivalry fell into a state of decadence as the code of honor no longer made sense. Finding themselves in a precarious situation, many older knights, mainly merchants, lost their dignity and began attacking and looting. Sometime later, chivalry disappeared altogether, and its decline inspired Miguel de Cervantes (1547–1616) to write his *Don Quixote*, the "Knight of the Woeful Countenance."

Three issues of general interest resounded throughout medieval Europe, brought and disseminated mainly by the troubadours: chivalric novels or romances; tales of King Arthur's court; and the quest for the Holy Grail. Many of these texts were written down, and some manuscripts can still be found in libraries. Literature about the Grail was so popular that *Parzival* and *Titurel* were among the first works printed after the introduction of the printing press by Johann Gutenberg (c. 1390–1468) in the mid-15th century. They were written mostly in medieval French and German, and were subsequently translated into modern languages. Some of these translations maintained their poetic form; others were transcribed into prose. Because they were translated by different people, there are naturally some differing interpretations; not all the translations are exactly alike.

In medieval times people did not have surnames, and we know many personalities by their Christian names followed by the name of their city of origin. Thus, for example, the writer Chrétien de Troyes was a native of the city of Troyes; Wolfram von Eschenbach came from the city of Eschenbach; Philip of Flanders was the feudal lord of that region. When no potential for confusion exists, it is customary to use only an author's first name, as in the phrase "Wolfram's work."

CHAPTER 2

Works Relating to the Grail

> If master Chrestien of Troyes has done wrong
> By this story, Kyot, who sent us the authentic tale,
> Has good cause to be angry.
> – Wolfram von Eschenbach, *Parzival* (B. XVI, 827)

he first known writings of the troubadours date back to the late 12th century. Before that, the stories were passed on orally by the minstrels, who sang and told them during long winter nights on their court visits. Previously transcribed writings may have existed, but we are not aware of any; they have disappeared or been lost or destroyed, intentionally or not. Actually, most known medieval texts were written over a short period of time (about fifty years). This period coincides with the violent persecution of some faith streams considered heretical by the Church of Rome. Although the quest for the Grail is profoundly Christian, it clearly has little to do with the Church itself. The Church either ignored the quest or did not want to know about it; ecclesiastical literature does not mention the Grail.

Several texts that mention the Grail have an enigmatic character, implying secret knowledge and initiation. Later works, written from the 14th century onward, sometimes do and sometimes do not reveal traces of secret doctrines.

There are several ways to order these writings; one way is according to the relative importance given to the Grail. In one group of texts, the focus is on King Arthur's Round Table. The search for the Grail is part of the content, but the text mainly recounts chivalrous adventures and feasting in Arthur's court. It is important to distinguish between Arthur's knights and the knights of the Grail, which will be done in a later chapter. In the texts about Arthur's community, the Grail is something distant, mystical, accessible only to those who have transcended the human condition. The imagery is vague, and one has the impression that the authors are not really aware of the true meaning of the Grail. In this sense, they bear some similarity to the romances of chivalry, the first known accounts describing heroes' acts of bravery and their achievements and accomplishments in the outer world, with no references to the Grail. These accounts hardly ever mention King Arthur and his court.

In a second group of texts, the Grail appears as central reference: The most important part of the story is the search for the Grail. The writings in this group are dense and profound, and contain highly symbolic features. One gets the impression that the authors wanted to transmit spiritual truths to posterity, in the form of stories and imaginations. These are more esoteric writings with a more intimate atmosphere, describing the personal development and growth of the characters involved.

A third group consists of texts dealing with some of the characters mentioned by Wolfram von Eschenbach in his *Parzival* (which belongs to the second group), such as *Lohengrin*, which describes the life of this hero, a son of Parzival who is called to serve the Grail as a knight and as such is sent to help Queen Elsa of Brabant. *Klingsor* (or *Clinschor*) describes a magician of that name who, through magic, poisoned the spear which caused the incurable wound in Anfortas, King of the Grail. These two writings are by anonymous German writers of the 13th century.

The principal Arthurian texts in which the Grail is given less importance and the adventures of Arthur's knights predominate include the following. *Merlin*, written in French by Robert de Boron in the late 12th century, is the story of the magician of the same name, from his fantastic conception and the gifts he obtained thereby, to his deeds, ending in the curious choice of Arthur as king of the Britons with Merlin acting as his advisor.

The Quest of the Holy Grail and *The Death of King Arthur*[7] were written by anonymous French authors of the 13th century. Their most important features are events at Arthur's court, the heroic achievements of knights, and, eventually, the quest for the Holy Grail.

In 1470 in England, Sir Thomas Malory wrote *The Death of Arthur*. The mention of death in its title, and also in the title of the abovementioned work by the anonymous 13th-century author, is related to the decline of chivalry. Walter Johannes Stein[8] cites studies by H. Oskar Sommer, who succeeded in tracking all sources used by Malory except for those in chapter 7, a chapter totally distinct in its character. Stein solves this puzzle by pointing to the alchemical nature of the chapter. He claims that Malory based it on the writings of Basilius Valentinus,[9] a most remarkable alchemist of the 15th century.

The facts, adventures, and even names in the writings mentioned above have nothing to do with those mentioned in those writings in which the Grail is the central focus. For example, in *The Quest of the Holy Grail* there is a knight who, toward the end, wins the Grail, becoming its king. His name is Galahad and he has two companions, one of whom is called Perceval. However, this work has nothing in common with the *Perceval* of Chrétien de Troyes or the *Parzival* of Wolfram von Eschenbach. In both the latter writings, Parzival is the hero who becomes King of the Grail after undergoing a long period of inner development. One should not, however, consider these differences extraordinary; we must try to understand each work according to what it reveals.

Several works in which the Grail is the focus have reached us since medieval times. One work that mentions the Grail, though it is not about

---

7 Anonymous, *The Quest of the Holy Grail*; Anonymous, *The Death of King Arthur – Romance of the Thirteenth Century*.
8 W.J. Stein, T*he Death of Merlin: Arthurian Myth and Alchemy*.
9 We do not know for sure the dates of his birth and death. As in one of his writings he mentions that antimony has other uses in addition to printing, we can be sure that he was alive after the introduction of printing by Gutenberg (about 1450).

the quest, is the introduction to the first prose novel written in French (c. 1230–1240): *Estoire del Saint Graal*, or *Le Livre Du Graal*, which some modern authors call *Le Grand Saint Grail* to differentiate it from the homonymous work by Robert de Boron (see below). Like the latter, the former also describes an esoteric Christian stream dating back to Joseph of Arimathea. The author is unknown, and the story takes place in the 8th century, the year 717 AD. It reports that a very devout hermit fell asleep during the Good Friday vigil and had a vision in which Christ appeared to him and revealed the mystery of the Trinity, giving him a palm-sized little book written by Him, which contained the story of the Grail. On Easter Sunday the booklet mysteriously disappeared and the hermit received instructions on how to find it again.

There follows a description of the painful and laborious path of initiation which the hermit had to undertake. Finally, he found the booklet on the altar of a chapel. Again Christ appeared to him and told him to copy the text of the book until Ascension Day, and that after His resurrection, He had written nothing else besides this one little book on the Grail. Julius Evola states that "opening the case that contains the Grail means to enter in direct contact with Christ."[10]

The best-known works focusing on the Grail are the following four, listed in chronological order. They were written over a period of about a hundred years. *Perceval or the Romance of the Grail* was written in French around 1180 by Chrétien de Troyes, at the request of Count Philip of Flanders.[11] Despite being the first such known text, it is a mature work. Surely its contents had already been transmitted orally for a long time, and Chrétien was the one who wrote it down. It consists mainly of a narrative about Perceval and the young knight's adventures and natural development. There are many references to the Church, church services, priests, and monasteries. One important feature is the book's

---

10 J. Evola, *The Mystery of the Grail*.
11 According to Konrad Sandkühler, who translated it from medieval French into German, Chrétien named his text *Perceval Le Conte du Graal*.

sudden and pointless ending. It is assumed that the author must have died while the work was in progress. His followers tried to finish writing it but were not very successful, introducing a large number of chivalrous adventures and consigning the Grail to secondary importance.

Around 1190 Robert de Boron, author of *Merlin*, wrote *The Story of the Holy Grail*, also known as *Joseph of Arimathea*.[12] This writer had intended to write a trilogy whose third volume would be called *Parzival*, but only fragments of it have been found (his third work was *Merlin*). In *The Story of the Holy Grail*, Robert de Boron described the trajectory of the Holy Chalice used by Christ at the Last Supper, until its arrival in Glastonbury.

The most complete work, *Parzival*, on which our current study is based, was written in medieval German between 1203 and 1217 by Wolfram von Eschenbach. It consists of more than 25,000 rhymed verses, 827 stanzas of 30 lines each. It shows a certain similarity to the *Perceval* of Chrétien de Troyes; moreover, Wolfram quotes this writer as one who inspired him. As in those days the same content was sung by many minstrels, the resemblance is not unexpected.

But, besides "master Chrétien de Troyes" (B. XV, 827), Wolfram quotes another writer who inspired him: Kyot from Provence, a quite enigmatic figure. According to Wolfram, Kyot found in Toledo, Spain, a pagan manuscript written by a certain Flegetanis, known for his wisdom. His knowledge of the movements of the stars was so great that in a celestial constellation he discovered an object whose name, the Grail, was written in the stars. Now these were the enlightened men of an era dating back to Babylonian, Chaldean and Egyptian cultures, who, it was said, knew how to read the stars; therefore it is possible that this book contained old esoteric knowledge—meaning that in the pre-Christian era there was already knowledge of the Grail. Kyot then

---

12 The original name in medieval French is *Li Romanz de l'Estoire dou Graal*, in the plural, which seems to indicate the intention to include other writings in the work.

deciphered the pagan text, and this, according to Wolfram, is the origin of his narrative. (B. IX, 453) Kyot inserted into his work something found in no other writing dealing with the same theme: aspects of Arab and Jewish tradition. That is why this work transcends the regional character of other writings and has a more cosmopolitan nature. At the end of the book it says:

> If master Chrestien of Troyes has done wrong by this story, Kyot, who sent us the authentic tale, has good cause to be angry. (B. XVI, 410)

Gerhard von dem Borne calls attention to the fact that both Chrétien de Troyes and Robert de Boron made reference to other inspiring books.[13] According to Chrétien, Count Philip of Flanders personally handed him the book he was to base his writings on. Robert de Boron claimed that he would not have dared to—nor could he have—written such things if he had not had the "great book" in which prominent scholars had written "great secrets, which are called Grail." Presumably these are special books passed from hand to hand in secret, possibly due to heretical content. Apparently the Manichaeans (a heretical group of the 3rd and 6th centuries) produced very valuable manuscripts, clearly written, artistically illustrated, and largely destroyed by the Church. However, more recently, in 1907, Manichaean manuscripts in Chinese were found in the Gobi Desert, and in 1930 some were found in southern Egypt, in Coptic writing.[14]

The fourth of the best-known works was written by Albrecht von Scharfenberg in German around 1270. The title is *Der jüngere Titurel* [The Later Titurel]; there are fragments written by Wolfram which were considered the "oldest *Titurel*." Albrecht describes the life of Titurel, a noble and very pure knight who was called to build the castle

---

13 G.v.d. Borne, *Der Gral in Europa*.
14 E. Hutchins, *Parzival, an Introduction*.

and temple of the Grail. Many of the characters from previous poets reappear in this work, with clearer and more realized destinies: This is true for the figure of Titurel, and particularly so in the case of Sigune and Schionatulander. In Wolfram's *Parzival*, Schionatulander appears only after his death, wherever Sigune is mentioned.

Rudolf Meyer states that until the 15th century, nothing that was written added any new material to the former texts and, by the end of that century, with the advent of the Reformation and Humanism, interest in this type of content began to decline;[15] it declined further in the centuries of the Enlightenment (17th and 18th). Only in the 19th century were the Grail and its secrets resurrected and the ancient images restored to their former glory. It was as if a layer of cold intellect had started to melt.

It was at this time German composer Richard Wagner (1813–1883) composed his opera *Parsifal*. He wrote both the lyrics and the music, keeping to the whole plot with only six main characters. The work is one of great depth and beauty. It is his last opera, completed in 1882, a year before his death. He conceived the main idea based on the tradition of Robert de Boron: The Grail was the cup used at the Last Supper.

As Wagner did not understand that Wolfram was describing Parzival's path of self-development, he declared that the medieval author had been superficial, simply describing one adventure after another. To be able to understand some of the differences between Wagner and the medieval writers, one must consider what Rudolf Steiner and other authors have revealed, in many books and lectures, about the development of humanity.[16]

---

15 R. Meyer, *Der Gral und seine Hüter*.
16 For more details see, among other works: Rudolf Steiner, *Theosophy* and *An Outline of Esoteric Science*; Rudolf Lanz, *Noções Básicas de Antroposofia* and *Passeio através da História na luz da Antroposofia*.

According to Steiner, the period following the catastrophe that resulted in the sinking of Atlantis, which he named the post-Atlantean age, is divided into seven cultural epochs. The first and most remote post-Atlantean cultural epoch was Ancient India. During this period, humanity still lived in spiritual spheres, considering the physical-sensory world an illusion, "Maya." In the following period, the evolution of humanity took place mainly in Ancient Persia. At this stage humanity was already relating to the physical-sensory world: It is the epoch when humans started to grow plants (grains and fruit trees) and domesticate animals. These first two epochs still lie in prehistoric times.

Then followed the Babylonian-Egyptian-Chaldean cultural epoch, in which the next evolutionary stage of humankind took place. During this time, human beings perceived the outside world through their senses, while at the same time feeling the inner self to be their true nature, thus differentiating between body and spirit. The fourth epoch is called the Greco-Roman period, when human beings gradually recognized themselves as autonomous individualities. Obviously there were also other important contemporary cultures in addition to those mentioned, but for our Western civilization these were the most important ones.

Currently, humanity has arrived at the fifth post-Atlantean epoch, or the present stage of civilization. During this period, our relative separation from the spiritual world has resulted in our denial of its existence, and the development of a science based solely on the sense-perceptible world. However, each separation carries within itself the desire for reunion; thus, one can already observe in many people a yearning that goes beyond the merely physical and tends toward the spiritual.

After the current fifth cultural epoch, two more will follow. In each of the epochs so far, humanity has developed, and will continue to develop, a new quality. In the third, fourth, and fifth epochs, humanity developed attributes of the soul, with features called by

Steiner respectively "sentient soul,"[17] "rational" or "intellectual soul,"[18] and "consciousness soul." Thus, from the Hellenistic period to the 15th century, humanity was developing soul qualities related to reason or the mind. One can observe during this period the birth of rational thought, philosophy, and the desire to better understand the phenomena of nature, among other characteristics nonexistent till then. From the early 15th century on, humanity reached a new evolutionary stage.

Our challenge is now to achieve self-awareness and freedom through conscious perception, using the thinking forces developed previously. Its corollary is always individual responsibility for what we do. The ultimate goal of this evolutionary stage is to achieve the ability to exercise true, selfless love. The medieval authors lived toward the end of the epoch of the rational soul, while Wagner was fully immersed in the period of the consciousness soul. In reality, Wolfram's hero, though he lived in the Middle Ages, achieved qualities more pertinent to the consciousness soul age, which is our current time.

In Wagner's *Parsifal*, Klingsor, the magician, has a significant role. He tries to involve Parzival in his magic circle by having a woman seduce him. Another feature of the opera is the presence of a single female character whom Wagner names Kundry. However, this is not Cundrie the Grail messenger, whom we meet in Wolfram's work. The former displays traits of several other women described by Wolfram. In the opera, when Parzival finally reaches the Grail, he arrives with Kundry, who has managed to overcome her lower, instinctive nature, unlike Wolfram's character. Wolfram also mentions the magician Klingsor

---

17 According to the Merriam-Webster online dictionary, *sentient* means "responsive to or conscious of sense impressions; aware; finely sensitive in perception or feeling."

18 The term *Gemüt* in the German original has no precise translation in English. It refers to a state of feelings, of warmth, a state of the soul. *Gemütseele* has therefore sometimes been translated as "natural soul" (in the sense of natural propensity), and sometimes also as "feeling soul." But do not mistake it for the soul of sensations or sentient soul, developed in the previous epoch.

only marginally, in episodes concerning Gawain. According to the explanation given by Franz E. Winkler,[19] Klingsor did not know how to handle the Grail lance, which represents divine wisdom, as he was not prepared to do so; therefore, when he stole the lance he transformed it into mere human knowledge, totally separate from its divine origin. Now this is the knowledge that has reigned within humanity since the 15th century, and which gave rise to materialism.

One can understand the difference between the older works and Wagner's opus: He lived completely in the materialistic wave of the mid-19th century, while the 13th-century writers, knowing nothing about this, could only glimpse its future outcome. That is why they mention Klingsor only indirectly as the representative of materialistic rationalism. One very important aspect presented by Wagner is Parsifal's recapture of the lance, which does not happen in the medieval texts. Moreover, both in Chrétien's and Wolfram's works, Klingsor (or rather, Clinschor) appears to have been the builder of Schastel Marveile, the enchanted castle featured in the story of Gawain, a knight in Arthur's court.

This castle was built by magical forces. In this sense Klingsor appears as an anti-Titurel, whom divine forces made responsible for the construction of the Grail Castle and Grail temple. Wagner's Parsifal follows a path on which profound feelings have a predominant role: He follows the path of mysticism, not the path of knowledge. At the end of the opera, he is the hero who "acquires knowledge through compassion."

It is also worth mentioning that, in an article, Richard Seddon ranks these works differently.[20] He bases his argument on Rudolf Steiner's lecture of February 6, 1913, in which Steiner relates these writings to the cultural epochs described above. The Arthurian legends relate to the mysteries of the sentient soul; the myths of the Grail correspond to the development of the rational soul; and the legends of

---

19 F.E. Winkler, *The Mythology in Richard Wagner's* Parsifal.
20 R. Seddon, "The Matter of Britain" in *The Mystery of Arthur at Tintagel*.

Parzival correspond to the development of the consciousness soul (the present time).

Seddon also states that the Roman Church had to get rid of all content deriving from the ancient mysteries, so that each human being could ultimately have the opportunity to approach the Mystery of Christ in complete freedom. Therefore, to obscure these esoteric legends, the Church began to spread fictitious tales. One example of Parzival's importance being diminished at the time was a Cistercian tale that recounts how Perceval failed to reach the Grail. This is achieved instead by Galahad, a faithful son of the Church, who dies without having brought any benefit to humankind.

Perhaps it is opportune to add a few more considerations about the differences between the writings of Chrétien de Troyes and Wolfram von Eschenbach, and the fact that the latter said he had based his work on that of Chrétien. The authors Emma Jung and Marie-Louise von Franz make reference to the fact that Wolfram "formulated the material consciously, according to an idea," while they had the impression that Chrétien was closer to the original, which is why they based their writing especially on Chrétien although they also referred to Wolfram.[21]

According to Walter Johannes Stein, the differences between *Perceval* and *Parzival* are based on the different points of view of their respective writers.[22] Chrétien de Troyes based his story on a book he had received from Count Philip of Flanders (1142–1191), son of Dietrich (c. 1099–1168) who had participated in the Second Crusade (1147–1149). His wife Sibyl (1112–1165) was the sister of Baldwin III (1130–1162), the king of Jerusalem who, in agreement with the Patriarch of Jerusalem, offered some of the blood of Christ collected by Joseph of Arimathea to Dietrich when he returned to Europe. This relic was taken to the city of Bruges in Belgium. Dietrich's successor, his son Philip, inherited the relic. He also owned the book mentioned by Chrétien. What inspires

---

21   E. Jung and M.-L. von Franz, *The Grail Legend*.
22   W.J. Stein, *The Ninth Century and the Holy Grail*.

Chrétien is the blood of Christ, which is something physical, material, corporeal. Therefore, it can be said that he described the microcosmic aspects related to wisdom in human beings. Rudolf Steiner says that nowhere else is the description of what happens in the soul when it experiences the human microcosm so wonderful as in the work of Chrétien, when he describes the arrival of Perceval at the Castle of the Grail, which corresponds to penetration into the secrets of the human body.

Wolfram, however, gives more importance to the book by Kyot, which contains the wisdom of the stars—that is, macrocosmic wisdom. Wolfram's claim that Kyot could not read was perhaps an indication that he did not want his work to be considered only a book. Rather, it was a revelation achieved by someone able to interpret the macrocosm.

CHAPTER 3
Wolfram von Eschenbach's Parzival

> I am Wolfram of Eschenbach and something of a minnesinger.
> – Wolfram von Eschenbach, *Parzival* (B. II, 68)

According to Eileen Hutchins, Dante's *Divine Comedy* and Wolfram von Eschenbach's *Parzival* are considered the major written works of the Middle Ages.[23] While the former presents portentous images of life after death, Wolfram emphasizes the human being's longing to bring spiritual values to life on earth. Hutchins says that Wolfram stands out as a poet because of his reverence for love in marriage and because he highlights the role of women, both in happiness and in sadness.

About the Author

Little is known about the life of Wolfram; most of what is known is deduced from the comments he inserts in his writings. Joachim Bumke states that the name Wolfram was quite common at that time, and that there were several regions called Eschenbach.[24] Researchers have concentrated mainly on two, both located in Bavaria. The one near Ansbach seems to correspond more to the town of origin of *Parzival*'s author, which is why since 1917 its official name has been "Wolframs-Eschenbach," or "the Eschenbach of Wolfram." What led scholars to give preference to this location are quotes from Wolfram, such as his claim of being Bavarian and his relationship with the Count of Wertheim, who owned land in that town. Other places mentioned by Wolfram are

---

23 E. Hutchins, *Parzival, an Introduction*.
24 J. Bumke, *Wolfram von Eschenbach*.

located in the vicinity of this Eschenbach. In addition to the Count of Wertheim, he also seems to have had contact with a gentleman of Durn, who owned the castle of Wildenberg. This castle, however, is located in the westernmost region of Germany near the Rhine Valley. There is a belief that Wolfram must have written part of *Parzival* there; however, while writing the work, he went into the service of the Landgrave, Hermann I of Thuringia, the most important supporter of German literature of his time. It was at his castle—Wartburg in Eisenach—that the famous minstrels' dispute, known as *Der Sängerkrieg auf der Wartburg* [The Dispute of the Troubadours at Wartburg—see pp. 328–329], took place in 1206–1207; Wolfram was a participant. During the time he served the landgrave, he wrote other parts of *Parzival*. In its pages he claims to be a knight, and seems to consider this more important than being a poet; there are doubts, however, as to whether he really wielded weapons. In *Parzival* he says,

> I haven't a letter to my name! No few poets make their start from them: But this story goes its way without the guidance of books. Rather than that it be taken for a book I should prefer to sit naked in my tub without a towel—provided I had my scrubber! (B. II, 69)

Many researchers interpret this passage as making fun of other more intellectual writers of the time, who considered him ignorant. On the other hand, some scholars claim that Wolfram had no knowledge of Latin, which would reveal the lack of an ecclesiastical education. Others disagree. At the beginning of the 13th century, it was virtually impossible to write in German using Latin letters (as opposed to the Gothic script) without prior knowledge of Latin, and the *Parzival* manuscripts are in Latin letters. It is almost certain that Wolfram could speak French, though he makes little reference to writings in that language compared to the large number of German writers he mentions (not always positively). All experts emphasize, however, that he was highly knowledgeable. Because his writings demonstrate comprehensive knowledge in so many areas (natural sciences, geography, medicine, and astronomy, in addition to his theological reflections), it is believed he was self-taught. His style involves the listener or reader directly; his personal comments, usually very humorous, as for example about his poverty or lack of a wife, establish an intimate relationship with his audience. Although written in the early 13th century (between 1203 and 1217), the story takes place in the 9th century, as will be seen.

Rudolf Meyer says Wolfram did not really intend to write a book on the inevitability of ever-increasing intellectualism.[25] He wanted to speak to people's hearts, because the path to the Grail is an initiatory path, as will be seen. This content can only be truly understood if it is renewed in the hearts of those who listen to (or read) it. We need to transcend, to go beyond the mere written words.

Summary of the Work

> I have yet to meet a man so wise that he would not gladly know what guidance this story requires, what edification it brings.
> – Wolfram von Eschenbach, *Parzival* (B. I, 15)

This summary concentrates mainly on the important passages for further analysis. Some passages will be cited verbatim, either because of their importance or to better illustrate certain points. Wolfram begins by writing about the two colors of the magpie, a white-and-black–feathered bird, and, relating these colors to heaven and hell, he writes:

> Infidelity's friend is black all over and takes on a murky hue, while the man of loyal temper holds on to the white. (B. I, 15)

This polarity can be found throughout the work.

---

25 R. Meyer, *Der Gral und seine Hüter*.

After the introduction, Wolfram tells of a noble knight, Gahmuret d'Anjou, who, being a second son, after the death of his father should have served his older brother, heir to the family property. Young Gahmuret, however, was eager to prove his courage and boldness, and with his brother's consent he left his paternal land in search of adventures. He came to Baghdad, where the caliph was being harassed by enemies. Gahmuret decided to fight alongside the caliph's men, and, with his help, the enemy was defeated. To demonstrate his gratitude for the services rendered by the young knight from the West, the caliph suggested he remain in Baghdad, but his eagerness for adventures was not satisfied and once again he went on his way.

When he reached the town of Patelamunt, in the country of the Moors called Zazamanc, he saw that it was besieged by two armies. Queen Belakane had refused to marry the Moorish prince Isenhart unless he showed his love for her in combat. As fate had it, he lost his life in a fight, and in revenge his subjects declared war on the queen. At the same time, a Christian army led by a Scottish vassal of Isenhart's joined the fight against the queen. Thus, facing eight of the town gates were the Moorish troops, and standing in front of another eight gates was the Christian army. Gahmuret decided to help Belakane, Queen of Zazamanc, who was black, as were her subjects. The noble knight defeated the enemies and eventually married the beautiful Queen Belakane. As a reward for his deeds he was promised a tent, armor, a sword, and Isenhart's diamond helmet, "of hard, thick adamant." (B. I, 38)

After some time, Gahmuret once again felt like going out in search of adventures and, discovering that a ship ready to sail to Europe was in port, he abandoned his wife in secret, leaving a letter in which he explained that he was leaving her because she was a pagan. At that time she was pregnant, and later she gave birth to a boy whom she named Feirefiz. As the mother was black and the father white, the son's skin "was both black and white." (B. I, 40)

44 Chapter 3

Arriving in Spain, Gahmuret, who was also a nephew of King Arthur, heard of the death of his brother, meaning that he was now the heir to his father's property. He also learned that a beautiful, widowed young queen named Herzeloyde was organizing a tournament and promising the winner her kingdoms and her hand in marriage. Gahmuret went to the tournament, where he arrived in great pomp to general admiration. Even in the preparatory fights that usually preceded the tournament, he showed such courage and valor that he was already considered the winner. The tournament proper was canceled. When the hero was in his tent with his squires, pages and other friends, the queen and her entourage came to offer him the winner's prize. She had already fallen in love with him by then. Gahmuret told her that he was married to a Moorish queen, to which she replied: "You must give up the Mooress in favor of my love. [...] In the Sacrament of Baptism there is greater virtue." (B. I, 57)

Gahmuret and Herzeloyde ended up married and were very happy together, when a messenger from the Caliph of Baghdad arrived, asking the knight for help, as once again he was being harassed by enemies. Gahmuret asked his wife for permission to help his friend. Although she was rather unhappy at this separation, she agreed with his departure for the East.

After six months, awaiting the return of her beloved husband, she had a tormenting nightmare: "For now she marveled at how she was mothering a serpent which then rent her womb and how a dragon sucked at her breasts and flew swiftly away and vanished from her sight!" (B. II, 62)

This time, luck abandoned Gahmuret. During a pause in the battle, he took off his diamond helmet to drink water and cool off, and an enemy poured a magical potion into the helmet which "grew softer than a puff-ball." (B. II, 63) When the noble knight returned to battle, an enemy lance fatally pierced his helmet. Before he died, however, he asked his squire to take the tip of the deadly spear to his wife, and also asked that all his pages and squires stay under the protection of Herzeloyde.

When Herzeloyde received the news of the death of her beloved, she swooned in pain and sorrow. On recovering, she was comforted by the knowledge that she was carrying in her womb Gahmuret's child, soon to be born. Fifteen days later she gave birth to a boy who already showed signs that he would become a great knight.

Fearing that her son would meet the same fate as his father, Herzeloyde decided to isolate herself with the boy and a few servants in the forest of Soltane, to bring him up far from the court and its culture of chivalry. She forbade words like "knight," "chivalry," and the like to be spoken in front of him.

So the child grew up in the forest, in perfect harmony with the conditions of nature. His mother gave him bows and arrows to shoot birds and other animals. Being very sensitive, he was moved by birdsong to the point of breathlessness. Realizing this, his mother sent her servants and peasants out to silence all the birds. When the boy saw that they were trying to kill birds, he asked the queen what they were doing. She came to her senses, exclaiming that she was transgressing the commandments of God. The boy then asked about God, and Herzeloyde answered:

> "My son, I shall tell you, just as it is. He Who took on a shape in the likeness of Man is brighter than the sun. [...] Pray to him in need. His steadfast love never yet failed the world. Then there is one called Lord of Hell. He is black, perfidy cleaves to him. Turn your thoughts away from him and treacherous despair." (B. III, 71–72)

One morning the boy was hunting in the forest when he heard the sound of approaching hooves. He brandished his hunting spear, thinking this might be the devil himself, the one his mother had mentioned. But he was willing to face the devil, and stood ready. Then three galloping knights came near, their armor gleaming in the morning sun, and the young boy believed they were gods, according to his mother's description. So he fell to his knees, asking them for help. Then a fourth knight appeared who seemed to be in a great hurry. He asked the boy whether he had seen two gentlemen who had abducted a maiden and were, therefore, not worthy of being called knights. These words assured the boy that he was standing before God, since this luminous figure was trying to help a maiden in trouble. Kneeling again, he asked the help of this "God." The prince, however, explained that he was not a god but a knight, who only followed divine commandments.

The boy then asked what a knight was, and who could confer such an honor. The prince replied that this was King Arthur's prerogative, and noting the boy's bearing and assuming him to be of noble descent, he commented that if he went to the court of King Arthur he could certainly become a knight. In his innocence, the boy then asked the knight what kind of creature he was, with his whole body in a mesh impossible to unravel. After receiving the explanation of how chainmail protects one against spears and swords, the young boy ventured to say that if the deer wore something similar, he would not be able to kill them. The knights took their leave, commenting that God would have created a perfect human being in this boy, had He also given him the ability to think.

From that moment onward the boy had only one desire: to become a knight. He ran back to his mother to tell her what had happened. She was so shaken by his account that she fainted. Regaining consciousness, she tried hard to dissuade him, but without success. She then provided him with "fool's clothing" and gave him just "the wretchedest nag" (B. III, 75), believing that once he was subjected to scorn and mistreatment he would soon return to her. As until then she had never told him of the existence of a world beyond the forest, before his departure she gave him some advice, to prepare him for a life among men. She recommended that, if he had to cross a river, he should look for a place where the waters were crystal clear. He should greet everyone kindly, and if he met a wise old man willing to teach him, he should follow his advice.

He should also win the ring and the kiss of a maiden. She explained that two of the realms that belonged to him by inheritance (Valois and Norgals) had been conquered by Lähelin, a knight who had killed or imprisoned many of his subjects.

The next day the young man set off happily for the court of Arthur. His mother went with him for some of the way, but was soon unable to continue. The boy was so happy that he didn't even look back, and therefore did not see that Herzeloyde had fallen. Seeing her beloved son depart, her heart had broken in pain, causing her death.

After riding for a long time, he came to a stream "which a cock would have crossed with ease" (B. III, 76), and whose waters were dark because of the shadow cast by the surrounding vegetation. Obeying his mother's instruction to cross a river only where the waters were crystal clear, he continued along it until nightfall. He slept there and the next day he found a stretch of clear water where he could cross.

Shortly thereafter he came to a meadow, where he saw a beautiful tent. On entering it he came across a maiden who was asleep. It was Jeschute, the wife of Duke Orilus of Lalande. Seeing a ring gleaming on her finger, he remembered his mother's instructions, took off the maiden's ring, and gave her a kiss. In desperation she urged him to return her ring and go away, but the youth was very hungry, and seeing a meal that the duchess had prepared for her husband, he unceremoniously devoured everything. She begged him for her ring and urged him to depart, so, keeping the ring, he kissed her once more and went away with gentle words as his mother had taught him.

Before long, Duke Orilus returned to his tent, noticing horse tracks in front of it. Upon entering he found his wife in tears. She told him what had happened but he did not believe her, thinking that she had betrayed him. Outraged, he said he would no longer consider her his wife but rather the least of his servants, so she would get no new clothes nor would her horse be fed. Thus it was that Jeschute fell into disgrace.

Meanwhile the young man went on his way and, following his mother's advice, kindly greeted everyone he met. Suddenly he heard the despairing weeping of a woman. Approaching the place it came from, he saw a maiden with a dead knight in her arms. After greeting her as his mother had taught him, he wanted to know what had happened and who had killed the knight, offering to avenge his death. Acknowledging his sympathy, the maiden asked him his name, to which he replied: "*Bon fiz, cher fiz, beau fiz*[26]—that's how I used to be called at home." (B. III, 81) Hearing these words, she immediately knew who he was and said, "You are Parzival, and your name means 'Pierce-through-the heart'" (B. III, 81), revealing that she was his cousin Sigune, whose mother, his mother's sister, had died when she was born. Then she told him about his father, Gahmuret, and about the two realms conquered by Lähelin. Lähelin's brother Orilus had just killed the noble prince, her fiancé, who had been defending Parzival's lands.

In view of these revelations, Parzival's desire to avenge the dead knight increased further, and he asked Sigune to point him in the direction Orilus had gone. She, however, knowing how unprepared he was and fearing for his life, pointed in a different direction.

That's how he came to the city of Nantes, where, in front of the city gate, he came across a knight whose armor, horse, and harness were all red. His hair, clothes, shield, shaft and tip of his spear, as well as the blade of his sword, were also red. The knight was Ither de Gaheviess, also known as the Red Knight. After returning Parzival's gentle greeting, he asked the young man if he were entering the city, and would he take a message to King Arthur, whose court was located there. The Red Knight was holding a golden goblet that he had stolen from the Round Table, and he was challenging the knights to combat because he claimed the right to their lands, which his uncle, King Arthur, would not agree to. The Red Knight also asked Parzival to convey his apologies to Queen Guinevere for having inadvertently spilled wine on her dress.

---

26 "Good son, dear son, handsome son."

Entering the city, the young man was soon the laughingstock of all the people he encountered, but a page named Iwanet took pity on him and led him to court, where Parzival was amazed to see "so many Arthurs," not knowing which one could make him into a knight. The page led him to the king. After greeting him according to his mother's instructions, Parzival delivered Ither's message and added that he would like to receive armor from the king's hands, preferably like that of the Red Knight. Until then Ither had been part of the Round Table and was respected and liked by all, so none of the knights wanted to face him in combat. Parzival, desiring armor very much, volunteered for the fight. Arthur and his whole court noticed that the handsome young man was surely destined for great things, but also recognized his naïveté and inexperience; therefore, Arthur initially denied his request. However, Sir Kai the Seneschal,[27] a very rough character, convinced the king to allow the young man to face Ither so that in case he lost, there would be no embarrassment to the court.

Leaving the royal palace, where many knights and maidens were assembled, Parzival heard the loud laugh of a lady and then the sound of a punch. It was the maiden Cunneware, who had sworn that she would only laugh when she saw a knight who "held the palm or was destined to win it." (B. III, 86) Seeing Parzival, she laughed. Kai was so furious to see her break her promise before a fool, when so many noble knights had passed through the court, that he could not hold back and beat her with his staff. Realizing the humiliation Cunneware had suffered, Parzival felt sorry for her and promised to avenge her.

When he reached Ither, Parzival challenged him to hand over his horse and armor, adding that no knight in the court was willing to fight him, hence the two of them would have to make do. At this, the Red Knight reversed his spear and hit Parzival so violently with its shaft that he fell off his mount. According to the rules, combat was over and Ither had won. Parzival, however, was unfamiliar with these rules. Furious, he

---

27 The court's steward or administrative supervisor.

took his hunting spear and threw it at his unprepared opponent. The spear hit his face shield, went through the noble knight's eye and lodged in his brain. He fell dead from his horse, the victim of a treacherous act. Parzival tried to roll the dead man over to take his armor off, but without success. In the meantime, the page Iwanet approached; he began to extract the dead knight from his armor to put it onto Parzival, whom he asked to strip off his clothes.

The young man refused to take off the clothes his mother had given him, so he put Ither's clothes and armor on over them. Iwanet strapped on his sword but did not allow him to take his hunting spear, saying it was not a weapon a knight should wear. He quickly taught the young man how to use the sword, shield and lance, and helped him onto the horse. Before leaving, Parzival remembered to ask the page to return the goblet to the king, and to tell him that one of his knights, who had mistreated the lady who had laughed because of Parzival, had dishonored the king.

Arthur's court greatly lamented the death of Ither, even more so as it was such a dishonorable death. Traveling onward, Parzival covered "in that one day as far as an old campaigner, minus his gear, would never have attempted had he been asked to ride it in two!" (B. III, 91) It was dusk when he spotted a tower in the distance. Proceeding in that direction, he had the impression that additional towers were rising from the ground just like the grain planted by his mother's servants. When Parzival arrived at the castle, tired, his shield swinging back and forth counter to all the rules of chivalry, the lord of the castle, an elderly knight by the name of Gurnemanz, was resting in the meadow under a lime tree in front of the majestic building. As was his wont, the youth kindly greeted the noble knight, adding that his mother had advised him to accept the teachings of an elderly man. Gurnemanz released his hawk, and soon several pages and squires appeared and led the guest to the castle to care for him.

Initially Parzival did not want to dismount from his horse, and much persuasion was needed before he did so in order to be taken to a room. There he was disarmed, and then the squires noticed his fool's attire and some wounds on his body. Dismayed, they reported all this to the lord of the castle, who went to his guest and personally cared for his injuries. Then dinner was served, which the hungry youth devoured greedily, to the host's great amusement. When Gurnemanz suggested that it was time to go to bed as Parzival must be tired, he answered that he had risen very early that day, and that his mother would certainly be asleep at this hour.

The next morning, Parzival's training to become a knight began. First, Gurnemanz advised him not to mention his mother so often, but to keep her image in his heart. In addition, he was advised not to speak thoughtlessly. He must also help those in need but judge wisely, keeping to the middle ground between generosity and greed.

The master also advised him to control his unseemly behavior and refrain from unnecessary questions. He instructed him to be merciful, sparing the lives of defeated opponents, and always, after taking off his armor, removing the rust stains from his hands and face so as to present himself in a dignified manner, since the ladies would notice such details. Then he advised him regarding proper behavior toward women. After all these instructions, Parzival started to learn to ride, to handle various weapons, and to fight. The youth showed amazing skill and dexterity in handling weapons.

Gurnemanz had become very fond of his pupil and wished for him to marry his daughter Liaze, but after two weeks Parzival decided to leave because he felt prepared to do great deeds. Gurnemanz was saddened and told the young man that he had lost his three sons in combat, and was now losing his fourth. Parzival, however, replied that he would need to prove his worth before deserving the beautiful Liaze. It was in this climate of disappointment and sadness that Parzival left behind his master and the inhabitants of the castle.

Parzival was restless and confused. He allowed his horse to lead the way, and was thus led to the kingdom of Brobarz. It was already getting dark when he came to a river he had to cross. The road led to the city of

Pelrapeire at the river's mouth, by the sea. The young man noticed that the surrounding fields lay devastated, and the bridge leading to the city was in such a precarious state that his horse refused to cross it. Parzival had to dismount and lead the animal by the reins to the other side. The city gate was closed, and he knocked on it vigorously. From a window above, a young woman shouted that they already had enough enemies, to which the young knight replied, offering to help with whatever they needed.

After a while he was allowed to enter the city, where he saw a crowd of thin, weak, pale people, which made a terrible impression on him. The reason was that the city was under siege, there was no more food, and the inhabitants were starving. They looked hopefully to the healthy knight and welcomed him. Some squires helped him out of his armor, and at the well he washed off the rust stains. He was given a rich garment and was taken into the presence of the queen, whose name was Condwiramurs. She received him warmly in the great hall, and all present looked in fascination at the two radiant young people sitting side by side. Remembering that Gurnemanz had recommended that he refrain from unnecessary questions, Parzival sat in silence and the queen started the conversation.

The last of the food supplies was distributed among the starving population, and the guest was led to a room where a soft bed had been prepared for him.

During the night he awoke to hear someone weeping, and the candlelight revealed the queen in tears, kneeling before his bed. He rebuked her, saying that she should kneel only before God. Settling down in his bed, she told him that she had taken over the throne after her father's death and had refused to marry King Clamide, who had become furious and had taken revenge with the help of his seneschal Kingrun, devastating her kingdom and besieging the city of Belrapeire. The following day Kingrun, who had already killed many of the queen's knights in single combat, planned to launch a new attack, but all the men of the kingdom were weak and hungry and would be overwhelmed. She would then be forced to marry Clamide. However, to prevent this she planned to throw herself from the top of the tower.

Parzival promised to protect her from Kingrun and Clamide by challenging Kingrun. Early next morning he took his weapons and waited for his opponent before the town gate. This would be his first real fight. The struggle was violent, the two horses fell to the ground, and the combatants jumped out of their saddles and began to fight with swords. Finally Kingrun, who had been considered invincible, had to surrender to Parzival, who remembered Gurnemanz's teaching and was merciful toward his opponent. He sent Kingrun to Arthur's court, where he must place himself at the service of the maiden Cunneware. Moreover, he must tell the king that he who had sent him would only return to court after avenging the insult suffered by this young lady.

Parzival returned to Pelrapeire, where the inhabitants awaited him, overjoyed that he had been spared. Kingrun's army, having witnessed his defeat, panicked at the loss of their leader. The queen herself helped Parzival take off his armor, and embracing him, said that she was willing to marry her liberator. The population applauded him and asked him to become their ruler. At that point, the watchmen on the tower saw two boats approaching by sea. When they anchored it was discovered that they were bringing provisions. Parzival ordered that all the goods be brought in, and he distributed them personally and sparingly among the inhabitants, as he feared that they might fall ill by stuffing themselves after such a prolonged period of starvation.

After three days, the wedding of Parzival and Condwiramurs was celebrated. Meanwhile, Clamide was nearing Belrapeire with the intention of taking possession of the town and the queen. On discovering that Kingrun had been defeated and Condwiramurs was married, he challenged Parzival to a duel. The fight was fierce; after the horses fell down exhausted, the knights turned to their swords. Sparks leaped from their helmets and their shields were reduced to shards. Clamide began to lose strength and was overcome by Parzival. Blood trickled from his mouth and ears. Once again the winner was merciful, and Clamide, too, was sent to Arthur's court to serve the maiden Cunneware. Parzival sent another message to the king, saying he would only return to his presence after making reparations for the insult suffered by the young lady.

This time Belrapeire was definitely free. Parzival ordered that the fields be tended again. The kingdom prospered, and he was beloved by his subjects and lived happily with his wife. One day, however, he asked her for permission to visit his mother, because he wanted to know how she was faring and wished to tell her what had happened to him during his absence from home. Saddened by the separation but recognizing the good cause that moved him, Condwiramurs allowed his departure. He left Belrapeire alone, having dispensed with pages and squires.

Parzival rode all day, and in late afternoon he arrived at a lake where he saw a boat. In it sat a richly dressed man, fishing. The knight asked the fisherman where he could find shelter, and was told that within a radius of thirty miles there was no housing at all except for his castle, which was of difficult access. Nevertheless, he described the way there, adding that even with such detailed directions Parzival could easily get lost. If he managed to get to the castle, however, Parzival would be his guest that night.

Parzival followed the fisherman's directions and suddenly found himself before a huge castle. He asked for the drawbridge to be lowered, which was done only after he added that the fisherman had sent him. Entering the castle courtyard, he noticed the tall grass and wondered whether any tournaments had taken place there lately. He was very well received by the inhabitants of the castle, who led him to a room where he was disarmed. After removing the rust stains, a valet put around his shoulders a precious silk mantle which the queen of the castle had put at his disposal.

Finally he was taken to the great hall, where he saw pomp and luxury never experienced before. There was ample room for four hundred knights. The king, dressed in a sable-lined robe and fur cap, was reclining on a settee in front of three marble fireplaces, in which crackled a fire of fine timber. His face expressed great affliction. He soon asked the guest to take a seat close to him and then:

> A page ran in at the door, bearing—this rite was to evoke grief—a Lance from whose keen steel blood issued and then ran down the shaft to his hand and all but reached his sleeve. At this there was weeping and wailing throughout that spacious hall, the inhabitants of thirty lands could not have wrung such a flood from their eyes. The page carried the Lance round the four walls back to the door and then ran out again, whereupon the pain was assuaged that had been prompted by the sorrow those people had been reminded of. (B. V, 123–124)

Then Parzival witnessed another scene, at once mysterious and impressive: Several groups of maidens, richly dressed, came in carrying objects which they displayed in front of the king, such as golden candlesticks with lighted candles, ivory pedestals, large torches, a precious-stone tabletop which had been chiseled from a "garnet-hyacinth! Very long and broad it was, and the man who had measured it for a tabletop had cut it thin to make it light" (B. V, 124), and two sharp silver knives. Finally came the queen, carrying on a green *achmardi* (brocaded silk) "the consummation of heart's desire, its root and its blossoming—a thing called 'The Gral', paradisal, transcending all earthly perfection." (B. V, 125) She set it down in front of the king. Then a hundred squires raised bread before the Grail, distributing it among those present; and immediately the food and drink that each one desired appeared before the Grail.

Parzival observed this miraculous phenomenon and had the urge to inquire about it, but remembered that Gurnemanz had recommended that he refrain from asking unnecessary questions. It was then that a squire approached him, carrying a very valuable sword which the king was presenting to Parzival. The king uttered the words: "Sir [...], I took this into the thick of battle on many a field before God crippled my body." (B. V, 127) Then Wolfram comments, "Alas that he asked no Question then! Even now I am cast down on this account! For when he was given the sword it was to prompt him to ask a Question." (B. V, 127)

After the banquet, everything was gathered up. The maidens took back what they had brought, and Parzival, following them with his eyes, saw behind a door they passed "the most handsome old man he had ever seen or heard of, whose hair [...] was more silvery even than hoarfrost." (B. V, 128)

After the king had wished him a good rest, Parzival was taken to a room where a magnificent bed had been prepared. His sleep, however, was plagued by nightmares in which he was the target of innumerable spear and sword blows. When he awoke, sweating all over, he saw that it was dawn. He wondered why there were no pages to help him dress, and fell asleep again. The sun was high when he awoke for the second time. He saw his armor and the two swords at the foot of the bed, but no servant, so he dressed himself. The palace seemed empty. Walking through the rooms, he met no one.

In the courtyard, his mount was prepared for departure, alongside his shield and spear. Parzival noticed that the grass had been trampled on, the tracks moving toward the outside of the castle, and he imagined that the knights had left for combat. He mounted his horse and went to the open gate. As he was coming to the end of the drawbridge, it was suddenly raised so that his horse almost fell into the moat. Parzival turned to see what was happening, but the page who had raised it only replied: "Damn you, wherever the sun lights your path! [...] You silly goose! Why didn't you open your gob and ask my lord the Question? You've let slip a marvelous prize." (B. V, 131). Parzival asked for more explanation, but the squire remained silent. Without understanding what was going on, the young knight decided to follow the tracks of the knights to join them and fight alongside his host. The tracks, however, gradually disappeared, and Parzival was lost in the forest.

Shortly afterward, the young man heard the weeping of a woman, and moving toward it he came across a maiden sitting under a linden tree, holding the embalmed body of a knight. She did not recognize him, nor did he at first recognize her as Sigune. She asked where he had spent the night. He said it was in a castle nearby. She did not believe him, because into that impenetrable forest hardly anyone not belonging to the Grail ever entered, and he bore the insignia of a strange knight. She told him that within a thirty-mile radius there was no dwelling except for the castle called Munsalvaesche,[28] and then she told him about the family that ruled Terre Salvaesche. One of the sons, called Trevrizent, had decided to live in isolation and dedicate his life to penance while the other, the king himself, called Anfortas, was so ill that he could not stand or walk, which was why the whole community was immersed in deep sorrow. She also said that if her young interlocutor had been accepted by the community, the king must have been freed of his suffering.

Parzival then described what he had seen in the castle, and as she listened she recognized him as her cousin and revealed to him who she was. He noticed that Sigune had lost all her youthfulness and suggested that they bury the deceased, but she rejected his suggestion. When Sigune saw that he held the sheathed sword of the Grail, she revealed its secret: "The sword will stay whole for one blow, but at the second it will fall apart." (B. V, 134)

Sigune then told him what he must do to restore the sword: Before dawn, he must take the parts to the place where it had been forged. In high spirits, she remarked that if he had asked the king the right question, he was now the luckiest person on earth. However, upon learning that he had not asked any question, she was outraged and said he was damned and dishonored; it would have been better that she had never set eyes on him. Realizing that he had committed an error, Parzival wanted to redeem himself, but Sigune fell silent and gave him no indication of the direction in which he should ride.

---

28 Wolfram von Eschenbach uses the term *Munsalvaesche*. Some authors interpret it as it being Mount Silvaticus, the Wild Mount, and others believe it signifies Mons Salvationis, Mount of Salvation.

Lost in the impenetrable forest, he noticed a new horse track. Following it, he came to a very thin, tired, starving animal. It carried a woman in rags. As soon as Parzival greeted her, she recognized him, claiming that it was his fault that she was in such a miserable state. He replied that since he had become a knight, he had never offended any lady. He offered her his cloak but she urged him to leave, as further on there was a knight who had been her husband, and if he saw them together he would kill them both. The young man thought it would be cowardly to leave, and prepared for combat. Noticing that someone was talking to Jeschute, the Duke of Orilus spurred his mount, immediately starting the fight without the formalities of a challenge. Orilus's coat of arms was the dragon, and Parzival had the impression that he was fighting a hundred dragons on the duke's shield, helmet, cloak, and saddlecloth.

The fight was violent, and Jeschute feared for the lives of both knights. Their swords clanged and sparks flew off their helmets, with neither of the heroes having an advantage over the other. Finally Parzival managed to throw Orilus off his horse, and jumping from his own mount, he slammed his opponent against a tree trunk, so that the duke had to admit defeat. Parzival now demanded that he reconcile with Jeschute, but Orilus replied that this was impossible because she had betrayed him. Parzival also demanded that the couple go to Arthur's court to serve the maiden Cunneware, who had been humiliated because of him. He insisted upon the couple's reconciliation, threatening to kill Orilus. Fearing for his life, the latter agreed.

In that same place there was a hermitage, where Parzival saw a shrine. Of his own will, Parzival put his hand on it and solemnly swore to the innocence of this noble lady, saying that it had been he who, still foolish and inexperienced before becoming a knight, had invaded the duke's tent and stolen Jeschute's ring. Then he returned the ring to Orilus, who put it on his wife's finger and covered her with his cloak. Soon after, they left for Arthur's court, where Orilus presented himself to serve Cunneware, his sister, saying that it was the Red Knight who had made this demand when he defeated him in combat. Meanwhile, Parzival, without realizing it, took a multicolored lance which lay next to the shrine.

After hearing so many wonders about the Red Knight who had sent so many knights vanquished in combat to serve Cunneware, King Arthur went out to look for him, because he wanted to invite him to join the Round Table. As a precaution, for he knew the Grail was near, the king forbade all his knights to get involved in any combat without his previous consent. One night, one of his falcons did not return to camp and, although it was "not the time for snow" (B. VI, 147), there was a blizzard. Sensing a human presence, the bird settled near that person, who was Parzival. The next morning Parzival noticed that the road had disappeared under the snow. Even so, he rode on until he reached a clearing, where he found a flock of wild geese. The falcon that had accompanied him dashed down onto the birds, digging its claws into one of them, but the bird was able to free itself. From its wounds, however, three drops of blood fell on the snow. This vision left Parzival in a state of ecstasy, as the drops of blood in the snow reminded him of his sweet wife. And so he stared at them as if hypnotized, ignoring all that was going on around him.

A squire of Arthur's court, sent in search of the falcon, crossed the same clearing and noticed a strange knight, lance in hand, as if daring someone to fight. Back in camp, he reported that a knight was challenging the Round Table. Segramors, who was always willing to fight, volunteered for combat. Arthur consented and he galloped into the forest. Arriving at the clearing, he found his opponent in a totally oblivious state. Segramors challenged him, but the strange knight did not move, deep in thought, dominated by passion for his wife. Arthur's knight spurred on his mount and lunged toward Parzival, whose horse, noticing the arrival of another horse, turned around so that the Red Knight lost sight of the drops of blood in the snow.

Regaining consciousness, Parzival just had time to place his spear in position. The clash of the two knights was so violent that Segramors was thrown off. Parzival immediately turned back to the three drops of blood in the snow, oblivious of the fact that his opponent's horse, freed from his heavy weight, had galloped back to camp. Meanwhile the knight walked back to camp, becoming his companions' laughingstock.

Keie, the king's steward, conveyed the news of Segramors' defeat and asked for permission to go and fight against the stranger. Receiving consent, he armed himself to the teeth and, arriving at the clearing, immediately called out his terms for surrender, saying that the challenger would soon lie sprawled in the snow. Parzival, however, was still in a trance, totally absorbed in his passion. Keie's first attack made the Red Knight's mount change position, and so he again lost sight of the drops of blood. Regaining consciousness, he took up his combat position as the steward was already at full gallop. With his spear, the latter opened a large crack in Parzival's shield, but he retaliated with such violence that rider and mount went down. The horse died and the rider broke his right arm and left leg. Then Parzival again turned to the drops of blood in the snow, tormented by his memory of Condwiramurs. Keie was carried back to camp, where many lamented his bad luck.

It was then that Gawain, King Arthur's nephew and one of the noblest knights of the Round Table, asked his uncle's permission to confront the stranger. He went unarmed to the clearing. Instead of challenging Parzival, Gawain greeted him kindly, but the stranger did not return the greeting. Being knowledgeable in everything related to love, Gawain assumed that the stranger was overcome by passion. Following the direction of his gaze, he noticed the drops of blood in the snow and immediately covered them with his cloak. Parzival, awakening from his trance, deeply regretted having lost sight of his beloved wife, and suddenly realized that his lance was broken. Gawain told him that it had been broken in combat, which Parzival took as an insult since he had no memory of a fight.

After Gawain introduced himself and invited the Red Knight to accompany him to Arthur's court, the hero became gentler, yet he declined Gawain's offer, saying that he could not go there without having first avenged the outrage suffered by the maiden Cunneware. So Gawain told him that revenge had been accomplished, showing him Keie's dead horse and Parzival's spear lying there in pieces. Under these circumstances, Parzival agreed to go to the Round Table, where he was greeted kindly by those present, mainly Cunneware, who thanked him for all he had done for her.

Then a great feast was held, during which Parzival, having won everybody's esteem and admiration, was happily welcomed to the Round Table. The merrymaking, however, was interrupted by the arrival of a figure whose description, ever so fantastic, will be given in the words of Wolfram himself:

> [...]She was mounted on a mule as high as a Castilian, a dun, with its nostrils much incised and with marks of the searing-iron such as proclaim the galled steeds of Hungary. Great care had gone into the making of her costly bridle and harness. The beast's gait was not open to cavil. She herself did not look like a lady. Oh why did she have to come? Whatever the cause, she was there, and there was nothing to be done about it. She brought suffering to Arthur's company.
>
> She was so talented that she spoke all languages—Latin, Arabic and French. She was on easy terms with such learned matters as dialectic and geometry, and she had mastered astronomy. Her name was Cundrie, her nickname "The Sorceress." Her mouth suffered from no impediment, for what it said was quite enough. With it she flattened much joy upstanding.
>
> In appearance this learned damsel did not resemble those whom we call fine people. This hailstorm so destructive of happiness had donned a fine fabric of Ghent such as bridal gown are made of, bluer even than azure and made up into

a travelling cloak well cut in the French fashion. On the underside next to her body there was good brocade. A hat of peacock feathers from London, lined with cloth-of-gold—the hat was new, its ribbons not old—hung down over her back. [...] A plait of her hair fell down over the hat and dangled on her mule—it was long, black, tough, not altogether lovely, about as soft as a boar's bristles. Her nose was like a dog's, and to the length of several spans a pair of tusks jutted from her jaws. Both eyebrows pushed past her hairband and drooped down in tresses. In the interests of truth I have erred against propriety in having to speak thus of a lady, yet no other has cause to complain of me.

Cundrie's ears resembled a bear's. Her rugged visage was not such as to rouse a lover's desire. In her hand she held a knout,[29] the lashes of which were of silk, the stock of ruby. This fetching sweetheart had hands the colour of ape-skin. Her fingernails were none too transparent, for my source tells me that they looked like a lion's claws. Seldom (or never?) were lances broken for her love. (B. VI, 163–164)

She walked over to where King Arthur sat, saying that his attitude covered the Round Table with shame, ruining its prestige because he had accepted in their midst someone false who seemed to be a knight, but was not. Then she went up to Parzival, cursing him and saying that shame should cover his magnificent appearance and that if it depended on her, he would never rest or live in peace. She asked him why he had not rid the Fisher King of his suffering when he had been before him, showing a little compassion.

"You feathered hook, you viper's fang! Did not your host present you with a sword you never deserved? By your silence you acquired great sin [...] Moreover, you saw the Gral carried into your presence, the keen knives of silver and the Bloody Lance! You ender of joy, donor of sorrow." (B. VI, 165)

---

29 Whip.

Then she said that Parzival had a brother, Feirefiz d'Anjou, a son from his father's first marriage, who was King Arthur's nephew. This young knight of great worth, whose skin was mottled, had conquered a huge kingdom in the East. Then she highly praised Herzeloyde and Gahmuret, adding that Parzival's fame had become exactly the opposite of his father's.

This is how the Round Table came to know the identity of the Red Knight. Leaving him aside, Cundrie turned back to Arthur, challenging the knights to seek the highest fame and love by liberating the Schastel Marveile,[30] where four hundred maidens and four queens were imprisoned. She left without saying farewell, crying bitterly.

All were dismayed. The women in Arthur's court burst into tears. Parzival, however, examining his actions, accepted responsibility for his error. Before anyone could recover, a knight in beautiful armor came in, asking for Arthur and Gawain. He accused Gawain of treacherously killing his master, the King of Ascalun, and said he had come to challenge him to single combat, to be held within forty days in the capital of that kingdom. The accused should prove his honor and loyalty. Gawain replied that he did not know exactly why he needed to fight and was not happy at having to do so but, as his honor was being questioned, he accepted the challenge. Before leaving, the stranger introduced himself as Kingrimursel, Prince of Ascalun, and promised Gawain that he would not be mistreated in his kingdom.

Still astounded at the new accusation, the nobles tried to comfort Parzival and Gawain. Clamide then approached Parzival, telling him how he had suffered on losing Condwiramurs. He asked him now to intercede with Cunneware so that she would not regard him as her prisoner, which he had been since Parzival sent him, but would accept him in marriage. Parzival agreed willingly. He then released the knights from their commitment of friendship and loyalty, which he had received when he was admitted to the Round Table. From that moment

---

30 Enchanted Castle.

on, he would know no happiness till he reached the Grail again, even if it took his whole life. He also requested that King Arthur protect Queen Condwiramurs and her realm. When he left, Gawain wished him God's protection, to which Parzival replied:

> "Alas, what is God? [...] Were He all-powerful—were God active in His almightiness—he would not have brought us to such shame! Ever since I knew of Grace I have been His humble servitor. But now I will quit His service! If He knows anger I will shoulder it." (B. VI, 172)

He ended by advising his friend to also trust no longer in God. Thus Parzival departed from the Round Table. Soon after, Gawain also left Arthur's court to present himself to Kingrimursel in Ascalun.

※ ※

On his journey to Ascalun, Gawain was at the top of a hill when he saw a huge army moving toward him. He was most unwilling to face all these knights, but there was no escape. He saw many knights and young noblemen, but was unable to recognize any coat of arms. It was an army totally unknown to him. Carts pulled by donkeys, loaded with arms and supplies, rolled on behind the horsemen. A large number of women, acrobats and vagabonds followed. Through a squire, Gawain learned that this huge army had been summoned by King Melianz and was heading for Bearoche to fight Lyppaut, a vassal and foster father of this same king. The squire informed him that before his death, Melianz's father had entrusted Lyppaut with his son's education. Now Lyppaut had two daughters, Obie and Obilot, the latter still a child.

When Melianz asked Obie if she would like to marry him, she rejected his proposal with great contempt and pride. Hurt and angered by her attitude, he decided to take revenge, because he thought that the way Lyppaut had educated his daughter had made her so arrogant. To no avail his foster father tried to prove her innocence, as Melianz was blind with fury. He armed many knights, forcing them to engage in this combat against Lyppaut.

Having heard all this, Gawain was undecided as to what stand to take. If he got involved in the combat he might miss the deadline for the duel with Kingrimursel. Yet, if he just remained a bystander, he would risk his prestige. Eventually he decided to head for Bearoche.

Arriving near the vicinity of Lyppaut's castle, Gawain noticed some very distinguished ladies on the high wall. From where he was, he could hear their conversation. They wished to know who the approaching people were. Lyppaut's older daughter, Obie, soon expressed her opinion, declaring that they were merchants, to which the smaller one replied: "Sister, you turn him into what he is not and you should be ashamed for it! Clearly he is not a merchant. He is of such a magnificent appearance that I will elect him my knight." (B. VII, 182) Gawain's squires found some trees along the wall and decided to rest in their shade.

Although it was obvious that our hero was a gentleman, Obie insisted on his being a merchant, humiliating the noble knight who was listening to the conversation. Then she sent a servant to ask the merchant if perhaps he had beautiful dresses to sell. When the servant came near, Gawain glared at him and ordered him to withdraw immediately, which the young man did without delay. The older daughter even made other attempts to humiliate Gawain until her father, the Lord of Lyppaut himself, went out to meet the foreigner. He recognized in the stranger a very valiant knight and asked him to join his army. Gawain explained the reason for his journey, which was to defend his knightly dignity in single combat; therefore he should not engage in other fights, although it would please him to share Lyppaut's victory or defeat. The lord of the castle continued to insist and Gawain promised to reconsider. When little Obilot, who had expressed the desire to ask the knight to put himself at her service, heard about this, she went to look for him and very cleverly arranged it so that he agreed to fight for her. As was customary, the little lady wanted to offer a gift to her knight, but she only had dolls. Her father ordered her a new dress, and one of its sleeves was offered as a talisman to Gawain, who fixed it on his shield.

The next day there was intense fighting between the two armies. Gawain threw many opponents, taking many prisoners. When he noticed in the middle of the enemy some Britons whose coat of arms belonged to the son of Arthur, he avoided fighting them. Despite fighting bravely, the knights of Lyppaut were retreating. King Melianz defeated all he confronted and eventually challenged Gawain, who managed to wound the king, though he kept on fighting. When his disadvantage became evident he surrendered, and that determined the end of the battle, with the defeat of Melianz's army.

Gawain was the one who stood out among the men of Lyppaut. On the enemy side, it was an unknown knight in red armor. He had joined the army only three days before and made many prisoners of his opponents. Seeing his master imprisoned, he addressed the men whom he himself had subdued, promising to give them freedom if they obtained the release of King Melianz. If they failed, they would have to win the Grail for him. As they had no idea where to find the Grail, he told them to go to Belrapeire and swear obedience to the queen of the country, giving her the following message: "Tell her that the man who fought Kingrun and Clamide for her sake is consumed with longing for the Grail and of course again for her love." (B. VII, 200)

The prisoners of the Red Knight headed first to Castle Bearoche, where they found Lyppaut and his men with their own prisoners, including King Melianz, all at table, recovering from the hardships of combat. When they reported what the unknown knight had ordered them to do, Gawain recognized immediately that they had been taken prisoner by Parzival. In his heart he thanked God for not having had to face his friend, as they had both fought anonymously. As for the release of Melianz, Gawain put the prisoner's fate into the hands of his lady, the little Obilot. She demanded that the king take her sister Obie for his wife. The latter, regretting her previous attitude, cried heartfelt tears in view of the injury Gawain had caused to Melianz. Lyppaut was very happy, as all he wanted was this marriage. Then Gawain said his farewell, to Obilot's great sorrow, and headed toward his greater quest.

On approaching the city of Schanpfanzun in the kingdom of Ascalun, Gawain saw a group of five hundred knights coming in his direction across an extensive plain. Arthur's noble knight was courteously received by King Vergulacht, who said he was willing to stop the hunt if his guest so desired, but then added that he would surely find his own way into town. Gawain left the decision to the king, who said that his sister lived in town and would certainly receive him with dignity. Vergulacht ordered one of his knights to accompany the guest to the city and ask his sister Antikonie to entertain him until his return from the hunt. Antikonie received the stranger with much kindness, and before long they were talking animatedly.

The conversation was already becoming more intimate when they were surprised by an old knight who, on recognizing Gawain, urged his warriors to take up arms. He screamingly accused Gawain of murdering the king and now wanting to rape his sister. The stranger was totally disarmed and asked the maiden what he could do to defend them, because a crowd was already hurrying toward the castle. Antikonie suggested they take refuge in a tower. The girl begged the crowd to retreat, but the outcry was such that no one heard her. The people were already approaching the tower when Gawain pulled the bolt off the door to use it as a sword. Antikonie found a huge chessboard, which she passed to him to use as a shield. She herself began to throw the heavy chess pieces at their enemies.

When Vergulacht arrived he saw an angry mob attacking Gawain, and he encouraged his subjects to further aggression. At that moment Kingrimursel appeared: the knight who had challenged Gawain in Arthur's court and had assured him that he would not be harassed in his country until the completion of the duel. Kingrimursel drove the people out of the tower and hurried to Gawain's side, promising him his protection. Given this situation, the king called a truce, as he needed some time to reflect on the best way to avenge the death of his father.

At his council meeting, Vergulacht said that he had faced a knight who defeated him in combat and that, to save his own life, he had had to agree to the task of going in search of the Grail. If he did not succeed, he would have to submit to the Queen of Belrapeire. The king was advised to transfer the assignment to Gawain, with the following argument: If the young knight lost his life in Ascalun, this would be a great discredit to the king, for he would have allowed his guest to be attacked in his country. The decision was taken to the noble hero, who was wondering why Parzival had been there. Gawain took on his task willingly and left, unattended, in search of the Grail.

୨୦ ৎ৬

(At this point, Wolfram talks again about Parzival.)

For many years Parzival roamed lost in the forest, passing through many lands, facing many challengers in knightly combat. One day he saw a hermitage in the forest and went to the window to inquire where he was. The shrine was inhabited by a woman wearing the costume of a penitent, bending over a coffin in which lay the body of her embalmed fiancé. Unknown to him, it was Sigune, who, out of a deep sense of loyalty, had renounced happiness and chosen to live in solitude, spending her days in prayer. When Parzival spoke to her, she invited him to sit on a bench outside the hermitage. The young man asked her how she could survive in such loneliness, and she answered that her nourishment came from the Grail. Every Saturday, Cundrie, the messenger of the Grail, brought her enough food for a week. Parzival was astonished to see a ring gleaming on one of her fingers, as hermits abstained from earthly love. Sigune then told him that she had been engaged to a noble knight in her service who had been killed in combat by Orilus. She had received this ring from him and remained faithful to her beloved.

That is how Parzival realized that he was with Sigune, and when he removed the helmet and chainmail covering his face she recognized him as well. She wanted to know what his relationship with the Grail was now, and he replied that he had given up everything, his domains and his beloved wife, because his only concern was the Grail, which he had not yet been able to find again. He emphasized that he himself was responsible for his destiny. Sigune then remembered that Cundrie had just been there a short while ago to bring food, and seeing how much her cousin had matured, she suggested he follow in the footsteps of the Grail messenger's mule. For a while he followed the footprints, but soon lost them in the forest. Again, he had to give up hope of reaching the Castle of the Grail.

A little later a knight approached him, warning him that he was near Munsalvaesche, a kingdom where intruders were not welcomed. If the stranger insisted on going further, the knight would have to stop him; it would be a fight to the death. Parzival accepted the challenge, and both spurred their mounts, approaching each other at full tilt. The thrust of Parzival's lance was so strong and sure that the Grail knight was thrown off his horse, rolling down a deep gully in the mountainside. However, the young hero's mount could not come to a halt and also plummeted off the cliff. At the last moment, Parzival was able to grasp the branch of a cedar tree. His horse lay dead at the bottom of the abyss, while his challenger was climbing up through the trees on the opposite side.

Not far from the Red Knight stood his opponent's mount. Having lost his own, Parzival seized the Grail horse and, saddened, continued riding through the forest, this time undisturbed by other riders.

The young knight was still lost in the extensive forest when it began to snow. He saw an elderly knight approaching in the company of his wife, his two daughters, and some knights and squires. All were dressed in rough clothes and walked barefoot in the snow. Parzival led his mount to the edge of the path in order to give way, and asked them why they were walking in such poor clothes. The old knight, named Kahenis, replied gently but regretfully that the young man was armed on such a saintly day when he should, in fact, be barefoot. Parzival justified himself by saying that he had lost count of the days, weeks, months and years since he had stopped serving God. He had been told that God helped people but, in his case, he had been forsaken, and God had even allowed his public humiliation. The gray knight asked if he meant the God born of a virgin who had died on the cross that very day, Good Friday, for the salvation of humankind. Then he advised Parzival to look for a hermit whose dwelling was nearby, who gave good advice and could even absolve his sins.

The old man's daughters asked their father to welcome the young knight to their property, and he was immediately invited to accompany them. But Parzival was not comfortable joining them, as he was the only one armed and on horseback. Besides, he did not share their veneration of God. So he warmly declined their kind invitation and took his leave. This meeting, however, made a deep impression on him and he turned his thoughts to God, saying to himself:

> "What if God has such power to succour as would overcome my sorrow? [...] If he ever favored a knight and if any knight ever earned His reward or if shield and sword and truly manly ardour can ever be so worthy of His help that this could save me from my cares and if this is His Helpful Day, then let Him help, if help He can." (B. IX, 231)

Then he let go the reins of his horse, and the horse led him back to the place where once, after defeating Orilus, he had assured him of Jeschute's innocence and demanded his reconciliation with his wife. Parzival also noticed along the way the still-fresh footprints of the gray knight and his entourage.

In that region lived Trevrizent, a hermit who did penance, prayed, and meditated, renouncing food and drink so as to approach the heavenly forces and fight the temptations of the devil. Seeing the young armed knight, he rebuked him for his outfit on that day, but then invited him to sit by the fire. After dismounting, Parzival said that he had met some pilgrims in the forest who suggested that he look for the wise man; then he asked the hermit for advice, saying he was laden with sins. Trevrizent acknowledged that the penitent family was that of Kahenis, a prince who every year made a pilgrimage to his hermitage.

As soon as they had entered the cave and Parzival had stripped off his armor, he asked the old man if his arrival had not frightened him; but the latter said animals scared him more than men. He told Parzival that once he, too, had been a knight. After leading the horse to a secure location, Trevrizent took the young man into a part of the cave where a fire was burning. Parzival was freezing and exhausted after such a long time lost in the woods. Free of his armor and wearing simple clothes borrowed from his host, he soon felt better.

It was inside the cave that he saw the shrine on which he had sworn Jeschute's innocence. He also remembered inadvertently having taken a lance with a painted shaft that was leaning there. On reporting the incident to the hermit, he learned the exact time that had elapsed since then: "It is now four-and-a-half years and three days since you took it." (B. IX, 235)

Then the young knight said that during all this time he had been wandering back and forth, unhappy, living only to fight and hating God, whom he considered responsible for his misfortune. Trevrizent then tried to convince his young interlocutor of every human being's need to deserve divine help, for God is always ready to help anyone who is about to succumb to the forces of darkness. He said that the earth, created by God, was tainted when the blood of Abel, killed by his brother Cain, penetrated it. Since then there has been disharmony among human beings. However, by his sacrifice, God had redeemed humankind. He said that human beings were free to decide between love or divine wrath, suggesting that Parzival had chosen whichever seemed more convenient to him. Parzival thanked him for the revelations about God, but he justified his attitude, saying that he had gone through extremely difficult situations. Then Trevrizent encouraged him to talk about what troubled him, saying that he was not only willing to listen to him, but also to help in any way he could.

Parzival then told him of his intention to get to the Castle of the Grail, and the immense longing he felt for his wife. The hermit praised his fidelity, but considered him unwise to be engaged in the search for the Grail, for he could only reach the Grail if he were predestined for it. He added that he knew this from his own experience. On discovering that his host knew about the Grail, the young knight wanted to hear more about it, though without mentioning his own visit to the Grail Castle.

Trevrizent said that in this castle lived honored knights whose nourishment came from a stone called Lapsit Exilis. This stone possessed some miraculous powers. If a phoenix landed on it, it went up in flames and was reborn to a new life. If a dying man contemplated the stone, he would not die nor lose his color within that week. If anyone contemplated the stone for two hundred years, he would only have his hair turn white, as it had the power to maintain youth and vigor. The stone was also called "the Grail." Every year on Good Friday, a dove came down from heaven and deposited on it a small wafer, which caused to appear all manner of food and drink that anyone could wish for. Besides, the Grail could call anyone to its service. On its upper edge was a mysterious inscription with the names of selected girls and boys; once a name was read out, it disappeared. The chosen ones were always young, pure adolescents. After hearing these explanations, Parzival said that he had always been brave in battle and that God should summon him in service of the Grail, so that he could prove his abilities.

Trevrizent replied that presumptuous attitudes were not allowed there, recommending that he cultivate modesty and adding that pride usually led to a fall. Then the host started to talk about the King of the Grail, Anfortas, who was in great distress as a result of his pride. Contrary to the rules of the Grail, he had let himself be seduced by a woman who had not been designated for him by the Grail, and he had suffered terribly due to this failure. Then the host reported that the Mysteries of the Grail had been preserved because to date no intruder had managed to reach the castle, so well defended by the knights. However, there had been one exception: One day a fool had appeared who had not been summoned. He had left eventually, covered in sin, because he had not even bothered to ask the king the reason for his suffering, though it was so intense and so obvious.

Next, the old man referred to a knight by the name of Lähelin, who had killed one of the knights of the Grail in a duel at a nearby lake and had seized the defeated knight's horse. Trevrizent then asked his guest if, perhaps, he was not that same Lähelin, as his mount had the same sign of the Grail.

Parzival said that he was the son of Gahmuret, who had died in combat and added that, although he was not Lähelin, he had also plundered the possessions of a dead man. Then he told the old man how, before becoming a knight, he had killed Ither and seized all his belongings. The hermit was very shaken by what he heard and spoke to the young man saying: "Dear nephew [...] You have slain your own flesh and blood." (B. IX, 242) He explained that Ither was Gahmuret's nephew, therefore his blood relative, and that such a death, in reality, could only be redeemed by his own death. Besides, Trevrizent continued, Herzeloyde had also died of grief at seeing her son leave. This was how Parzival learned of the death of his mother, and that he himself had caused this tragedy.

Then the old man enlightened Parzival about his family relationships, telling him among other things that, due to the premature death of Frimurtel, the Grail King, the eldest of his five children, Anfortas, had to take his father's place though still very young. Of the three sisters, one died while giving birth to her daughter Sigune, who was then brought up by Herzeloyde, the second sister. The third one, Repanse de Schoye, was the guardian of the Grail.

About the suffering of Anfortas, Trevrizent said it was caused by a wound in his groin: A poisoned spear had hit him during a duel which the king had fought, impelled by love. His opponent was a pagan whose aim was to gain hold of the Grail by force. Although wounded, Anfortas was able to defeat him. However, the poison of the spear was so powerful that none of the potions known at the time could heal him.

Trevrizent had then decided to give up his life as a knight and devoted himself to penance, prayer and fasting, in order to intercede with God for his brother, while the latter had to continue occupying the position of King of the Grail. As he was in the presence of the Grail, he would not be allowed to die. On the other hand, it meant no relief for his suffering; on the contrary, it was increased. Messengers had been sent to all corners of the world to bring all kinds of medicine, but none managed to diminish the king's torments.

Once, when the community begged for help kneeling before the Grail, some wording had appeared on the edge of it saying there would be a knight who, moved by compassion, would ask for the reason of the king's suffering and so ensure his healing. However, this young man could not be encouraged to ask, because then his question would have no effect and the pain would only increase. The question would also only be effective if asked on the first night.

If he were healed, Anfortas would not reign again; the youth would inherit the kingdom. In fact, after a while such a knight had appeared, but it would have been better if he had never come, for, even though he witnessed all the suffering, he postponed the question and, missing his great opportunity, he departed covered with guilt.

After a long silence, the host suggested that they seek some roots and herbs to feed the horse and themselves. After the frugal meal, Parzival filled himself with courage and said to his uncle:

> "My Lord and dear uncle, […], if shame would let me reveal it I would tell you of a sad misfortune that befell me. I beg you of your courtesy to pardon my misdeed […]. I have erred so greatly that if you assent to my being punished for it, farewell to consoling hope.
>
> "The man who rode to Munsalvaesche and saw all the marks of suffering and who nevertheless asked no Question was I, unhappy wretch! Such is my error, my lord." (B. IX, 248)

Despite the impact and pain caused by his nephew's revelation, Trevrizent said that God had not abandoned Parzival, for he, Trevrizent himself, would be the mediator of divine counsel. The fact that Parzival had reached the Grail Castle undisturbed by guards and having survived so much hardship for so long, was certainly due to God's intervention.

Parzival stayed with his uncle for a fortnight. In addition to giving him some explanations, Trevrizent encouraged him to do penance and face the future. At the time of parting, Trevrizent said: "Give me your sins [...], I shall vouch for your penitence before God. And do as I have instructed you: Let nothing daunt you in this endeavor." (B. IX, 255)

※ ※

(Here Wolfram once more interrupts the story of Parzival and continues with the story of Gawain.)

A year had gone by, and in the meantime the true murderer of king Vergulacht's father was discovered, and Gawain was declared innocent.

One morning, riding through a lush green plain, he saw, under a linden tree, a woman holding a badly injured knight in her arms. She asked Gawain for help and the latter managed to revive the knight through some treatment of his own. The knight thanked him profusely and asked whether Gawain also wished to prove his knightly worth in Logroys, though he discouraged him, saying that he himself, on getting too close to the city, had had to fight with Lischoys Gwellius and had received his wounds as a consequence. He said that the fights were to the death. Gawain dressed the knight's wound, then mounted his horse and went to Logroys.

Soon he sighted a magnificent castle, and, riding toward it, he came across a beautiful lady by a fountain. He was enraptured by the maiden's beauty. She was Orgeluse of Logroys. Gawain greeted her kindly, proclaiming that he would like to remain in her company, to which she answered that it would be best if he turned away, as the desire to be close to her would cost him dearly. Besides, there was no place for him in her heart. He need not perform chivalrous deeds and expect any reward, as there would only be dishonor there. Even so, Gawain wanted to put himself at Orgeluse's service to obtain her love. She reiterated that he would face only difficult situations which would result in disgrace. As he kept insisting, she asked him to proceed on foot to get her horse for her: It was tied up in a not-too-distant orchard, where he would meet people singing and dancing, but he should go directly to the horse and bring it back. She pledged to hold on to his horse, as there was nowhere to tie it; but when the knight gave her the reins, she said with much disdain that she would not touch them where he had held them.

The noble hero left and soon found the orchard, where ladies and young knights danced happily. When they saw him coming they lamented his situation with great sadness, saying to one another that Orgeluse's love, false as she was, would land the youth in great trouble and that it would have been better had he not heeded her. However, he moved on to where the horse was. Beside it there was an old knight who burst into tears when he saw Gawain approaching and said:

> "If you are open to advice you will let this palfrey be.
> However, nobody here will stand in your way. Yet if you have
> always done what is wisest you will leave this horse alone. A
> curse on My Lady for this way she has of causing so many
> fine men to lose their lives!" (Seeing that Gawain would not
> give up, he continued:) "May He Whose hand made the sea
> all briny succour you in your need! Take care lest My Lady's
> beauty make a mock of you, for with her sweetness goes much
> sourness, as in a hailstorm lit by sunshine." (B. X, 514)

After saying goodbye, Gawain returned to the lady of his heart. He expected to be received more favorably, but she tried to dissuade him from his wish to serve her. When he wanted to help her mount, she refused his help and jumped up into the saddle. She ordered him to ride ahead. Going through a flowery meadow, Gawain spotted a plant whose roots' therapeutic power was known to him. He dismounted and dug up the plant. Orgeluse never stopped mocking him, saying that in addition to being a knight he was also a doctor, earning his living concocting drugs. He said he had come across a wounded knight and, if he met him again, this root would help him to regain his strength.

Soon they saw a squire coming toward them to convey an urgent message to his mistress. When Gawain looked at him more closely he "was struck by his monstrous appearance.—The proud squire was called Malcreatiure, and Cundrie la suziere was his comely sister." (B. X, 263) He was riding a weak horse that limped along on four legs. He impudently said some strange words to Gawain who, angered, grabbed the monstrous figure by the hair, pulling him off the saddle. Malcreatiure's hair, however, was like a hedgehog's bristles, and wounded the hands of the knight. Orgeluse did not hide her amusement at this situation.

Soon they arrived where the wounded knight lay. Gawain gave him the root, and the knight, noticing Orgeluse's presence, advised his benefactor to leave her. She was the reason that he himself had been involved in a risky fight. Then he asked Gawain to help his companion to mount her horse and then help him onto the animal's rump, so they could continue on their way. Very helpfully, the noble gentleman helped the woman to mount and before he realized what was happening, the other knight jumped onto Gawain's horse, galloping away with the woman. Once again Orgeluse was very much amused, laughing heartily as she said:

> "I took you for a knight. Soon after, you turned surgeon. And now you are reduced to footman. [...] Do you still desire my love?" (B. X, 523)

dy sent her squire to perform a task and he went on foot. Gawain examined the squire's mount, but it proved too weak to carry him. Nothing remained but to follow on foot, once more becoming the target of Orgeluse's jesting. Finally they came to an uninhabited region, where they saw a splendid castle such as had never been seen before.

Gawain noticed about four hundred ladies on the ramparts. The road leading toward it was wide and took him to a wide river along a meadow, where jousts took place. The castle stood on the opposite bank of the river.

The noble gentleman noticed that a rider was coming toward them. Orgeluse warned him that this was an opponent to be confronted in single combat, and that she would bet on Gawain's defeat in front of all the ladies of the castle. Then she called a boatman and entered his boat with her horse, ordering him to take her to the other side. She forbade Gawain to accompany her. He even asked when he would see her again, to which she replied that this would only be possible if he came out a winner of the contest. Then she left. The knight Lischoys Gwellius was already approaching at a fierce gallop, but Gawain, even though he was now mounted on Malcreatiure's poor horse, managed to throw him in an intense clash. Both drew their swords and fought fiercely. Finally, Gawain managed to strike down his opponent and demanded surrender. However, Lischoys had never been defeated and was not prepared to surrender. He would prefer death. Yet Gawain did not dare kill him, and Lischoys insisted on not submitting to the winner.

Gawain allowed his opponent to get up and both knights, exhausted, sat on the grass to rest. Having lost his horse, Gawain decided to take over Lischoys' mount. To his utmost surprise he recognized his own horse, which had been stolen by the wounded knight! The next moment, Lischoys, already rested, grabbed his sword and attacked Gawain. Again the fight was very fierce and again Gawain threw his opponent, who would rather die than submit to him. But Gawain did not want to kill him for no reason. It was then that the boatman, who owned the meadow, came to claim tribute: He wanted the loser's horse. The winning hero managed to convince the boatman that the mount belonged to him, and proposed that instead of the horse he take the defeated knight, which the boatman accepted. Then the boatman invited Gawain to spend the night at his house, which he accepted gladly. Even though he had won, Gawain was sad to have lost sight of the woman he loved. He was very well received and taken care of at the boatman's simple dwelling, getting his deserved rest.

The next day, when he awoke and looked out of the window, Gawain again saw the magnificent castle of the previous day and, although it was still too early, he observed many ladies on the castle ramparts. When he saw the boatman's daughter he asked her who those ladies were. Full of fear, the young woman replied that, despite knowing who they were, she had been ordered to maintain secrecy. Gawain insisted and the girl began to cry, attracting the attention of the host who was coming near. Gawain then asked the host about this matter. The boatman also begged his guest not to ask anything, because there was no way to describe the misery that reigned there. Given this response, Gawain wished to know why his question caused such embarrassment and the host replied that if the youth knew what went on in there, he would be very concerned. As the noble knight kept insisting, the boatman said:

> "I cannot help being very sorry indeed, my lord, that you insist on asking. [...] I will lend you shield, now arm yourself for battle. You are in the Terre Marveile (Enchanted Land), and the Lit Marveile (Enchanted Bed) is here. My Lord, the perils up at Schastel Marveile (Enchanted Castle) have never yet been attempted. Your life is hastening deathward! If you have known adventures before, whatever your past feats, that was child's play compared with this." (B. XI, 281–282)

Gawain replied that he would never forgive himself if he did not try to save the ladies he had heard about, and he asked his host for advice. The boatman then told him that many ladies were kept prisoners in that castle, and that all the knights who had tried to rescue them had been killed. The winner of this trial would be the new ruler of that country, and lord of all the beautiful ladies from different lands. Then he reaffirmed that Gawain had already proven his worth by defeating Lischoys. He continued his report, saying that the day before, he had ferried the knight who had killed Ither before the gates of Nantes, and that this knight had left with him five horses he had won in combat; he had asked only about the Grail. Gawain then asked if that knight had heard the facts about the castle. The host denied it, as he himself had tried to conceal it in the same way that he had just tried to hide everything from Gawain.

The young knight armed himself and took the shield offered by the boatman, as there was almost nothing left of his own shield after the fights of the previous night. The boatman told him to leave his horse with a peddler whose tent stood in front of the Schastel Marveile gate. Gawain should buy something and pledge his horse as payment. He should not enter the castle on horseback. The ladies would remain invisible to him, and the whole palace would seem empty. The dangers would begin at the precise moment when the knight entered the castle. During the trials, he should not be without the protection of the shield and sword for one moment, because just when he thought he had been through the worst, something even more intense would still be ahead. The host and his family were very sad when the young hero took his leave.

Arriving at the castle gate, Gawain saw the merchant's stall and acted in accordance with the boatman's advice. He left his mount in the peddler's care and entered the palace, whose magnificence would stun anyone. He walked through various rooms, richly ornate, but not a single soul was in sight. Through an open door he saw a room with a floor as smooth as glass, so polished that Gawain could barely stand. Here was the Lit Marveile, whose feet rested on wheels made of rubies. It slid along the floor at "swifter than the wind." (B. XI, 286) At one point, when the bed was close enough, the knight jumped onto it. It was then that the bed began to spin and slide precipitously, colliding with the walls and causing a crash like peals of thunder. Although he was lying down, Gawain had to remain alert. To protect himself from the noise, he covered himself with the shield and placed his fate in God's hand.

Suddenly the bed stopped right in the middle of the room. On the walls were five hundred catapults, which through an ingenious mechanism hurled large pebbles at the knight. Fortunately his shield was big and strong, so that this scourge did not cause much damage to the hero; only a few reached him. When the throwing of stones stopped, five hundred arrows flew at him. Even though he was protected, some pierced the shield and his mail.

Gawain thought the punishment had now ended, but a door opened and a huge man of Herculean build, ugly and terrifying, came in. In his hand he carried an enormous mace, and came up close to the bed. But Gawain sat as if nothing had happened, so the thug retreated and retired, enraged. Then, through the same door, a huge hungry lion burst into the room, the size of a horse. He threw himself onto the knight, who was alert and protected himself with the shield so that the lion's claws stuck in it. The animal wanted to pull away, but Gawain cut off one of its paws with his sword. Although wounded, the beast still attacked the young man. In a single jump it tried to throw itself onto its opponent, but the latter buried his sword in its chest. The lion staggered and fell to the floor, dead. While Gawain wondered what else could still befall him, he was stricken by extreme weakness. He lost consciousness and fell onto his shield, with his head on the lion's body.

A beautiful young woman had secretly been observing the scene and saw the bloodstained floor, the lion and the knight lying as if dead. Fearfully, she went to the wise Queen Arnive to tell her what she had seen. Very apprehensive, the queen assessed the situation and sent two young women to see if the hero was still alive. After removing his helmet, they held some sable fur in front of his nostrils and noticed that it swayed weakly, so he was still alive. They wetted his mouth and he regained consciousness. Gawain asked for someone to tend to his wounds and, in case he still had to face more trials, to fasten the helmet on his head and withdraw; but he was informed that his trials were over, and he had come out victorious! The maidens returned to Arnive and the other ladies with the news that the hero was alive.

The joy of all the women was immense. The wise old queen ordered a bed for the sick knight and brought some precious healing ointments to treat his wounds. Four maidens were told to extricate him carefully from his armor, and, if he could not walk, to put him to bed. The queen committed herself to his treatment because, were he to die from his injuries, she and her court would also be affected by this misfortune, and their survival would be a "living death." (B. XI, 29). Then she placed an herb in his mouth to cause a deep and refreshing sleep. It was night when he awoke and found himself surrounded by many ladies, who took turns in his care. They all wanted to serve him, for he was the cause of their happiness. After taking a light meal, he went back to sleep to recover.

The next day Gawain woke up feeling much better. He put on the clothes left next to his bed and went out to explore the castle. He climbed a narrow spiral staircase and came to a hall where he found a circular column, large in diameter and sparkling, which reflected the surrounding landscape. The hero stood there contemplating that wonder. Some places he seemed to recognize. Then Arnive, the queen, came in accompanied by her daughter and two granddaughters, and introduced them to Gawain, saying they were of royal descent. She scolded him for being out of bed, as his wounds were not totally healed. Although the queen's granddaughters were beautiful maidens, Gawain thought only of Orgeluse. He asked Arnive why that column was so special and what it was for. The Queen replied that it shone day and night, and one could see in it all that was going on within a six-mile radius.

Then the noble hero recognized in the column Duchess Orgeluse riding alongside another knight, who gave signs of wanting to fight. Although Queen Arnive begged Gawain not to fight because he was not fully recovered and because Orgeluse's companion was known for his bravery, he sent for his armor, to the great sorrow of the ladies, who feared the worst.

The hero was still very weak, but withstood the weight of the shield. He asked the boatman to take him across the river because his opponent was already waiting for him in the meadow. The expertise of this knight was fighting with the spear, and in his challenge he proclaimed that the winner would be he who first overthrew his opponent. He had never been thrown. The onslaught was violent, but Gawain was able to bring him down in the first clash. The horse of the losing party was given to the boatman.

Orgeluse, however, continued to humiliate Gawain, suggesting that the deeds he had accomplished must have seemed to him like simple chivalrous exercises. She also said that he should go back to the castle to be pampered by the ladies. If, on the other hand, his love was so great that he wanted to put himself at her service, he would have to face a fight with an opponent chosen by her. She also ordered that he should bring her a crown made of the branches of a certain tree. If he were successful, Orgeluse would consent to be courted by him.

Together they rode through the forest of Clinschor, past an open field, and reached a gorge. On the other side was the tree Orgeluse craved. This tree was the property of a man who had destroyed her happiness. There was no bridge across the gorge to the place where the tree was. The lady just said, "(M)ay it rest in god's hands! There will be no need to drag matters out, urge your mount to one spirited leap from here and you are over *Li gweiz prelljus* (the perilous ford)." (B. XII, 302–303)

Approaching the gorge, Gawain heard the roaring of a waterfall whose waters had dug a deep path among the rocks. He spurred his mount to take the great leap, an impractical feat. Seeing him jump, Orgeluse burst into tears, for both horse and rider fell into the gorge.

However, Gawain managed to cling to the branch of a tree, and emerging from the waters, grabbed his spear and succeeded in reaching the shore. The horse was fighting against the current, and at a point where it was weaker the hero, making a huge effort, was able to rescue it. Gawain went up to the tree and took the coveted branch, when a handsome knight appeared in front of him. It was King Gramoflanz, to whom the tree belonged. He was very proud and would only fight two opponents simultaneously. To fight only the knight who had affronted him would not bring him honor. Nor did Gawain feel honored to face him in that particular situation, for he was unarmed.

Noticing the intruder's shield full of holes, the king concluded that he was the knight who had been victorious in the trials of Schastel Marveile. He told Gawain that he had been in love with Orgeluse and had killed her lover and kidnapped her. She had not forgiven him, continuing to be hostile toward him. He knew that she had been the one who had seduced the stranger and sent him so that the two of them would meet in life-or-death combat.

Gramoflanz revealed that he was in love with another woman, but his amorous aspirations depended on the unknown winner of the trials, the new ruler of Terre Marveile, where his beloved was. He asked the intruder to take a small ring to his beloved as proof of his love. He then said that there was only one man in the world with whom he would fight in single combat: It was the father of the man who had killed his own father. This man was Gawain, son of King Lot and nephew of King Arthur, whose deeds were widely recognized by all. Gawain then revealed who he was, and discovered that Gramoflanz's heart longed for his sister Itonje.

They agreed that the duel would take place within sixteen days before a select audience. Gawain should, therefore, send messengers to King Arthur asking him to come with all his entourage. Gramoflanz offered to teach Gawain another way to cross the river by the only existing bridge, but he preferred to return through the Wild Crossing. This time the horse crossed without major problems, and both reached the other side safely.

Orgeluse came up to Gawain and confessed her love, to which he replied that he did not believe her words because, until then, she had doubted his honor as a knight; however, he would willingly forget everything, provided she promised never to underestimate any knight. He also said that he would prefer to renounce his love rather than continuing to be humiliated by her. Crying bitterly, Orgeluse then told him her story, hoping to be forgiven. Her beloved Cidegast, a pure and noble knight, had been killed by Gramoflanz. The offenses directed at Gawain were part of the tests he had to face to prove his love for her. She had brought him there to take revenge on Gramoflanz, who had caused her so much grief. Gawain then told her of the arranged duel in which he intended to punish Gramoflanz, and he forgave Orgeluse.

Together they returned to Schastel Marveile. As she was still weeping, the happy knight asked her the reason for such sorrow. She replied that, with her heart deeply wounded by the death of her beloved, she had tried by all means possible to seek revenge on that proud king. To see him dead, she had even accepted the services of another king, who owned some strange and valuable objects; his name was Anfortas. While he was in her service he had been struck by misfortune, and therefore she had fallen into deep despair. She had been so distraught that, to be left in peace by Clinschor, she had given him all the treasures Anfortas had given her, on condition that she could give her hand in marriage to the winner of the trials of Schastel Marveile. If the winner refused her, the gifts would again return to her. Yet, as Gawain had forgiven her, these gifts would belong to them both.

Orgeluse also said that Clinschor was initiated in black magic and, thanks to his hidden powers, could subjugate both men and women. To maintain his good reputation, he allowed her knights to compete in his territory (Terre Marveile). She had managed to find many brave knights who had put themselves at her service to fight Gramoflanz, but so far none had succeeded in defeating him. In fact, any man who saw her would immediately desire to serve her, except for one. This warrior wore red armor, and as soon as he arrived in Logroys he had caused trouble for her knights. Five of them, sent after him, were defeated in the boatman's meadow, and their horses were given to the boatman.

Then Orgeluse went out to meet him and offered him her kingdom and her hand in marriage; however, the warrior replied that he preferred to be faithful to his wife, who was much more beautiful than she. Offended, she wanted to know who his wife was, and received the following answer: "She whose looks are so radiant is called the Queen of

Belrepeire. My own name is Parzival. I do not want your love: The Gral bids me seek other troubles." (B. XII, 310) Then he left.

When Gawain and Orgeluse were close to the castle he had won in combat the day before, they saw a large number of knights carrying magnificent banners, moving toward the gate in great haste. They seemed to be preparing for a confrontation, but the duchess explained that it was Clinschor's army, awaiting the hero's arrival to give him a warm welcome. Meanwhile, the boatman arrived to take them across the river and soon they entered the palace, where they were warmly welcomed by the knights and ladies of Schastel Marveile. Queen Arnive, helped by some of her ladies, came to treat the wounds of the hero. He wished to send a message, which was promptly done: A worthy squire was asked to go to Arthur's court and tell the king, and him alone, that Gawain asked him and all his retinue to leave for Joflanze where, in sixteen days, Gawain would have to defend his honor as a knight in fierce combat. No one else should be told the name of his lord, or the reason or destination of his trip.

After a deep and wholesome sleep, Gawain went into the great hall where Orgeluse was in the company of the four queens. He asked a damsel which of them might be Itonje, the beloved of Gramoflanz, and sat down beside her. In the conversation that followed, he delivered Gramoflanz's message: He was determined to serve her and expected to receive help and comfort from the love she might perhaps dedicate to him.

When she confirmed that she was Itonje, daughter of King Lot, Gawain said that he was willing to act as an intermediary between her and that knight, and gave her the ring sent by Gramoflanz. She blushed and confessed that she loved the king as well. She had stayed with Orgeluse and the other knights in obedience to them, but she hated them deeply, for as they served the duchess, they had been complicit in the attempt to kill her loved one. Gawain withheld from her the fact that they were siblings. During the dinner that followed, all the ladies and knights imprisoned in the castle by Clinschor met for the first time.

One day Gawain wished to talk to Arnive. They sat in a bay window from where they could watch the river. The noble knight asked the wise queen to reveal the miraculous deeds related to the castle and the reason Clinschor had devised all his magic. He remembered to thank the queen for the care he had received, saying that he owed her his life.

Arnive told him that the spells encountered in Schastel Marveile were rather simple when compared to some in other parts of the world. Clinschor had been born in Terre de Labur and was descended from a family that dealt in magic. He ruled in Capua, near Naples, where he was well known. He once seduced Iblis, the wife of the king of Sicily, who avenged himself by emasculating her lover in one stroke. Full of hatred as he could no longer enjoy the pleasures of the body, Clinschor decided to learn black magic. He hated all people and enjoyed destroying their happiness; in fact, this was his primary pleasure. He had seized a cliff and the surrounding land in an eight-mile radius, spreading fear and terror until the king who owned the land, the father of Gramoflanz, gave it to Clinschor as a gift. There he built the Schastel Marveile. He then publicly announced that whoever could succeed in the trials of the Enchanted Castle would become owner of the castle and the adjacent lands, and would never be harassed by the magician.

Arnive then revealed that all the prisoners of the palace, the ladies and knights, were now subjects of the winner, and asked Gawain to free them and allow them to return to their pagan lands. She added that in the past she and her daughter had been queens, and that since their imprisonment they had been unhappy, waiting for the day of liberation. The noble Gawain assured her that soon she would again know happiness.

Through the window they now saw a large army approaching, spreading out across the meadow. Gawain rejoiced when he recognized Arthur, the uncle who had raised him. He had come to give him support in the fight which would take place in a few days. But Queen Arnive was also very surprised when she recognized the heraldic symbols of the

Britons, as she had once been the queen of the Britons. In fact, she was King Arthur's mother.

Much to the surprise of the inhabitants of Schastel Marveile, the foreign army pitched their tents in the meadow. On the journey there they had had to face the local army of Logroys, but Gawain had told these men to help only if the castle were attacked. The next day Arthur's army continued their journey to Joflanze, and Gawain made sure that his councilors followed and found a place where he could pitch camp. In the afternoon he went there, accompanied by his subjects. To reach their destination, they had to pass through the ranks of Arthur's army. Before his tent they stopped their mounts, and Gawain was happily received by Arthur and Guinevere. The king also invited his traveling companions to enter the tent, asking him to introduce them. Great was the amazement and joy when Gawain presented to Arthur his own mother, Arnive, her sister, and two of his nieces (Sangive, Gawain's mother, and his two sisters). The next morning Orgeluse's army arrived as well, so that the plain was filled with tents, and all, ladies and gentlemen, looked forward to the imminent combat.

On the morning of the appointed day, when all were still asleep, Gawain decided to try on his armor to make sure that his wounds were sufficiently healed for him to be able to use it without fear. Then he asked his squire to prepare his mount, for he intended to do some preparatory exercises. It was then he saw a knight who carried a branch from Gramoflanz's tree. Gawain thought that Gramoflanz was already there in person, and considered it shameful that his opponent had arrived before all the ladies and gentlemen who had come to watch the fight.

So it was that before daybreak, a fierce battle took place. Both knights proved greatly worthy in the use of their weapons. When the horses fell exhausted under their weight, the combatants drew their swords, and soon the ground was covered in shield shrapnel. There was no one to intervene as there were only the two of them. At that point King Arthur's messengers came to the site and were dismayed by what they saw, as Gawain was almost succumbing to his opponent's blows. Had it not been for their interference, he would have been defeated. On recognizing him they called his name, and on hearing that, his opponent threw away his sword, exclaiming:

> "Accurst and contemptible! [...] fortune must have abandoned me for this infamous hand of mine ever to have known this battle—how grossly it has blundered! I accept the blame. Misfortune has come out and parted me from Fortune, and so I display my old blazon again, as so often in the past! To think that I have been attacking noble Gawain here! So doing, I have vanquished myself and waited for Misfortune, Fortune having fled from me the instant battle was joined." (B. XIV, 344)

At these words, the stunned Gawain wondered who his opponent was. He replied: "Cousin, I shall make myself known to you, at your service now and always. I am your kinsman Parzival!" Before fainting, Gawain managed to say:

> "Your hand has overcome us both. Now regret it for our sakes.
> If your heart be true, you have subdued yourself." (B. XIV, 689)

Shortly after Gawain recovered, ladies and knights started arriving to watch his fight with King Gramoflanz. When the king arrived, he learned that a violent fight had just taken place simply because the knights in question had not recognized each other to begin with. Reaching the place where the two combatants were and seeing Gawain exhausted and wounded, the King postponed the combat till the following day. Parzival, who was still prepared, proposed to fight instead of Gawain, but Gramoflanz rejected his proposal. Gawain and Parzival returned to camp so that the former could receive proper care. Soon the news spread that Parzival, of whose remarkable deeds all had heard, was among them.

He himself, however, did not wish to meet the ladies and knights, remarking that many of them had been present when he was cursed by Cundrie. He did not want to embarrass them by his presence. Nevertheless he was very well received, and all praised him. After being readmitted to the Round Table, Parzival went to Gawain, proposing to fight in his place the following day; after all, he, too, had stolen a branch from Gramoflanz's tree. But Gawain did not agree to this. When everyone retired for the night, Parzival decided to mend his armor which had been badly damaged in the fight, and left it at the foot of his bed.

Next morning, Gramoflanz, who resented having arrived late the day before and also resented another man having taken a branch off his tree, let it be known that he was prepared early for the fight. He left alone to reconnoiter the land, and was annoyed that Gawain was not in a similar hurry. In the meantime, without anyone noticing, Parzival armed himself, took a strong spear and went to the battlefield where the king was waiting expectantly. Without exchanging a word, they started to fight. It was an extremely violent fight. Meanwhile, Gawain was also preparing for combat. As he and his entourage were arriving on the battlefield, they heard swords clashing. On approaching, they could see that Gramoflanz, who refused to face just a single man, seemed to be attacking many knights at once, though there was only Parzival. With the arrival of the ladies and knights the fighting was interrupted and, as the king had done the previous day, Gawain now granted him a day of rest, postponing the fight to the following day.

It was only then that Itonje, Gawain's sister and Gramoflanz's beloved, learned that the combat would be between these two knights. In desperation, she asked her grandmother, Arnive, for help, and the latter confided in Arthur, who had also won the heart of her niece. Seeing that there was true love between Itonje and Gramoflanz, King Arthur promised to prevent the fight. He then invited Gramoflanz to see him later that day, promising the visitor total security. He also planned to try to convince the Duchess Orgeluse to forget her old enmity. Gramoflanz was very happy with the invitation and prepared to meet King Arthur. Orgeluse, having fallen in love with Gawain, no longer wanted to avenge the death of Cidegast and was willing to reconcile with Gramoflanz. When the latter arrived, he was very well received, and with the due intervention of several people, total reconciliation was achieved among all the affected parties. As a result, the duel was canceled and the wedding of Gramoflanz and Itonje took place.

While happiness reigned in the camps, Parzival ached in sadness and longing for Condwiramurs. Unable to stay there any longer, he armed himself, saddled his horse and rode away at daybreak. He entered an extensive forest and came to a clearing, where he came across a foreign knight who was certainly an infidel. His armor was highly ornate with precious stones, bespeaking wealth and power. Both spurred their mounts and their clash was violent. Chips of broken spears flew through the air, but despite the impact, neither of them was thrown off; they continued to fight with swords. Soon the horses were tired out, so the knights jumped out of their saddles. Neither of them had ever faced such an intrepid opponent.

The infidel's blows were so violent that Parzival seemed to falter. Recovering his strength, he struck such a blow on his opponent's helmet that his sword, the one that had belonged to Ither, broke. The foreigner stumbled and fell to his knees but raised himself immediately. Noticing that his opponent was unarmed, he stopped fighting, because to win under the circumstances would not be honorable. He proposed a truce to allow them to recover their strength, recognizing that Parzival would have been the winner if his sword had not broken. The stranger even threw his own sword into the bush, to be on equal terms when they took up combat again.

Both sat on the grass, and the infidel asked the name and family crest of his brave opponent, as he had never faced such a fierce fight. However, Parzival refused to answer because the request seemed to him more like an offense. Then the other replied that, even at risk of being misunderstood, he would identify himself first. He said: "I am Feirefiz Angevin, with such plenitude of power that many lands pay tribute to me!" (B. XV, 371) Initially Parzival was angry, because Anjou belonged to him; however, he then remembered hearing that he had a brother on his father's side in the land of the infidels. He asked the other to uncover his head so he could see his face, promising not to touch him until he had replaced his helmet.

The foreigner asked how this same brother had been described, and Parzival answered that his skin was stained black and white. Hearing this, Feirefiz exclaimed: "I am he!" (B. XV, 372) The two heroes pulled off their helmets and all hostility between them vanished. Overjoyed at this meeting, both brothers praised each other for their courage, skill with weapons, bravery and nobility, and Feirefiz said he had undertaken this journey to meet Gahmuret, his father, who, he had heard, excelled any knight. Parzival then revealed that he had never seen his father either, for he had died in combat before his birth. The infidel was visibly saddened, lamenting the loss, but on the other hand glad to have discovered a brother; and said:

> "[…]—my father and you, and I, too were but one, though seen as three distinct entities […]. On this field you were fighting with yourself. I came riding to do battle with myself and would gladly have slain myself." (B. XV, 374)

Feirefiz had sailed in very close with his powerful fleet, and invited Parzival to join him. The latter, however, explained that not far from there, King Arthur was encamped with all his court. If his brother could leave his fleet for a couple of days, Parzival would take him to the Round Table, where Feirefiz would meet several relatives. He agreed to the proposal and soon they were on their way. Meanwhile, news of a violent fight, seen in the magic column of Schastel Marveile, reached Gawain's camp. Shortly afterward, the brothers arrived. Their weapons bore the signs of the terrible combat they had been involved in. After being disarmed, the foreign knight was the object of general curiosity because until then, no one had ever seen a person with black and white skin. Parzival immediately introduced his brother, who was very well received by all. His rich attire attracted favorable attention. King Arthur invited Feirefiz to join the Round Table, and he readily accepted. The following day there was grand feasting.

They were all gathered happily when they saw a richly dressed damsel approaching, wearing a black velvet cloak on which the Grail crest was embroidered in gold. She kept her face hidden by a thick veil. Her horse was also magnificent. Everyone was surprised and curious, wondering who she was. She was taken to King Arthur, whom she greeted warmly. Then she addressed the community in French. She asked them to disregard the punishment she thought she deserved, and asked them to listen to what she had to say. Turning to Parzival, she jumped off her mount and knelt down weeping in front of him. She begged him not to deny her his welcome and to forgive her. Arthur and Feirefiz gave him all their support, and Parzival forgave her unreservedly. Then the lady, whose appearance denoted great nobility, stood up, tore the veil that covered her face and threw it on the ground. They all recognized Cundrie, becoming even more surprised that she wore the Grail crest.

> For she still had the same features which so many men and women had seen approach the Plimizoel. You have heard her visage described to you. Her eyes were still as they used to be—yellow as topaz; her teeth long; her mouth bluish like a violet. Except that she hoped for praise, she need not have worn that expensive hat on the meadow beside the Plimizoel, for the sun would have done her no harm—its treacherous rays could never have tanned her skin through her hair! (B. XV, 387) [...] She began her speech at once in these terms. "O happy you, son of Gahmuret! God is about to manifest His Grace in you! I mean the man who Herzeloyde bore [...]. Now be modest and yet rejoice! O happy man, for your high gains, you coronel of man's felicity.
>
> "The Inscription has been read: You are to be Lord of the Gral! Your wife Condwiramurs and your son Loheragrin have both been assigned there with you. When you left the land of Brobarz she had conceived two sons. For his part, Kardeiz will

have enough there in Brobarz. Had you known no other good fortune than that your truthful lips are now to address noble, gentle King Anfortas and with your Question banish his agony and heal him, who could equal you in bliss?" (B. XV, 387)

Then she advised him not to commit excesses so as not to run the risk of being excluded from the community, for the Grail does not tolerate people who are not authentic. Parzival was elated with happiness and asked how he could reach Munsalvaesche. Cundrie replied that he could choose just one man to accompany him and that she herself would lead them there. Parzival asked Feirefiz to accompany him, and he promptly agreed. Before they left, the heathen nobleman sent messengers to his ships, because he wanted to reward all who were there, from the most noble to the minstrels, by giving them some of his rich treasures.

As Cundrie was leading them, they arrived at the Grail Castle quite easily and were received with great honors. Parzival and Feirefiz disarmed and went immediately to the room of King Anfortas, who was suffering from terrible pain. Even so, he received them amiably. Then he asked Parzival to urge the ladies and gentlemen of the castle to give their consent for death to relieve him of his suffering. To achieve this he need only to be deprived of the vision of the Grail for "seven nights and eight days." (B. XVI, 394) Parzival asked where he could find the Grail. Kneeling before it, he prayed for help for the sick king. He then stood up and asked solemnly: "Uncle, what ails you?" (B. XVI, 394) Anfortas' wound healed immediately and his face regained life and brightness. He had fully recovered.

As the message in the stone indicated that Parzival would be the new king of the Grail, he was soon invested with this role, and Condwiramurs was advised that her grief would soon be over. She went to Munsalvaesche accompanied by a large entourage. She camped in the same forest clearing where, years ago, Parzival had been oblivious to the world while contemplating the three drops of blood in the snow. With a small number of knights the new Grail King rode all night, arriving at the camp at dawn. He entered the tent of the queen, who was sleeping next to their children. The joy of reunion was immense. Some time later, Parzival informed his subjects that he had been called to succeed the King of the Grail, and would leave with his wife and Lohengrin to Munsalvaesche. His other son, Kardeiz, would be the sovereign of all their lands when he came of age.

On the way to the Grail Castle, Parzival asked his companions whether they knew where the hermitage of Sigune was. As they would ride not far from it, he decided to make a small detour to see it. Upon arriving, they found Sigune dead, in an attitude of prayer, leaning on the coffin of her beloved. Parzival ordered that her body be placed in the same coffin as Schionatulander, and then they were buried.

Late in the evening the delegation arrived at the Grail Castle, all lit up by many candles. All greeted the new queen with great joy. Later, the ritual of the Grail took place. The community was only allowed to participate on very festive occasions. When Parzival had first visited the castle, the maidens brought in a great variety of objects and food and put it all before Anfortas; this time they placed everything before Parzival and Condwiramurs. During the meal, Feirefiz was very impressed by the fact that the table was always full of food, and asked Anfortas how this was possible. Anfortas then asked if the guest had not noticed the Grail right in front of him, but the infidel answered that he could only see some green fabric which had been brought in by Repanse of Schoye, for only those who had been baptized could see the Grail.

Feirefiz was so enraptured by the beauty of Repanse of Schoye that he fell deeply in love. He wanted to marry her, which would only be possible if he accepted baptism and renounced his gods. He agreed to this and was baptized the following day, witnessed by many knights who had gathered for the occasion. The baptismal font was inclined toward the Grail and soon filled with water. As soon as he was baptized, Feirefiz could see the Grail. Then his wedding to Repanse of Schoye was celebrated.

After these ceremonies, an inscription appeared in the stone which read as follows: If a knight of the Grail were summoned to reign in a foreign country, he would have to forbid people to ask questions about his name and origin. If, despite this, the questions were still asked, he would have to leave that country immediately. After a few days, Feirefiz decided to return to his country in the East. He insisted on inviting Anfortas to accompany him, but the latter replied that he wished to lead a humble life dedicated to the Grail.

After settling in India, Repanse of Schoye gave birth to a boy who was named John. He became known as Prester John. From then on, all the kings of India were called John. Feirefiz spread Christianity in his country as he had found out about it in the Grail Castle.

Wolfram ends the story of Parzival at the apex of his life. But the story still continues, revealing that Lohengrin, Parzival's son, was called to serve the Grail and grew up to become a courageous knight. At that time reigned in Brabant, Antwerp, a noble princess who refused all suitors who came to ask her in marriage, claiming that she would only marry the man for whom God had predestined her. Her subjects were already rebellious due to this situation when Munsalvaesche sent the expected knight. He arrived riding on a swan, which confirmed that he was destined by God to marry the princess. Before the wedding ceremony, however, he spoke up so that everyone could hear him, requesting that she never ask his name and origin. Such a question would jeopardize their happiness because he would have to leave, according to the will of God. For many years they lived happily together. He reigned wisely and with great courage over Brabant and the couple had several children. One day, however, Antwerp ended up asking the fatal question, and then came the swan to take Lohengrin back to the Grail Castle.

CHAPTER 4
The Structure of *Parzival*

> This my story does not fit the principles of bookish knowledge.
> – Wolfram von Eschenbach, *Parzival* (B. I, 115)

One of the aspects that interests literary scholars is the structure, the shape of a text. In the case of Wolfram's *Parzival*, the most widely accepted edition is Karl Lachmann's edition. After researching the 13th-century manuscript classified simply as "D," which is in St. Gallen (Switzerland), I discovered that Lachmann divided the work into sixteen books. Bernd Lampe, however, based on his own research and citing other authors, disputes this division.[31]

Analyzing the initial capital letters of that manuscript, the latter authors concluded that the work consists of 24 chapters, as this is the number of initial capital letters of chapters. In his opinion, therefore, this division seems to have a more organic and flowing character. Each stanza of thirty verses begins, in sequence, with a smaller initial letter. It is not for us here to pursue such specialized details.

It is very intriguing that, regardless of the number of books or capital letters, Wolfram gave the story of Parzival an amazing structure. It is an open question whether this was deliberate or was only revealed as a result of subsequent analysis. In this chapter the sections dedicated to Gawain's adventures will not be considered. The story of Parzival does not begin with him: Wolfram reports in detail the adventures of Parzival's father, Gahmuret, including his first marriage to the black queen, Belakane and their son, Feirefiz, whose "skin was mottled black

---

31 B. Lampe, *Graalssuche und Schicksalserkenntnis*, vol. 1, Parzival.

and white." (B. I, 57)Then he reports on Gahmuret's second marriage to Herzeloyde and his death in Baghdad. (Interestingly, none of this is mentioned by Chrétien in his *Perceval*.) Parzival was born shortly after his father's death. This part (B. I and II) can be considered a kind of PROLOGUE, as it deals with the hero's *ancestors*.

Next follows the story of his CHILDHOOD (beginning of B. III). Fearing that her son might become a knight and meet the same fate as his father, Herzeloyde withdrew with him and a few servants to the forest, where she brought him up isolated from the court and the world. The child grew up in the midst of nature, very pure and naïve, learning to hunt and getting to know his surroundings. He lived in perfect harmony with his environment and never knew his name, his origin, or the code of chivalry. In this sense, one can say that he was in a state of unconscious perfection. One of the knights whom the boy met in the forest said: "God would have made you perfect if he had also distinguished you with a mind." (B. III, 124) According to Chrétien, the riders commented that the boy was "like an animal." They awoke in him the desire to leave home to become a knight, which is why his childhood ended after the meeting in the forest.

Leaving home began a new phase in Parzival's biography (middle of B. III). Ill-prepared to face the world, he acted and spoke exactly as his mother had taught him to before he left, and therefore caused a lot of misery wherever he went. The first such event was his mother's death, which occurred as she watched him leave; then Jeschute's misery, followed by Ither's treacherous death. This period can be called Parzival's YOUTH.

Parzival acted impulsively and had no defined goals. He let himself be carried along by his horse and just wanted to satisfy his own selfish wishes. The result was an accumulation of unconscious guilt though he thought that he was acting properly, according to his mother's instructions.

Next came the LEARNING phase, when Parzival received from the old knight Gurnemanz all the necessary lessons to become a citizen of the world and a brave knight, worthy and noble. He acquired good habits and began to develop his mind (toward the end of B. III). This *social education* directed toward the *outer world* was completed by Condwiramurs, his wife, with whom he learned about affection and love between two people of opposite sex, which also meant home and family. The story could have ended here, as he had already achieved what he had set out for: to become a knight, prove his worth, and win a wife. (B. IV) Although he was living happily with Condwiramurs, he went away to "find out how his mother was faring." (B. IV, 223).Without knowing how exactly, he arrived at the Grail Castle, where, strictly following Gurnemanz's instructions, he failed to ask the question that would have healed King Anfortas. He did not immediately realize his mistake and was surprised to find the castle empty on waking the following morning. Nor did he understand the reason that he was insulted by a servant who almost made him fall off the drawbridge when he was leaving the Grail Castle.

When he met his cousin Sigune again, she asked him about the question he should have asked. Discovering that he had not asked it, Sigune at first told him off and then refused to teach him anything else. Parzival still could not figure out what had really happened, and most certainly this disturbed him. The culmination of this situation came with the curse of Cundrie, immediately after he had been accepted to Arthur's Round Table. So Parzival was in great *doubt*, going through a CRISIS period during which he almost lost faith in God and denied him his service (B. V and VI). His doubts only cleared much later (B. IX).

When the narrative returns to Parzival (earlier in B. IX) he had a new encounter with his cousin Sigune, who noticed that during that time span he had matured considerably due to intense suffering. (A little later, Parzival would discover from the hermit, Trevrizent, that he had been wandering through the woods for "five years, six months and three days" (B. IX, 460) since he had defeated Duke Orilus. This event had occurred shortly after he left the Grail Castle.) What happened to the hero during that phase, of which we only know superficially that he became involved in many struggles and fights? It was, in fact, a time of isolation. He rode alone in the woods, always lost, relentlessly trying to find the Grail Castle. All this suffering had the effect of greatly increasing his LEARNING. However, contrary to his gentlemanly education oriented toward the outer world, this second learning was totally turned *inward*. He underwent a *self-education* process and was preparing himself to receive further necessary help.

It has not been mentioned so far that, as Parzival became aware of his mistakes, he tried to compensate for them whenever an opportunity arose, thus redeeming himself. On reaching the hermitage of Trevrizent (B. IX), he still did not know of the death of his mother, nor was he fully aware of his failure in the Grail Castle. Besides, he was unaware that Ither, the knight he had killed in cowardly fashion and whose horse, armor and other belongings he had taken, was his cousin on his father's side. Trevrizent informed him of all these facts, giving him plenty of advice and explanation, and when Parzival departed, Trevrizent took upon himself Parzival's sins before God. It can be assumed, however, that this was due to the death of Herzeloyde and the error committed before Anfortas, both of whom were siblings of the hermit.

There remained one last fault which could only be redeemed by someone with ties of consanguinity with the victim, that is, with Ither. When Parzival's sword broke in his fight with Feirefiz, his half-brother (B. XV, 744) could have killed him. But being merciful and even recognizing Parzival as the winner was evidence enough of forgiveness (even if it was unconscious), as Ither was a cousin of both knights. This fight was not revenge for a crime committed, but real forgiveness. This phase in Parzival's life can be called PURIFICATION, for *he had all his other sins forgiven*. Next comes the stage of REALIZATION: Parzival now longed to rediscover the Grail Castle and put himself at King Anfortas' service. (B. XV, 778)

Having gone through a long path of self-education and finally achieving purification and freeing himself of any guilt, he regained *perfection*, but now *consciously*. So he was summoned "to become the King of the Grail." Through performing in complete freedom an act of selfless love that would not bring him any other benefit, he healed Anfortas.

The work ends (toward the end of B. XVI) with the story of the birth of Parzival's nephew, the son of Feirefiz and Repanse of Schoye known as Prester John, a name which was "successively given to all Kings of India." (B. XVI, 822) In that country Feirefiz disseminated Christianity along the lines of the Grail. The text also describes the mission of the Grail knight, Lohengrin—son of Parzival—in Brabant. In an analogy with the prologue, the EPILOGUE deals with Parzival's *descendants*.

The chart below illustrates the above. The interdependence of different phases can be recognized, i.e., the sequence of events has an intimate connection. More surprising, however, is the correspondence between the right and left stages of the chart.

PROLOGUE
(ancestors)

EPILOGUE
(descendants)

1. CHILDHOOD
(unconscious perfection)

7. REALIZATION
(conscious perfection)

2. YOUTH
(accumulation of guilt)

6. PURIFICATION
(forgiveness of sins)

3. LEARNING
(external, social education)

5. LEARNING
(inner, self-education)

4. CRISIS
(confusion, doubt)

- While the PROLOGUE (quite extensive, in fact) is about the ancestors and Parzival's half-brother, the EPILOGUE reports in a nutshell what happens to the children of Parzival and Feirefiz, the descendants.
- In CHILDHOOD there is the description of the child that lives in full harmony with nature, but without any knowledge. It lives, in fact, in a state of unconscious perfection. In the corresponding phase, REALIZATION, Parzival reached conscious perfection.
- The hero's YOUTH is marked by an accumulation of guilt (one episode is even from a later phase). In the stage of PURIFICATION his remaining sins are forgiven. Some of them he was not even aware of. This forgiveness is only possible thanks to the intervention of others (Trevrizent and Feirefiz).
- Then there are two stages of LEARNING: The first refers to the social education, focused on the outer world, in which Parzival received the help of Gurnemanz and Condwiramurs. Mirroring it there is the phase of self-education which takes place entirely within, in Parzival's inner self, as he rides alone, isolated from the world by his own volition. The author does not mention anything concrete about this phase; the consequences, however, are evident.
- Finally there is the CRISIS, the only phase that has no parallel. It represents the turning point in the trajectory of Parzival. However, it is a phase full of doubts about his own destiny, about what he was taught, even in relation to God. Whenever there are doubts there are at least two paths to follow, i.e., the evident duplicity in the previously described phases is implied in this singular stage.

CHAPTER 5

Important Encounters and Events in the Life of Parzival

> "Yet kindly bear with me while I tell you (God) is innocent.
> God has not abandoned you. He advises you through me."
> – Wolfram von Eschenbach, *Parzival* (B. IX, 489)

Another way to analyze the life of Parzival is to take into account the events and decisive encounters in his life. Notably, when Parzival makes a mistake, he later has the opportunity to compensate for this failure in some way. There is almost always a resolution. When this does not occur, another person helps him to make amends. In other situations, the encounters determine some kind of development in the hero, or else take him toward a certain goal, or divert him from it. Parzival meets Sigune four times. Each encounter will be addressed separately. The figure of Cundrie and the meeting with Trevrizent will also be analyzed separately in more detail.

Summary of the Encounters

As a rule, the first major encounter one has is with one's mother. Parzival was no exception. The importance of *Herzeloyde* in his life was to isolate him from the world for fear that he might meet the same fate as his father Gahmuret, who died in knightly combat. Herzeloyde went to live with Parzival and a few servants in the forest where he was brought up away from court and society, without finding out anything about knighthood. Keeping him in extreme naïveté, she kept him from his destiny, which was to become a knight. At first, this maternal attitude seems to be totally selfish and repressive. It is possible, though, to see something positive in it. In the theory of Waldorf education, founded by Rudolf Steiner in 1919, all learning takes place at the expense of vital forces. Indeed, by keeping Parzival away from society for so long, leading an absolutely natural life, Herzeloyde gave him the opportunity not to spend certain forces he would have otherwise used up in a so-called normal life of academic learning.

It is during the early years that the basic attitudes of the human being are established, as they will remain throughout life. A young man can easily adapt to new living conditions, but his attitude to life is the one he developed in his early years. In the case of Parzival, the consequence of his upbringing was that he became a stranger in his time. Even though he adapted to the social rules, in his heart, in a certain way, he was always a stranger. This favored him, for example, during the period in which he wandered alone in the forest for many years, a situation in which many others would have succumbed. The deepest feeling of a person who is a "stranger in his time" is loneliness. Nowadays one can see that almost everyone considers him- or herself misunderstood, suffering to a greater or lesser extent from this inner loneliness, even when surrounded by other people. However, when Parzival saw the *knights in the forest,* he was so impressed that he immediately wanted to become a knight of King Arthur. This encounter made him return willingly, but with no preparation, to the destiny mapped out for him at birth as the son of kings.

His mother, desperate at not being able to prevent the fate of her son, died when she saw him leave. Parzival, however, was so anxious and happy to be on his way that he did not even look back when he left his home. Therefore he did not acknowledge the death of his mother, caused by his departure. Naïveté does not prevent someone from becoming "guilty without guilt," an expression which is not very easy to understand. In fact, he had provoked his mother's death, though he did not have the slightest intention of causing her any grief.

Today we usually associate guilt with the harm one inflicts on another person. In Parzival's case one cannot accept the argument that he was at fault; on the contrary, his mother could be found guilty, because in order to protect him, and for selfish reasons (to avoid another loss), she did not allow him to follow his destiny.

In his writings related to life after death,[32] Rudolf Steiner explains that, at a certain stage, a deceased person experiences in his or her soul the consequences of everything s/he did to others, be it good or bad. In other words, after death there is a period in which the soul is fully aware of all the acts (and also omissions) committed, for the soul feels the exact pain or joy caused to others. Then an immense desire arises to re-encounter the people concerned, so as to make up for the wrongdoing or allow something positive to continue. This resolution, however, can only occur in the incarnation on earth where the act was performed. This is what is called karma. Therefore, if someone is not aware of his or her own acts during life on earth, this will most certainly entail awareness in the afterlife. In any case, according to several writers, one must admit that from this moment on Parzival carried an *unconscious guilt*.

Riding aimlessly through the world, without knowledge, without any preparation except for some last-minute advice given by his mother before his departure, Parzival met a damsel sleeping in a tent. Jeschute had a ring which shone on her finger. Following his mother's advice to win the ring and the cordial greeting of a lady, he stole her ring and a kiss. As he was starving, he also devoured the meal that the noble lady had prepared for her husband, Duke Orilus. Satiated and satisfied with his achievement, Parzival did not realize that he had done anything wrong. Jeschute's life, however, was made miserable due to this episode because her husband, convinced of her infidelity, degraded her to the level of a servant. Jeschute's assertions about what had actually happened were to no avail, and Parzival carried another *unconscious guilt*.

Having obtained permission in Arthur's court to fight Ither, the Red Knight, Parzival went to meet him. When he left the hall he heard

---

32 See, among others, his works *Theosophy* and *An Outline of Esoteric Science*.

the laughter of a maiden and then the sound of a blow being struck. Lady *Cunneware* had made a promise: She would only laugh on the day she saw the greatest knight of all time. At the sight of Parzival she laughed, as she recognized this knight in him, even though he still wore the jester's garment his mother had made for him. Kai the Seneschal was so angry that she had broken her promise before this fool that he could not contain himself and hit her. Parzival, witnessing this even without knowing the reason, felt that this episode had something to do with him. He felt guilty and promised to avenge this insult. Here one could ask: Why did Parzival feel guilty? After all, this time he really had not acted incorrectly; he had done nothing wrong, but he still felt guilty. For what reason? It is true that his presence had triggered the events, and that is why he felt he had caused them. Yet, can one consider him guilty of something? Should he be blamed for the way he was, or that Cunneware recognized in him what he would become? In fact, she was the first person to believe in him, and therefore she had to suffer. This event also committed him to redemption, and Parzival left Arthur's court carrying *conscious guilt*, promising that he would not return before he had totally redeemed himself.

Next, there was the duel with *Ither*. Parzival intended to take this knight's armor, horse, and equipment. As he did not know the knight's code of honor—or any fighting rules at all—he was not aware that he was there to save the honor of the Round Table, challenged by the Red Knight. Therefore, when he told Ither that he had been sent by Arthur for that fight, he was soon thrown off the saddle by the experienced knight.

By the rules of horsemanship, he had lost the fight and was at the mercy of Ither; however, without any warning, and from the ground where he was lying, he shot a well-aimed arrow through the visor of Ither's helmet which "entered the eye, across the brain through to the nape" (B. III, 155), killing the Red Knight. Parzival did not even realize that he had committed murder. He craved the armor and the horse, and soon tried to extricate the dead knight from his gear to take possession of it. The death of that person had, for him, the same meaning as killing the animals he hunted in ambush in the forest of Soltane, and therefore he did not regret it. On the contrary, it seemed absolutely normal to him. So he added another *unconscious guilt* to his burden.

Parzival finally met an elderly knight, Gurnemanz, who taught him everything he should have learned before leaving for the world: various combat skills, the moral and ethical codes of knighthood—in short, how to become a knight. After this learning his master dubbed him a knight. He was now prepared to enter society and the world. Although Gurnemanz offered his daughter in marriage, which would probably have meant the end of Parzival's journey, the latter decided to leave his master's castle to prove his worth in accomplishing some deeds. Once again he did not perceive that, on abandoning Gurnemanz, he was hurting someone to whom he owed so much.

On offering his help to the Queen of Pelrapeire, Parzival had to confront *Kingrun*, the commander of the army of Clamide, the king who was besieging the city after having been refused by Condwiramurs. Parzival won this battle, and following the teachings of Gurnemanz by being merciful, he spared Kingrun's life. However, he sent him to Arthur's court to serve the maiden Cunneware. In this way he was trying to compensate for the outrage suffered by the lady, toward whom he felt guilty. It seems this was an attempt to *redeem himself of this conscious guilt*.

In return for this deed, Queen *Condwiramurs* offered him her hand, and in a few days the wedding was celebrated. So Parzival received an education in affection, for he had never known this kind of relationship between man and woman. When he was born his mother was already a widow and had isolated herself with him in the forest. Still, King *Clamide* was not satisfied and challenged Parzival to a duel. He came out victorious again, and sent the defeated knight to Arthur's court to serve Cunneware. This is another attempt to *redeem conscious guilt*. On the other hand, though, Parzival was not aware of Clamide's suffering at having his love rejected, besides believing his beloved woman lost forever.

Parzival could have stopped here and his life story would have ended with fame, honor and a wife, as was the case in the story of almost every other knight. However, following an urge to know how his mother was faring, Parzival went on his way again, with the permission of his wife.

Looking for a place to spend the night, he came to Munsalvaesche, the Grail Castle in Terre Salvaesche, where he was the guest of King Anfortas, who was ill and suffering great pain. During his stay in the castle, Parzival witnessed strange rituals. He noticed the people's great expectations of him, and had the desire to ask questions to find out "why this community of knights was so special" (B. V, 239), but he refrained from asking, remembering Gurnemanz's teachings. However, this was precisely Parzival's task on his first visit to the Grail Castle: Seeing the king's great suffering, he should have asked him what his suffering was, and the king would have been healed. Anfortas even offered him the Grail sword "to stimulate him to ask the question" (B. V, 240), but Parzival remained silent. Thus he loaded another *unconscious guilt* onto himself, becoming once again "guilty without guilt."

Again one must question whether he really committed an error, as he was faithfully following the instructions he had received, namely not to ask unnecessary questions. The question here, however, was not unnecessary. On the contrary, it would have meant salvation. Parzival did not have enough discernment to assess the nature of the question; besides, he had not yet acquired freedom. He continued to apply all the learning he had received, but in fact he needed to become independent. This would mean breaking away from such learning, if necessary. It is precisely this breakthrough that can lead to progress.

When one always sticks to established rules, there will never be transformation, development, and evolution; however, breaking away indiscriminately from all rules also does not necessarily lead to progressive evolution but can lead to chaos, to a setback. For proper evaluation, clear discernment, and total freedom are a must, and they are something humanity as a whole is beginning to learn. How often can someone claim really to have acted in total freedom? In general people's deeds originate in feelings, impulses, and desires, often determined by sense perceptions. On the other hand, every fully competent adult is responsible for his or her actions and, even if acting unconsciously, bears the consequences. That is, freedom, responsibility, and selfless love are connected. An example of this liability linked to selfless love is beautifully described by Antoine de Saint-Exupéry in his book *The Little Prince*: When he leaves his planet he feels responsible for the flower he loves. To act freely means to recognize the possibility of realizing two or more distinct actions at any time and, based on conscious reflection and considering the possible consequences of each action, to choose the most appropriate. To act freely one first has to achieve free thinking, and it is only in freedom of thought that the human being of the present time is free to reach truth.[33] In other words, a person is free not when he or she follows any wish (blindly following an unconscious impulse or any set rule) but when he or she consciously does what is necessary in any given situation. According to Rudolf Steiner, an action is free when it is exclusively an act of love for the action,[34] as Parzival experiences during his second visit to the Grail. To get there, he still had much to learn and develop.

In any case, consciously or unconsciously, Parzival was responsible for all the people he had made to suffer during his journey, being part of their fate. Actually, until that moment he had not yet experienced suffering. In his naïveté he was always happy. All he wanted, he had obtained without any effort. Whoever knows nothing about suffering

---

33 For more details see R. Steiner, *The Philosophy of Freedom (Intuitive Thinking as a Spiritual Path)*.
34 R. Steiner, *Knowledge of the Higher Worlds: How Is It Attained?*

cannot be compassionate. After all, to sympathize means to suffer with the other, endure together; and the hero had not yet completed his evolution and was still in the learning process. Riding alone and lost after leaving the Grail Castle, Parzival encountered Jeschute in rags, mounted on a thin and limping horse. Becoming aware of the consequences of his foolish attitude, he challenged Duke Orilus to combat. After defeating his opponent, he returned the stolen ring and demanded reconciliation (after swearing that Jeschute was innocent). Then he sent them both to Arthur's court to serve Cunneware. Restoring Jeschute's honor, he consciously *redeemed himself completely of the guilt* that he had taken on unconsciously when he was an inexperienced fool, and he continued to strive to compensate for the *feeling of guilt* he felt toward Cunneware.

During the episode of the three drops of blood in the snow—when he was bewitched by them, in a state similar to ecstasy or trance, i.e., unaware of what was happening around him—Parzival confronted three knights. The first, Segramors, had no influence on his journey. The second was *Kai*, King Arthur's Seneschal, who had beaten the maiden Cunneware. Even mesmerized by the three drops of blood in the snow, Parzival struck him, winning the fight. However, he did not notice what he had done, turning immediately back to the blood in the snow, dreaming of his beloved wife. What draws one's attention in this episode is that the only fault that Parzival *consciously assumed was redeemed when he was in a state of unconsciousness*. So he managed to rid himself completely of that guilt, and never again would he send defeated knights to serve Cunneware.

The third knight, *Gawain*, managed to release Parzival from his state of trance by covering up the drops of blood. The great importance of this is that Gawain helped Parzival, who was not yet free of his desires, to give up cherished images and have a life of feelings without losing his own identity, that is, without being overruled by his feelings. Now, in a way, Parzival had an obligation toward Gawain. He refused to accompany his liberator to the court of Arthur, as he did not feel ready to go. He said he still had to avenge the offense suffered by Cunneware due to his own failure; but Gawain then made Parzival aware that he had in fact defeated Kai, and so they both went to the Round Table.

Parzival's aspiration on leaving his mother's house, to become one of Arthur's knights, was now near fulfillment. If this had indeed happened he would never have returned to the Grail Castle; but he had been predestined to become a server of the Grail and not a knight of the Round Table. Therefore, during the ceremony that would seal his admission to that select group of knights—which might really mean the end of the story—*Cundrie*, a messenger of the Grail, appeared. After telling him who his father was, and that Feirefiz was his stepbrother, she cursed him for not asking the question that would have saved King Anfortas. Only then did he become aware of his guilt, and he decided to live in total solitude from then on, seeking the Grail Castle, where he intended to make amends for his mistake by putting himself at Anfortas' service and, if possible, remedying the situation. It was an act of great courage to acknowledge the guilt of which Cundrie accused him (for he could have ignored her and returned to Condwiramurs) and leave behind all he had won so far: fame, honor and a wife. From that moment on, he had a new goal to reach. One can say that with her curse, Cundrie protected Parzival from becoming a knight in Arthur's court and allowed him to follow his true destiny.

Before leaving on his new quest, Parzival had the opportunity to compensate for the suffering of Clamide, whose love for Condwiramurs had been refused. This noble king, whom Parzival had sent to serve Cunneware, had meanwhile fallen in love with the latter. However, he needed Parzival's consent to marry her. Willingly, Parzival agreed.

The curse of Cundrie made Parzival turn away from God, denying Him his service, dismissing divine protection, so to speak, not believing in it or in the benevolence of God. He remained solely dependent on himself. It must also be said that to be able to consciously believe in the divinity, one must first remove oneself from it. Until then, Parzival was simply following what he had been taught, so this was the time when his self-education began.

After a long time, during which he suffered and matured, Parzival faced a *Grail knight* in life-or-death combat. He defeated the knight but lost his horse and ended up gaining the Grail horse. This indicates that he was close to the domain of the Grail, as the knights of the Grail only went out to fight when they needed to protect the castle from intruders; they were never summoned for combat. Winning the Grail horse might mean that from then on he was near the Grail Castle. After all, a horse always tends to return to its stable. But there is another symbolic explanation: In mythology and Western folklore, the horse is considered a symbol of intelligence, of thought, as all great civilizations originated with people who bred and used horses. (Pegasus, the winged horse, symbolizes the thought that flies and jumps from one subject to another.) In this context, to win a Grail horse could mean the acquisition of the type of thinking inherent to the community of the Grail.

Rudolf Meyer provides yet another interpretation: He says that the seeker will follow a spiritual direction that takes him to the path leading to the spirit.[35] Parzival would now have a greater affinity (not just by blood, something he was not aware of yet) to the people in the Grail's service. In any case, the result of this encounter indicates not just the physical vicinity but also Parzival's mental and spiritual nearness to the Kingdom of the Grail.

The importance of the meeting with the penitent knight *Kahenis* and his family on Good Friday was a rapprochement with God. That the knight reprimands Parzival for wearing armor on that day calls attention to this fact. "Being armed" could mean being on the defensive, indifferent to divine revelations or a reunion with God. Indeed, the words of the knight touched Parzival's heart, causing a change in attitude. He had been through so much hardship and suffering that his pride and arrogance were already at least partially mitigated. Then he let go the reins of his horse, challenging God to make his mount take him where he could receive help, as proof of divine grace. Meyer

---

35   R. Meyer, *Der Gral und seine Hüter*.

interprets this by saying that the young knight had consciously given up continuing the search, assuming an attitude of serenity. He trusted his horse to follow the path; it was, as said before, a Grail horse.

Until then Parzival had not surrendered to the hidden wisdom which operated in the animal. In fact, the horse took him to the hermitage of *Trevrizent*, who had been a knight of the Grail; but when his brother Anfortas was wounded for letting himself be seduced by a woman, Trevrizent decided to make up for this deed. He abandoned his knightly activities, the joys of life, to become a hermit. In reality, he had no vocation to become a hermit, but had sought this life of renunciation, selflessness, and meditation only to try to help the Grail King. In this isolation he was able to develop, in addition to selfless love, great wisdom.

On entering Trevrizent's cave Parzival took off his armor, that is, from then on he was "unarmed," open to teachings about God. Thus, through his host Parzival not only received help and advice, subsequently returning to God, but even became *fully aware of all his faults* of which he was still partially or totally unaware. Only then did he find out about the death of his mother and Ither, the knight he had treacherously killed, who was his cousin on his father's side. On the other hand, the hermit said he had only managed to survive his many tribulations because he had God's protection, coming from the spiritual world. When after fifteen days Parzival took leave of Trevrizent, the latter took Parzival's guilt on himself before God. Trevrizent, the brother of Herzeloyde and Anfortas, against whom Parzival had become "*guilty without guilt*," was indeed able to forgive Parzival.

Gawain and Parzival met in combat, unaware of their identities: Gawain thought he was confronting Gramoflanz. Parzival broke up the fight, which he was winning, on discovering who his opponent was. As Parzival came out almost victorious, he was able to *extricate* himself from the power Gawain had exerted over him since the day when he liberated him from his ecstasy at the three drops of blood in the snow.

There was still the *forgiveness for the death of Ither*: Parzival won this in the fight with *Feirefiz*, his half-brother on his father's side, when, at a decisive moment in the fight, his sword broke and he was at the mercy of his opponent. Feirefiz, however, recognized the superiority of the other and saved his life. According to the teachings of Trevrizent, killing a blood relative could only be redeemed by the death of the one who had killed. As Ither was the nephew of Gahmuret, Parzival and Feirefiz had the same degree of relationship with him. So the broken sword can be interpreted as "Ither's revenge," as it was the sword Parzival used in combat (the Grail sword, a very special one, would break at the second blow—a different subject still to be dealt with). The gesture of Feirefiz was a kind of pardon, even if he did not have the knowledge of what had happened previously. In other words, a treacherous death (the victim, although armed, was taken by surprise) was forgiven by the magnanimity of the knight facing an unarmed opponent (whom he could have killed). Incidentally, if Feirefiz had killed Parzival, it would have meant more bloodshed among relatives. The fact that Parzival was forgiven, both by Trevrizent and Feirefiz, indicates that total purification is not always achieved only by one's own efforts, however great the efforts may be. The need to forgive shows that there is a need to help in others (the ones who forgive).

Free of all guilt, mature and in full consciousness, Parzival had his second encounter with Cundrie, again at the Round Table. This time she came to summon him to become the King of the Grail. She herself would lead him there, and he must take a comrade. His choice was Feirefiz.

When he arrived at the Grail Castle, Parzival at once asked to be taken into the presence of *Anfortas*. Kneeling before the Grail, he asked for help for the sick sovereign, and then he asked the question. Anfortas, healed of his suffering, arose instantly. Actually, Parzival did not know what the result would be. On the one hand, Trevrizent had told him that the King of the Grail would be cured if a young and naïve knight, moved by compassion, asked the question without being prompted to doing so. On the other hand, Cundrie, calling him to become the new King of the Grail, said that by asking the question he would heal Anfortas. Moreover, Parzival already knew the answer and Anfortas himself had asked him to have mercy and help him die: that is, not allow him to contemplate the Grail. Yet Parzival asked the question. This was an act carried out in complete freedom, imbued by true, selfless love, the fruit of the responsibility he felt toward Anfortas, knowing that he had been the cause of the continuation of the King's suffering. With this example, according to Steiner, an action can be considered free when it is taken *out of love for the action itself*, that is, when it does not come from an internal need or an unconscious impulse. After all, for Parzival himself, who had been rewarded beyond his heart's desire (not just to find the Grail but also to become King of the Grail) and had reached the pinnacle, to ask or not to ask the question would not have interfered in his further development. Yet having asked not out of curiosity, but out of true compassion and love, he exercised a healing power.

The following table summarizes the actions that led to guilt and the consequences that resulted in redemption or forgiveness:

GUILT	REDEMPTION or FORGIVENESS
Mother's death (unconscious)	Trevrizent (forgiveness)
Jeschute's misfortune (unconscious)	Combat with Orilus (redemption)
Kai hitting Cunneware (conscious)	Sending Kingrun, Clamide, Orilus (attempts at redemption), combat with Kai (unconscious redemption)
Ither's death (unconscious)	Combat with Feirefiz (forgiveness)
Clamide's sorrow (unconscious)	Clamide & Cunneware's wedding (redemption)
Not asking Anfortas the question (unconscious)	Trevrizent (forgiveness)

Once, in the first Waldorf School, founded in Stuttgart, Germany, in 1919, Rudolf Steiner visited the classroom where the teacher Walter Johannes Stein was analyzing Parzival with his students. He was asked why, in the text, some scenes were repeated (two encounters with Jeschute, two with Cundrie, two visits to the Grail Castle...), though the second time around they were more noble and pure. Steiner answered that the first time around such experiences are always ancient and, in a sense, not of much use, while the second time around these images are experienced as something new, renewed from the spiritual source, and consequently having a positive effect.[36]

Sigune

It has already been mentioned that Parzival met Sigune four times, each encounter having distinct characteristics. It is worth mentioning that in Chrétien's *Perceval* there is only one encounter, in which Sigune is holding on her lap her bridegroom who had recently died. When she asked Perceval his name, "[...] he who did not know his name suddenly knew it." It was Sigune who told the hero of his mother's death, and at Perceval's request she indicated the direction taken by the knight who had killed her bridegroom, so that his death could be avenged. Finally, seeing that he carried the sword that had been given to him by the Fisher King, she counseled him not "to trust it because it would fly into pieces!"

To understand them better, these encounters with Sigune will be taken up again as set forth in Wolfram's writing, stressing only the most important aspects.

At their first encounter, after Parzival had dishonored Jeschute, Wolfram writes that Parzival heard heart-rending weeping and, nearing the place it came from, he saw a young maid holding a dead knight on

---

36   W.J. Stein, *The Ninth Century and the Holy Grail.*

her lap. After he questioned her and offered to avenge the murderer, she asked him who he was. To her surprise, Parzival did not even know his own name. Hearing the nicknames which, according to him, his mother used to call him, Sigune recognized in him her cousin. Then she revealed his name and origin, and told him about the kingdoms that belonged to him.

When Parzival asked her about the dead knight, she said that he was her bridegroom, who had died in combat with the Duke of Orilus who wanted to take over Herzeloyde's lands, which were being defended by her lover. Parzival, realizing that the youth had actually died defending his own lands, decided to avenge him and asked in what direction Orilus had gone. Sigune, knowing Parzival's naïveté and inexperience and fearing that he would meet the same fate as her beloved, a brave and valiant knight, pointed in the wrong direction. But was it really the wrong direction? To earthly eyes it certainly was, with the intention of protecting him from certain death, but the direction she indicated would lead the youth to the court of Arthur, where Parzival had intended to go after leaving home. There he would find ways to improve himself, which really happened from the moment he arrived in Gurnemanz's castle.

A surprising fact in this encounter is the situation Parzival was in, totally different from that of his son Lohengrin, which will be told at the end of the story. Parzival did not know his name or origin, which had to be revealed to him by someone else. Lohengrin, on the other hand, had to hide his name and origin, and when asked about them, had to leave his wife and return to the Kingdom of the Grail. In Parzival's time, ancestry was very important. Yet, as his self-development progressed, his past, his origin, lost importance. All that mattered was the individual, regardless of his ancestors. Lohengrin is just such an example. When his wife asked his name and origin, she was not giving due value to his person, but going back to a time which was no longer valid and had nothing to do with him. So Lohengrin had to leave. Interestingly, the first major Wagner opera of a mythological nature was *Lohengrin*, and the last, *Parsifal*.

Parzival's second encounter with Sigune occurred shortly after he left Munsalvaesche, in search of the Grail knights who had left and whose tracks had disappeared into the forest. This time, Sigune was much changed. She had aged, withered, sitting on a tree trunk and holding the embalmed body of a knight. They did not recognize each other immediately. When Parzival asked her about the castle he had just left, she replied that within a thirty-mile radius there was no dwelling of any sort. Finally she recognized his voice, and he was saddened to see her in that state.

On discovering that Parzival had been to the Grail Castle, Sigune brightened in the expectation that he might have released Anfortas from his agony. Noticing that he was carrying the sword of the Grail, she told him about its miraculous power. She said something intriguing: This sword "supports the first blow, but breaks with the second." (B. V, 254) Then she revealed what should be done to mend it. She added that Parzival would be the luckiest person on earth if he had asked the proper question to rescue the King from his pain. When Parzival confessed that he had asked nothing, she became surly and despised him. Again he asked for directions because he wished to repent, placing himself at the service of the King of the Grail, but Sigune kept silent. Then Parzival left, lost in the forest again.

After recounting the first two episodes in the story of Gawain, Wolfram again takes up the story of Parzival, who had not yet found the Grail. Riding through the forest, he came to a clearing where there was a hermitage. He knocked on the window because the hermitage had no door, and a woman answered and he started to talk to her. Listening to the way she described certain events, Parzival recognized his cousin, who had spent her days in prayer by the embalmed body of her beloved, who lay in a coffin inside the chapel. When Parzival uncovered his face, she recognized him as well. Noticing that he had matured during his long period of suffering, she asked whether he had found the Grail Castle yet. When he said that he had not, she suggested he follow the tracks of Cundrie's horse, the Grail messenger who had just come by to bring her food.

The fourth encounter took place when Parzival, having been reunited with Condwiramurs, was returning to the Grail Castle. He came past Sigune's hermitage with his companions to tell her the good news. However, he found her dead, leaning over the coffin of her beloved as if in prayer. Parzival ordered that her body be placed in the coffin next to her beloved and be properly buried.

What is the meaning of Sigune? What does she represent?

From the description above, one can say that these encounters always occur after a very special event in Parzival's life, a turning point: after leaving his maternal home to face the outside world, after his first visit to the Grail Castle, after maturing and undergoing difficult self-development, and finally after being called to become the King of the Grail.

We may recognize that fundamentally, Sigune has two distinct functions. On the one hand she provides important information to Parzival—his name, his origin, the secret of the Grail sword—and she also assists him in his self-development. On the other hand, she points the way for him, sometimes sending him in the wrong direction, sometimes not giving him any direction at all, sometimes indicating a path even without its being requested. In a way, the wrong direction only seemed wrong to Parzival from his own point of view, because he wanted to avenge the death of Schionatulander by challenging Orilus. Sigune, however, knows that this is not his mission at that moment. The direction she indicated was crucial for the development of the future hero. When he was lost in the forest after their second encounter, he had the opportunity to undergo his process of self-development; once it was complete, Sigune was able to indicate the way to the Castle of the Grail. When he reached his goal and even exceeded expectations, as he was called to become the King of the Grail (his only intention having been to serve the wounded king), he found his cousin dead. He no longer needed information and directions. Sigune, therefore, represents his guide, his higher conscience, Parzival's higher self, guiding him always in the most suitable way for his evolution.

When describing the process of spiritual development, Rudolf Steiner said that the everyday self, which allows us to call ourselves "I" here on earth, must transcend the earthly plan in which it operates and consciously find the Higher Self and connect to it. During life on earth the Higher Self remains in the spiritual realm. It is also this Higher Self that stores our whole life plan, drawn up with the help of other spiritual beings before each person reincarnates. It acts in the unconscious, leading each person to the places where encounters or situations planned in prenatal life can occur. According to Steiner, the encounter with this Higher Self already occurs, although unconsciously, during sleep; but it is vital that one accomplishes it in full consciousness. If Sigune represents this Higher Self, then she is not an earthly being, but a supernatural, spiritual being, endowed with the infinite wisdom to provide guidance. One can say that when Parzival was called to become King of the Grail, he had the conscious encounter with his Higher Self. The Higher Self no longer needed to guide him in his life on earth (Sigune's death), for he had reached the level of development that allowed him to consciously unite within himself his everyday self and his Higher Self.

In Wolfram's fragment, *Titurel*, and in the homonymous work by Albrecht, there are more detailed descriptions of the personalities of Sigune and Schionatulander. Sigune's mother, sister of Herzeloyde, died in childbirth; so she was descended from the Grail line. Initially, her father took her to be raised by one of her uncles on her father's side, who had a young daughter, Condwiramurs. The two cousins grew up together until this uncle died. So Herzeloyde, her maternal aunt, took on her upbringing. Meanwhile, Herzeloyde had married Gahmuret, whose page, Schionatulander, came from Arthur's court and accompanied his master everywhere, having gone with him the first time Gahmuret went to the East.

Sigune and Schionatulander developed the pure love of children. The latter left to follow Gahmuret in his second trip to Baghdad, where Gahmuret died in his arms. Then Schionatulander avenged the death of the hero, killing the murderer in battle. Before returning to the West, taking with him—to give to Herzeloyde—the garments and the spearhead that had pierced Gahmuret's head, as his master had requested of him, he even made sure he was given a Christian burial. On his return, he took over the tasks of the deceased lord, including the defense of Herzeloyde's lands, as Orilus and his brother Lähelin wanted to take them away from her. Herzeloyde, however, did not receive him in Soltane after the birth of Parzival, as she did not want her son to know about the life of a knight.

Once Sigune and Schionatulander were near a forest when a dog appeared on whose collar many verses were written. The dog escaped before Sigune could read the entire text. Orilus eventually seized the animal and offered it to his wife Jeschute. To obtain the dog, Schionatulander confronted Orilus in a duel, which resulted in the former's death. Wolfram omitted all this in *Parzival*, when he introduced the dead young knight held on his bride's lap.

A very intriguing figure is that of this dead bridegroom, later embalmed, always near Sigune. Relating this figure to Parzival one can say that he had to die because he had taken on a task that, in reality, should have been Parzival's, if Parzival been educated in the outer world. On leaving his mother's house, sooner or later he would have had to confront this task, freeing Schionatulander. This is represented in his death.

As for Parzival's relationship with Sigune, one must keep in mind what was described above: The Higher Self does not act in the earthly sphere, but dwells and operates in the spiritual realm. Every human being who longs to connect with it in full consciousness must rise to the spiritual world. In Parzival's encounters with Sigune, the youth does not yet realize he is facing his Higher Self. The author seems to use a device to convey this situation: As this Higher Self is experienced unconsciously, acting from outside (or better said, from higher up), it is, so to speak, clothed in the image of his cousin Sigune, who dies when the experience becomes internalized, for then the Higher Self begins to operate in Parzival. However, even acting through Sigune, the Higher Self continues to be an entity that operates in the spiritual world, but it has the need to be anchored in the earth to be able to manifest itself. This is possible through the body of Schionatulander, which is embalmed so as not to suffer decay and remains unchanged.

The body is essentially pure earthly matter, devoid of life, soul, and spirit. It is the most earthly and physical part of the human being, and naturally decomposes at death, in accordance with physical laws, into its elements. As a representative of physical forces, it is related to the mineral kingdom, which is unchangeable and eternal. One can assume, then, that this image of Sigune, always close to Schionatulander, represents what is the most spiritual in the human being—the Higher Self, with which each person must unite in the spiritual world, together with what is physical, the physical body. Actually, so that in the course of the evolution of the earth and humanity the Self could manifest itself, the prerequisite was a mineralized physical body. Therefore, the most spiritual part of the human being, the Self, depends on the physical body. The goal of human evolution is the spiritualizing of this physical body.

To summarize, Schionatulander died when Parzival became a citizen of the physical world, and Sigune died when Parzival consciously became a citizen of the spiritual world. Actually, he consciously became a citizen of both worlds, and that is why he ordered them to be buried side by side in the same coffin, as Wolfram states.

Cundrie

Wolfram describes two encounters between Parzival and Cundrie, both of which took place in Arthur's court. The first took place shortly after Parzival was admitted to the Round Table with great joy and celebration. The complete description of Cundrie in the original (B. VI, 312–315) is quoted on pages 61–62 of this book; it includes fantastic elements merged with the wonderful qualities of this figure. The author interwove such features as the loyalty and learning[37] of this young woman with some animalistic aspects (her hair in long braids, rough, ugly, and coarse like pig bristles; her nose reminding him of a dog's snout; wild boar's teeth; hands like monkey paws, etc.) and rich clothes, silk from Ghent but of dazzling colors, a London hat, the woes that her presence would engender, the grotesque mount in its valuable harness, i.e., a mixture of very valuable things and horrendous ones.

At this encounter, Cundrie, also called "the witch," cursed the Round Table for accepting Parzival into their midst, and accused him harshly for not having asked the right question that would have freed Anfortas of his suffering. During her speech she also referred with high praise to Gahmuret and his other son, Feirefiz d'Anjou, and mentioned Herzeloyde with great respect. That is how Parzival learned of the existence of his brother, who, in Cundrie's words, presented a "singular aspect, for his skin was mottled black and white." During this encounter she seemed distraught and in despair.

The second encounter (B. XV, 778–781) began with much admiration at Cundrie's arrival. Once again her attire is mentioned,

---

37 "(...) she mastered all languages – Latin, French. She was on easy terms with such learned matters as Dialectics, Geometry and she had mastered Astronomy." The latter are three of the seven liberal arts of the Middle Ages, which were part of the intellectual and artistic education (the others were Grammar, Arithmetic, Rhetoric, and Music). There was also the education of the will through active exercises specifically performed by knights, and even the learning of techniques from craftsmen.

highlighting its wealth and fashion. She displayed the symbol of the Grail, as she was actually its messenger. Her mount and its harness were magnificent. Her face was veiled. Very polite and courteous, she first went to the king, then to Parzival, and asked everyone to intercede on her behalf so that the latter would forgive her, which then happened. Then she uncovered her face and everyone recognized her.

Wolfram reminds the reader (listener) of the ugliness of her features during the first encounter, even highlighting some features which had not been previously mentioned. These, however, were irrelevant after the auspicious news that she had come to reveal: It had been read in the Grail that Parzival had been called to be the new King of the Grail. She also reported that Condwiramurs had been called to become the Queen of the Grail, and that she had been pregnant with twins at the time Parzival left. Lohengrin, one of the sons, had been appointed to serve the Grail. The other son, Kardeiz, would receive the paternal kingdoms. Cundrie also said that even if Parzival had only come to heal Anfortas, he could still consider himself very fortunate; and she revealed that his question would cure the king.

What kind of symbolism underlies Cundrie's appearance? Some paintings by Hieronymus Bosch (c. 1450–1516) may shed light on this. Some figures are recognizably human but deformed by animal features. They are paintings of a strong surrealistic character. One must remember that animals are totally dominated by their instincts and also show fantastic wisdom. The intelligence revealed in each animal species from the moment of its birth must be deeply admired. On it depends the survival of the animal. Almost all animals, from birth or a few weeks after, are totally independent, not depending on any other being for their survival. However, this kind of physical intelligence specializes the animal in such a way that it becomes unable to act differently. Only on rare occasions is it possible to teach or, rather, train young animals, but only within their physical limitations. In contrast, the human being at birth is still a great embryo, totally dependent on other humans for survival, and only reaching full autonomy at the age of 21. Until then, s/he has the capacity not only to learn many things that depend both on the body and the creative intelligence detached from the physical element, but also to develop ways to overcome a total lack of specialization. Because human beings do not have a specialized intelligence of the body (instinct), we can develop, using our independent creative intelligence, tools or other means to compensate for our lack of physical expertise.

For example, though lacking appropriate apparatus for flying, the human being can build devices that resemble birds' wings. To swim faster, flippers come in handy. To dig holes as moles would, bulldozers do the job, and so on. But surely there are some very important survival instincts left, like hunger, thirst or the urge to run when danger threatens, among others. Moreover, certain people have spiritual qualities that are characteristic of certain animals, like the cleverness of the fox, the slowness of the slug, the involution of the oyster, etc. When these animal features predominate, they end up marking the person with that respective quality.

In the paintings of Bosch, these characteristics are portrayed, in this case, negatively—which makes the paintings so surreal. There are other paintings in which this painter portrays people with rather grotesque faces, though still human, which point to certain attributes of the soul, like pride, greed, brutality, among others. In such paintings the nobility and beauty of the human being are also deformed, acquiring inhuman traits.

One can find another clue in Rudolf Steiner's book *Knowledge of the Higher Worlds: How Is It Attained?* Steiner said that at some point in the path of self-development one achieves, in wakefulness and full consciousness, experiences that normally only happen during sleep. At such a moment, there is an encounter with a spiritual being whom Steiner calls the lesser guardian of the threshold, who, among other things, addresses the human being as if to say:

"Now, all the good and bad aspects of your past lives shall be revealed to you. [...] They are assuming an independent form so that you will be able to see them [...] And I myself am the entity that built this body from your noble and evil deeds. My ghostly figure was woven based on the ledger of your own life. I was until now invisible within you. [...] The hidden wisdom of your destiny continued to work within you to eliminate the ugly spots in my appearance. Now that I have left you, this hidden wisdom has also withdrawn. Henceforth it will no longer look after you. It will place the responsibility entirely in your hands. If I am not to fall into corruption, I must become a perfect and glorious being."[38]

We must remember that at the time of the first encounter between Parzival and Cundrie, the soul of the hero, although he had already learned a number of things and redeemed some of his faults—in fact, all those that he had been made aware of—was still burdened and tarnished by others: those faults of which he had become guilty without guilt. Of this unconscious guilt, one only becomes aware when one reaches the threshold of the spiritual world, either through initiation or after death. In the first case, Steiner's description of the guardian of the threshold suffices. We find here a concept that Wolfram reported in the form of images. Another important aspect is the fact that from the moment this being leaves the soul of the person in question, help is no longer possible. The person has to take self-development into his or her own hands. Indeed, shortly after this encounter the period begins for Parzival when, all alone and isolated, he achieves his self-education and interior development.

Later on, in the same book, Rudolf Steiner mentions the greater guardian of the threshold, whom a person meets during the self-development process after reaching a higher level of development, freer of earthly, sensory bonds. This second guardian appears as a very bright

---

38 R. Steiner, *Knowledge of the Higher Worlds: How Is It Attained?*, "The Guardian of the Threshold."

figure of indescribable beauty. Its words would be approximately as follows:

> "You have freed yourself from the sensory world. You have earned the right of citizenship in the spiritual world. [...] You have reached your present level of completion through the faculties you were able to develop in the sensory world, while still dependent on it; yet now comes a time when your freed forces must continue working upon this sensory world. So far you have freed only yourself. Now, as someone who is free, you can help to free all your fellow human beings in the sensory world."[39]

It seems strange that the grotesque figure of Cundrie is at the same time the messenger of the Grail. Often a blow of destiny helps a person change course to find a more appropriate path, rather than continuing on one's previous way. Had it not been for Cundrie's curse, Parzival would never have left the court of Arthur and become a Knight of the Grail, his true mission. This ugly woman is nothing other than the counter-image we carry within us when we are still led by desires and lust. Still, she is the messenger of the Grail, and once transformed, ugliness becomes beauty. The worst greed, when transformed into its opposite, is revealed as a magnificent force. In other words, Cundrie is the mirror of Parzival's soul. As he did not understand this fact in his first encounter, he took her words as a curse, not even realizing that in fact she was protecting him so he would not become Arthur's knight, but follow his true destiny.

At the second encounter with Cundrie, Parzival had already freed himself of all sins. He had transformed all his imperfections and was totally purified, and free of all earthly bonds. His freedom, however, was not enough. From now on he must help others to free themselves, and the first one was Anfortas.

---

39   Ibid.

Comparing these two excerpts of Wolfram's *Parzival* with Rudolf Steiner's descriptions, one notices that both deal with the same issue, described in language appropriate for each writer's time. The first elaborates a grand picture, understandable to people of the Middle Ages, while Steiner translated the same content into the conceptual language of modern humanity. The way he describes the two guardians of the threshold (the lesser and the greater), it follows that Cundrie could, in fact, represent these two spiritual entities, whom human beings encounter when they come to the threshold of the spiritual world, having purified the forces of thinking, feeling and willing, which are part of the soul.

Considering these findings regarding the figures of Schianatulander, Cundrie, and Sigune, who generically represent the physical *body*, the *soul* and the *spirit*, the immense esoteric wisdom contained in Wolfram's work may be startling. And, as will be seen in subsequent chapters, at the Council of Constantinople (869 AD) the Church decreed by means of a dogma that the human being consisted of body and soul only, and that the latter had some spiritual attributes.

Trevrizent: The Meeting on Good Friday

The encounter between Parzival and Trevrizent is the central aspect of Wolfram's work. In this long conversation between uncle and nephew, we observe a deepening relationship and a growing intimacy. It all began informally. Parzival, having been informed of the existence of a wise man, was looking to him for advice.

In the cave of the hermit, Parzival saw the shrine at which he had sworn Jeschute's innocence. When he asked how much time had elapsed since the moment of the disappearance of the lance he had taken without meaning to, the answer was that five years, six months and three days had passed. Discovering how long he had been wandering through the forest, he remembered the reason he had sought help: his prolonged suffering. He felt wronged and blamed God for his fate. He confessed he felt hatred toward God, for he had been told that He was all-powerful and benevolent to those who were faithful to Him, but although Parzival had always served Him faithfully, He had allowed such suffering and for such a long time. Trevrizent then gave him ample instructions, valid for any person:

Be unswervingly constant toward Him, since God Himself is perfect constancy, condemning all falsity. We should allow him to reap the benefit of having done so much for us, for His sublime nature took on human shape for our sakes. (B. IX, 236)

Then Trevrizent explained the appearance of evil on Earth, asking Parzival to think "consider what Lucifer and his comrades achieved" (B. IX, 236), who, moved by pride and envy, rebelled against divinity and were cast out of Heaven. In reality, he was trying to show Parzival that he himself was acting like Lucifer, rebelling against God, moved by pride and envy.

Gerard Klockenbring explains in an interesting way what envy is, suggesting that one should imagine that one is living next to a "more beautiful, quieter, stronger being."[40] This could be something wonderful for someone living in this situation, taking advantage of that being's qualities; however, one might also ask why this being had so many qualities and we did not. That would be envy. In fact, Parzival could not understand why everyone else lived well and he was the only one to suffer.

The hermit also said that after Lucifer had been thrown out of heaven into hell, his place was taken by human beings. Therefore, one can conclude that human beings are now polarized between heaven and hell, between good and evil, in order to develop our own freedom. Steiner said in his lecture of November 22, 1906[41] that through Lucifer,

---

40 G. Klockenbring, *El Santo Grial y el hombre moderno*.
41 In *Supersensible Knowledge*, GA 55.

the human being, once integrated with nature, acquired self-awareness and self-esteem (developed self-love), which lead to selfishness. Since then, humanity also acquired the knowledge of good and evil. However, to be aware of what is good, humanity also needs to be aware of what is bad. Without the existence of evil there can be no free choice of what is good, i.e., there cannot be freedom. In this context, evil and freedom are of common origin.

Then the hermit taught Parzival about Adam, the first human being, whose mother was Mother Earth herself, who was a virgin. When Cain, son of Adam, killed his brother Abel and his blood poured onto the ground, "her virginity was gone." (B. IX, 237) The act committed by Cain established discord among people. To compensate for this act of staining the Earth, God chose to take human form. He was born of a virgin and came to redeem humans' sins out of pure love of humanity. On explaining the meaning of the sacrifice of divinity to redeem humankind, the wise man was speaking of Christ, who bound Himself to earth and the fate of human beings. According to Steiner, one cannot deny God when one can find Him again through Christ.[42] It should be noted that the God Parzival hated was God the Father, and that the teachings of Trevrizent bound him to God the Son. After these explanations from his host, the young man gave up his hatred and anger. Klockenbring points out that Trevrizent only relayed these facts, without giving them a connotation of guilt. This would be in line with the attitude of God, who has the power to withstand evil thanks to His immeasurable strength in love. In fact, throughout this encounter between Parzival and the hermit, the latter never judges—he just regrets and suffers through the youth's attitude.

Then the young knight spoke of his personal aspirations: to win the Grail and return to his wife. Trevrizent praised him greatly for having remained faithful to her all this time, and encouraged him

---

[42] R. Steiner, *The Work of the Angels in Man's Astral Body / How Do I Find the Christ?* GA 182.

by saying that because of his faithfulness, he would probably reunite with her soon. Only true love substantiated by mutual respect could be sustained for so long. Yet the host considered the young man rather foolish for wanting to win the Grail, as he had been a knight of the Grail himself and knew that only predestined people could achieve it. Then he revealed to his guest the secrets of the stone (which will be described in the chapter "The Symbol of the Grail") and finished his report by referring to the angels who, during the struggle between Lucifer and the Holy Trinity, had remained neutral: They had to stay on earth looking after the Grail.

Trevrizent supposed that God would have forgiven them and reinstated them in His kingdom, because, from a certain time onward, the stone was guarded by human beings called by God especially for this mission. This information satisfied Parzival's curiosity in a way, although it reiterated the impossibility of reaching the Grail through his own will. Actually, the atmosphere during this part of the conversation remained quite impersonal and generic. Furthermore, the hermit was still unaware of the identity of his guest.

After hearing all this, Parzival told of his knightly deeds and added, "If God is any judge of fighting, He will appoint me to that place so that the Company there know me as a knight who will never shun battle." (B. IX, 241) His host scolded him for his pride and presumption, advising him to develop modesty, for "pride goes before a fall." (B. IX, 241) He then revealed that these same feelings had led the King of the Grail, Anfortas, to suffer great pain. He commented that to date only one person had managed to reach the Grail without being summoned, but had left full of guilt because he had not even asked his host the reason for his suffering, despite having witnessed his pain. Some time before, another knight, Lähelin by name, had come to the lake and challenged a knight of the Grail, who was killed in their fight—and Lähelin had taken over the opponent's mount. It was only then that Trevrizent expressed the desire to know the identity of his guest, whom he supposed to be a knight. After all, Parzival had come mounted on a Grail horse. After saying that he was the son of Gahmuret, the youth also confessed to having killed and robbed a knight, Ither by name, when he was very young and inexperienced. He knew how wrong this was, but he was shocked when the hermit told him that the knight he had killed was his blood relative, and the crime would, in fact, have to be paid for with his own death.

Then Trevrizent told him that he himself was Herzeloyde's brother and that her death had been caused by the departure of her child. That was how the youth heard of his mother's death. When their kinship was established, the conversation became more intimate and personal. In this atmosphere of intimacy, the uncle told his nephew everything he considered important for him to know about his family—both good and bad. He also told him that he had become a hermit in an attempt to heal Anfortas, his wounded brother, because many attempts by every imaginable means had not produced the hoped-for result. Finally, in desperation, the knights of the Grail had lain prostrate before the stone, seeking help. On the border of the stone an inscription appeared announcing the coming of a young knight. If he felt compassion and asked the question about the King's suffering, he would free him from his pain. However, he could not be warned and would have to ask the question of his own accord on the first night, otherwise it would have no effect. The hermit ended by saying that this knight had actually appeared, though it would have been better had he never set foot there, because, in spite of witnessing so much suffering, he failed to ask the vital question. That is how Parzival became fully aware of his past, and also came to a true understanding of Anfortas' suffering.

After thus building up the tension, Wolfram interrupts his story and talks about the frugal meal they both ate, after picking some roots and herbs and feeding the horse. Only then did Parzival gather his courage and confess that he himself was the knight who had been in the Grail Castle and had not asked the question, realizing that he had no hope of redemption. As already mentioned, at no time did the wise hermit blame his nephew for his acts. He only expressed his deep sorrow, and then sought to encourage the youth, who was shaken by all the information he had received: "God Himself will not abandon you. I counsel you in His Name. (B. IX, 249) He explained that on approaching the Grail Castle any person would put his life at risk. He also spoke about the destiny of the men and women who lived in that community.

What could have been a brief counseling session became a fifteen-day companionship, during which Parzival slept on the straw-covered floor and fed only on herbs and roots, like his uncle. The youth had one last question: the identity of the man who was in the room where the Grail was, and who radiated so much light. He learned that it was Titurel, his great-grandfather, the first to be called to guard the Grail. As he was constantly in the presence of the stone, he had not yet died, and continued to advise the community. Trevrizent encouraged the youth, advised him to do penance and, at the time of farewell, took his nephew's guilt on himself.

Steiner points out that the encounter with Christ is part of each person's destiny. One could say that this encounter with Trevrizent was part of Parzival's destiny, because only after this was he prepared to return to the Grail Castle in order to have his conscious encounter with Christ.

CHAPTER 6

General Considerations about Parzival

She was so talented that she spoke all languages —Latin, Arabic, and French. She was on easy terms with such learned matters as dialectic, and geometry, and she had mastered astronomy.
— Wolfram von Eschenbach, *Parzival* (B. VI, 163)

When one becomes acquainted with *Parzival* there is always the question of its origin: Is it a legend or not; is it based on reality—in short, how to consider this work.

If we research the locations described in the work, several are still familiar to us, such as India, Britain, and the cities of Toledo, Nantes, and Baghdad. Cundrie wears a London hat and clothing made of silk from Ghent. The vast majority of place names, however, are unfamiliar: Munsalvaesche, Zazamanc, Pelrapeire, Bearoche, etc. The fact that we do not know of such places today, however, is not evidence of their nonexistence in the Middle Ages, because their names may have changed, or they may have disappeared. So these considerations do not lead us to any conclusion.

Nor is much concrete data revealed when one searches through historical documents for evidence of the events or characters mentioned in the text; the only familiar names are those of King Arthur and Prester John[43] (son of Feirefiz and Repanse of Schoye). Historians mention the existence of a King Arthur in Brittany who lived in the 6th century, yet the facts known about him do not confirm that he is the King Arthur of the Round Table described by Wolfram and elsewhere in medieval literature. Richard Seddon mentions that the King of the Round Table,

---

43   Prester means "priest," from the Latin *presbyter*, meaning "elder."

surrounded by his knights, is a kind of figurehead for a lineage not limited to one person only, but to a whole series of leaders of the same impulse.[44] According to Julius Evola, the King Arthur role in itself might have been a symbolic, superhistorical character.[45] The name may even have been perpetuated as an indication of something transcendental. One can imagine, then, that "King Arthur" is comparable to other titles which have lasted for centuries, such as, for instance, Pope or Emperor— titles to which certain functions are attributed. Charles Kovacs points out that Arthur was the representation of the spirit of the Breton people.[46] For centuries, the heroes of the Round Table, commanded by various "Arthurs," protected the population from oppression and violence, and even before the advent of knighthood, they were already serving as knights. Possibly they even constituted a secret community with branches across Great Britain, each one led by an "Arthur."

It is important to point out that the stories of King Arthur were disseminated in the form of medieval French romances, whose authors no longer knew their true meaning. In general, the episodes took place in wild places: impenetrable forests and dangerous swamps. The King and Queen, with their twelve knights, represented the stellar order to be established in this wild land.

The name "Prester John" also appears in some documents in the Middle Ages, referring to someone of Moorish origin who lived in the East, leading a group of Christians. In *Parzival*, Wolfram says: "[Repanse de Schoye] bore a son named 'John.' They called him 'Prester John,' and, ever since, they call all other kings by no other name. Feirefiz had letters sent throughout the land of India describing the Christian life, which had not prospered so much till then." (B. XVI, 408) In some legends, the kingdom of Prester John is considered a center of sun worship. Steiner says that Christ is a sun being, therefore a community worshiping a sun

---

44   R. Seddon, *The Mystery of Arthur at Tintagel*.
45   J. Evola, *The Mystery of the Grail*.
46   C. Kovacs, *Parzival and the Search for the Grail*.

being might be related to Christianity. It is known that the Portuguese navigators in their travels to the East, besides looking for the sea route to India, also sought the whereabouts of Prester John, taking letters and gifts from the Portuguese king to offer him when they met.

Research has it that the story of Parzival takes place in the 9th century, for the following reasons:

a) There had always been belligerence between the West and the East. However, there was a short period in history, in the 9th century, when Harun Al-Rashid (763–809),[47] in a treaty signed with Charles the Great, facilitated travel for French pilgrims. Consequently it became easy to move between regions. Wolfram does not mention any difficulty that Gahmuret might have encountered on his trips to the East. Furthermore, the hero was well respected by the Caliph of Baghdad, who even asked for his aid on a second visit. After the death of this noble knight, the Caliph rendered him all kinds of honors. Gahmuret seems to have served as a mediator between the West and the East. He was a Christian, but had no prejudice, either racial or religious. He knew how to appreciate the culture and people of the Arab world. As a Christian he showed tolerance, as indeed did many people of his time, who rather quietly brought to the West the treasures of Eastern wisdom still lacking in Christian Europe. It is known that in Arab countries mathematics, chemistry, astronomy, and medicine had reached a high stage of development, while the West was still in the "Dark Ages."

b) When referring to Queen Herzeloyde after her death, Wolfram praises her nobility, purity, kindness, and modesty, "Alas, that we no longer have her kindred with us to the eleventh remove!" (B. III, 76) We can take this to mean that she had lived eleven generations before his own. Now in the Middle Ages, thirty years were counted as one generation. Wolfram wrote his work around 1210. Subtracting from that date 330 years (eleven generations), we arrive approximately at the year 880, i.e., the 9th century.

---

47   Persian caliph, supreme head of the Islamic civilization, then based in Baghdad.

c) Walter Johannes Stein[48]—the first teacher commissioned by Rudolf Steiner to teach the Parzival block[49] in the Waldorf School in Stuttgart—reports that, when he was in town, Steiner had the habit of visiting the school and attending some classes. Once he attended a class in which Stein was working with his students on an excerpt from Wolfram's *Parzival*. At one point, Rudolf Steiner asked the young people what period those events related to; and then he explained that according to the known facts, one could deduce it was the 8th and 9th centuries, since

> People were used to living with bloodshed. [...] From time to time, some luminous figures, in shining armor, crossed the immense and dense forests. Then the inhabitants of the villages in the forests hid, and would not come out to fight or plunder. Thus, in those times of bloodshed, these riders maintained some order through much killing.[50]

The center of these wandering knights was Arthur's court.

The 9th century is very important from both the political and religious point of view in European history. The Holy Roman (Germanic) Empire was built under Charlemagne (747–814), but began to crumble immediately after his death. The gap between East and West increased again and would widen some time later, with the Crusades.

In a lecture on April 16, 1921,[51] Rudolf Steiner made an analogy between the Crusades and the search for the Grail. According to his explanation, the Crusades referred to the earthly conquest of physical Jerusalem, while the search for the Grail endeavored to conquer the path to the spiritual Jerusalem described in the Book of Revelation.[52]

---

48 W. J. Stein, *The Ninth Century and the Holy Grail*.
49 In Waldorf schools, a "block" corresponds to a sequence of classes given on consecutive days for three to four weeks, focusing on one theme or subject.
50 R. Steiner quoted by Walter Johannes Stein, op. cit.
51 In *Materialism and the Task of Anthroposophy*, GA 204.
52 See R. Steiner, *The Apocalypse of St. John*, GA 104.

There were initially two religious streams within Christianity: gnosis, an offspring of Eastern initiation wisdom, of a more esoteric character, in which one tried to understand the Mystery of Christ, though this understanding was increasingly difficult; and the far Western religion, whose followers had no need to understand the Christ impulse, although they experienced it intensely in their religious services. Their greatest religious desire was to complete a pilgrimage to Jerusalem to visit the Holy Sepulcher. The Roman Church then introduced a third way, in which the esoteric content of Christianity was not to be understood as a suprasensory experience (as it was in gnosis), but should rather be laced with abstract concepts of a dogmatic character.

In the 9th century—the year 869, to be precise—the Council of Constantinople took place, and the human being, heretofore considered tripartite, i.e., consisting of body, soul, and spirit, was reduced to a bipartite entity, with the abolition of the spirit. Thereafter the Church established that the human being consisted of body and soul, and that the soul had some spiritual qualities (see chapter "Historical Currents Related to the Grail," section on the Catholic Church).

Our initial question thus remains without a concrete answer. Maybe we should be looking for it in a context that transcends the merely sensorial and rational. Perhaps in Wolfram's work, in the example of the character Cundrie, there are hidden meanings and realities presented to the great medieval public in the form of images and symbols, and not in the form of the clear concepts more familiar to Western people, or those with a Western education, in the 20th and 21st centuries.

One must bear in mind that humanity as a whole has undergone an evolution, and therefore the consciousness of the person of the Middle Ages was different from the consciousness of the modern person. That is why the Middle Ages, considered from a modern point of view, are sometimes called the Dark Ages. In his aforementioned work, Evola says, quoting Guenon, that folk tales, sagas, and legends may not even be of human origin, but may derive from a tradition going back to prehistoric times and a higher sphere of consciousness which, according to Steiner's spiritual observations, was still very present in so-called prehistoric humanity.[53] Evola considers the folklore in the cycles of Arthur and the Grail to be holdovers from ancient traditions about to be extinguished. It is also possible for archetypal realities of a higher order to incarnate in certain structures or historical personalities.

It is of course possible to study *Parzival* from a purely rational and sensory point of view, and this study will prove very interesting, providing a lot of data about the habits and knowledge of the time in areas such as mineralogy, botany, medicine (therapeutic procedures as well as herbs, minerals and animals with therapeutic properties), astronomy, alchemy, history, etc.

But there is something very peculiar about this work, and in this sense Wolfram is unique. He mentions three major cultural currents of his time, which meet and cross-fertilize: the Celtic, the Christian, and the Arabic. As already mentioned (see chapter "Works Relating to the Grail"), in many books and lectures Rudolf Steiner discussed the development of humanity in the post-Atlantean age. For those who lived in Europe between the 9th and 13th centuries, the Celtic culture represented the past, that is, the period when human civilization flourished in Babylon, Chaldea, Egypt (third post-Atlantean cultural epoch); the Christian culture and the Greco-Roman culture (fourth post-Atlantean epoch) accounted for the present; and Arabism the future, or our current, modern period (fifth post-Atlantean epoch).

Reference has also been made to Richard Seddon,[54] who classifies works according to the post-Atlantean cultural epochs and considers the Arthurian legends to be related to the Celtic mysteries (development of the sentient soul), the Grail legends with the development of Christianity in the West (development of the intellectual soul or personal character), and the legends of Parzival with the development of the consciousness

---

53 J. Evola, *The Mystery of the Grail*.
54 R. Seddon, "The Matter of Britain" in *The Mystery of Arthur at Tintagel*.

soul (the present). Rudolf Steiner explained this by saying that in the Arthurian legends, events are "presented as external images" which speak to the sentient soul. The most important aspect of the Grail legends is "to achieve understanding," "to permeate the rational soul or character with new knowledge."

However, as Steiner mentioned in his lecture of February 6, 1913, the legend of Parzival frees forces that aspire to something higher, the power of self-knowledge to be developed by the consciousness soul,[55] so that humanity can turn to the Mystery of Christ in full freedom (the meaning of this will be discussed later). Seddon says that the Roman Church set out to remove all content deriving from ancient mysteries, including the Christian mysteries. This was why the Church started spreading fictitious tales to obscure the esoteric legends, trying to hide, among other things, the real meaning of the work *Parzival*.

The Celtic culture derives from the Germanic culture which dates back to two to three thousand years before Christ. The Babylonian-Egyptian-Chaldean culture also began two to three thousand years before Christ and features several aspects in common with the Celtic-Germanic one, mainly in relation to astronomy and megalithic constructions. When, around the year 1000 BC, the Celts denied the intellectual impulse that had originated from the runic script,[56] a clear differentiation took place: From then on the Germanic culture—the birthplace of this script—fell into decay. This was manifested in the so-called "twilight of the gods." As the intellect developed, the Germanic culture lost touch with the spiritual worlds. Something similar had happened to the Eastern people. The advent of cuneiform writing in Babylon and hieroglyphs in Egypt heralded the doom of these civilizations—so much so that the culture of Western humanity began

---

55 R. Steiner, *The Mysteries of the East and of Christianity*, GA 144.
56 Writing in runes, letters of an esoteric alphabet in use by the Germanic people, dating back to the beginning of the 3rd century and later introduced in Scandinavia and the British Isles.

to develop in Greece with the philosophers around 600 BC. From then on, Hellenism influenced the whole of late Western civilization.

In the Far West, however, the Celts held to their worship of the sun and the moon, and their culture lasted for about two thousand years (i.e., from approximately 1000 BC up to a thousand years after the advent of Christ).

Rudolf Steiner mentions that, just as a river can go underground and surface again elsewhere, sometimes far from its place of origin, part of the contents of the Egyptian mysteries related to the wisdom of the stars resurfaced in the West in a modified form. This was the case with the Celtic mysteries, represented in a "humanized" form in King Arthur's Round Table.[57] An important aspect that differentiates the two cultures (Egyptian and Celtic) is that in the East, initiation occurred inside the temples, while the Celts went through the initiatory process outdoors, or rather in the shadows cast by their buildings; or, lacking those, services were held in clearings in the forests, where the trees projected the necessary shadows in a circle. W.F. Veltman states that during such initiations, a circle of twelve people worked together, each one developing a particular interior force or spiritual quality for the benefit of the group.[58]

The Celtic culture developed mainly in the Western regions of the European continent, but spread throughout Europe. The Celtic people were still very attached to the phenomena of nature. They had a great knowledge of plants and their healing powers, and built huge monuments that today we would call astronomical observatories. They gathered immense stone blocks (each weighing several tons), transporting them long distances (up to one hundred kilometers). It is a mystery how they managed to do this, as they had no knowledge of either iron or the wheel. These blocks were placed vertically, at regular intervals and in straight lines several kilometers long (the alignments

---

57 R. Steiner, *The Mysteries of the East and of Christianity*, GA 144.
58 W.F. Veltman, *Tempel und Gral*.

of Carnac in Brittany or Little England in Wales) or arranged in circles. Then other blocks were placed horizontally connecting the vertical blocks, as in the example of Stonehenge in England.

The orientation of the stones related to the course of the sun and its relationship with the earth, because the sun's obvious influence on the plant kingdom and everything living was well known; the moon played a smaller role. In fact, the layout of King Arthur's Round Table had its origin in this circular arrangement of the stones of the Druids. Today we still marvel at the baffling accuracy with which these centers were built; and they served not only as observatories, but also as shrines, holy places for worship, mystery centers comparable to those of ancient Egypt and Greece, and core centers from which radiated wisdom, art, and religion.

The initiated Celtic priests were known as Druids, and their knowledge encompassed fields like astronomy, architecture, theology, and medicine. As in ancient Egypt and Chaldea, where the priests were at the same time the monarchs of their people, the Druids were also Celtic rulers. The symbol of their priestly dignity was the inexhaustible cauldron of fullness and rebirth. During their initiation process, they spiritually accompanied some of the important events that were occurring in the universe, including, according to Steiner:

> [T]he impulse of Christ, at that time, was an entity that was distancing itself from the sun, and was thus living in all that was influenced by the sun's rays. So, even before the event of the Mystery of Golgotha, that is, the Mystery of Christ, Arthur's knights could take into their souls the Spirit of the Sun, the pre-Christian Christ [...].[59]

The starting point was the Round Table. It may sound strange to talk about the Round Table and its knights in the pre-Christian era, but this configuration exactly matches that of the twelve knights around

---

59 R. Steiner, *Karmic Relationships*, vol. 6, GA 240.

Arthur and Guinevere at the Round Table. As mentioned above, the circle of twelve entities developing specific strengths for the good of the whole was a metaphor very often in use during pre-Christian humanity. In a lecture on February 6, 1913, Steiner gave us a beautiful picture of this Round Table: The twelve most important knights surrounded by an army of others remind one of the countless stars around the zodiacal constellations.[60] These innumerable people received inspirations from the whole universe, while the twelve principal knights were inspired by the forces arising from the twelve zodiacal directions, each one associated with a constellation. The inspiration originating in the spiritual forces of the sun and moon was represented respectively by Arthur and Guinevere. What is revealed here is the stellar or star wisdom known to the Celts, which was only later expressed in the images and names of the Round Table, Arthur and Guinevere, in a kind of "humanization of the cosmos."

After a visit to Tintagel, Rudolf Steiner revealed that Arthur's knights had intensely combated the forces of evil and managed to save the impulses of esoteric Christianity, carrying them forward to a later age. In Tintagel, Arthur and his knights drew on solar forces which they carried in their campaigns throughout Europe, where they contended with the old, vile, demonic forces that still raged among the population. These battles were waged for the whole of civilization. In a lecture on Sept. 10, 1924, Steiner pointed to the fact that in the 9th century, the Cosmic Christ was much better understood by the culture of remaining European paganism (the Celts) than by official Christianity.[61]

Currently, the achievements of the Celts are considered acts of magic, because they can no longer be understood through the intellect. As they had not yet developed our modern intellectual type of thinking, the Celts most certainly retained forces which were subsequently lost with the acquisition of the intellect. What is currently known about

---

60 R. Steiner, *The Mysteries of the East and of Christianity*, GA 144.
61 R. Steiner, *Karmic Relationships*, vol. 4, GA 238

them comes largely from a time when these mysteries were already declining. Julius Evola refers to a Celtic text that says that the lineage of the *Tuatha dé Danann*, a mythical Irish tribe, brought with them four treasures closely related to the learning received in a particular mystery center: the *"lance of overcoming"* that would have belonged to Lug, the sun god; the *"sword of light*," invincible and inexorable; the *"cauldron of plenitude*," the contents of which magically sated all warriors; and a stone called the *"stone of destiny"* or *"royal stone"* because, like an oracle, it identified the rightful king, as in the case of King Arthur, by way of the sword in the stone. In the chapter "The Symbol of the Grail" it will be explained how these symbolic objects are related to the Grail.

The Celtic stream ceased to have importance in the world between the 8th and 9th centuries. In the story of Parzival it is represented by King Arthur (who can be seen as an initiate of the Celtic mysteries) and the knights of the Round Table, including Gawain.

Throughout the Middle Ages, Europe was dominated by Christianity, represented mainly by the Catholic Church. The Community of the Grail, although it appears to have had no ties with the official Church, represented Christian virtues of repentance, penitence, brotherly love, and forgiveness, besides also practicing Christian rituals like baptism; and there was the heraldic symbol of the dove, the symbol of the Holy Spirit. As will be discussed in the chapter "Historical Currents Related to the Grail," this community was close to a form of Christianity practiced by the early Christians: A more esoteric, spiritual Christianity, resisted at that time by the official Church. At the end of the Middle Ages there was a resurgence of the values that shaped the beginning of the fourth post-Atlantean cultural epoch, which reached its height in classic Hellenism. Between the 11th and 12th centuries the most important neoplatonic school was Chartres. Later, in the late Middle Ages and the Renaissance, Hellenism flourished again.

Belakane, the first wife of Gahmuret and the queen of a Moorish country, was a pagan. She and Feirefiz, their child, are the representatives of the third stream, Arabism. This stream approached the Iberian

Peninsula beginning in the 7th–8th centuries, with the Moorish invasions. Even after being expelled from Europe in the 15th century, the Arabs exerted a deep influence on cultural and scientific development in Europe, and thus influenced the whole Western continent. This Arabic impulse had its origin in the city of Gondi-Shapur, which was founded by the Sassanid (central Persian) King Shapur I (242–272) and soon became the spiritual center of the Persian Empire. Later, the region became known by its Syrian name, Lapeta. In the early days, the city was led by a hierarchy of magicians who had reactivated old Persian worship rituals. Later, Shapur II (336–380) developed the sciences; during this period, Greek medical writings were translated there. In the 5th century, the work of Aristotle was brought there and translated into Syrian. The famous Academy of Hippocratic Medicine of Gondi-Shapur dates back to those times; for centuries it was a center of all Greek, Syrian, Persian, and Hindu medical knowledge. In this center the scientific thinking of the present day was developed, denying any spiritual existence and based mainly on arithmetic, trigonometry, and algebra in relation to a natural world seen as lifeless and exclusively physical. Just as nature was considered devoid of spirit, the human being was not considered to have an individual self either.

Although Cundrie was the messenger of the Grail and therefore linked to that community, she was pagan by origin. On hearing of the Grail, Queen Secundille (who would later marry Feirefiz) sent some valuable gifts to King Anfortas, including "a pair of human wonders, namely Cundrie and her fair brother."[62] (B. X, 264) Wolfram wrote that Cundrie "was on easy terms with such learned matters as dialectic and geometry, and she had mastered astronomy" (B. VI, 163), referring to her pagan education based on Arabism. With the dissemination of Islam by the 7th century, this knowledge spread throughout the lands conquered

---

62 It should be noted that Wolfram was often quite ironic, and in this passage it is very clear, since the figure of Malcreatiure, Cundrie's brother, was as monstrous as she was.

by the Moors. The decay of Gondi-Shapur occurred beginning in the mid-9th century.

It is very important not to confuse Arabism with Islam.[63] Arabism preceded Islam by three to four centuries, and has to do with the cultivation of science, while Islam is a religion. One must also be careful not to confuse, at least initially, Baghdad with Arabism. Baghdad was founded in 762 exactly on the border between Persia and the Arab region, by Al-Mansur (712–775), who was of Persian origin. The ruler, the caliph, was a successor of the former Persian kings. Caliph Al-Mansur was the one who sought to establish contacts with the rest of the world, achieving a cosmopolitan government. It was during his time that a first delegation sent by the Frankish King Pepin the Short, father of Charlemagne, visited Baghdad. The predominant language in the city was Arabic, but the religion practiced was Zoroastrianism, the ancient Persian religion. In the person of Harun Al-Rashid, the highest representative of Arabism, Gondi-Shapur nurtured a strong enmity toward the rulers of Baghdad, as they threatened Al-Rashid's power.

It can be said that there was a confrontation between Arabism and Zoroastrianism. In 803, Al-Rashid ordered the destruction of Al-Mansur's dynasty. All family members were arrested and the caliph was beheaded. His head presented on a tray is like a counterimage of the Grail. It follows, therefore, that in an ingenious way Wolfram mentions these three currents in their actual historical interweaving. Even in a small detail this becomes evident: During the first encounter between Parzival and Cundrie, the author states that she "was so talented that she spoke all languages—Latin, Arabic, and French." (B. VI, 163). Latin was the language of the clergy, French was the language of the knights,

---

63 In the work of Pierre Ponsoye, *El Islam y el Grial*, the author confuses Arabism, Islam, and even the ancient pagan mysteries. The value of his work is the importance given to aspects mentioned only by Wolfram in relation to Eastern culture, and Ponsoye's huge commitment to reconciling Islamic, Christian, and Jewish esotericism to explain the esotericism of Wolfram's *Parzival*. The author seeks what these religions have in common on the esoteric level, recognizing their common origin.

and Arabic ("language of the pagans") was the language of the invaders from the East.

The importance given by Wolfram to these three streams is evident, as the entire Book I is dedicated to Gahmuret and his adventures in pagan countries. According to von dem Borne,[64] besides going to Baghdad, his travels took him to Morocco and Persia. This means that in the East he had contact not only with Arabism but also with Zoroastrianism, the ancient Persian religion.

Zarathustra, the great initiate and guide of the Persian people, taught of the dualism between the forces of light and darkness, good and evil, spirit and matter. Gahmuret justified leaving Belakane because she did not share the same faith, saying: "Madam, you can still win me, if you will be baptized." (B. I, 39) She then lamented the fact that her husband had hidden this desire from her, as she would have been willing to accept baptism. This same situation repeats itself, transformed, at the end of the book: Feirefiz, the son of Gahmuret and Belakane, accepted baptism so as to be able to marry Repanse of Schoye. In fact, Feirefiz's black and white spotted skin can be taken as a symbol of the light-and-dark polarity of Persian Zoroastrianism, which Wolfram presents in a variety of ways over the course of his story. At the beginning we read: "Shame and honor clash where the courage of a steadfast man is motley like the magpie." (B. I, 15) The magpie is a bird with white-and-black plumage.

One could also say that, from a spiritual point of view, we can see in this work the confluence of Zoroastrianism (prehistoric wisdom that envisioned the Christ as the great Sun Aura or *Ahura Mazdao*), Arthurian Christianity (macrocosmic, with wisdom that spoke of a Sun Being approaching the Earth and of the Mystery of Death and Resurrection which was about to happen), and the Christianity of the Grail (microcosmic, with the advent of Christ and the Mystery of Death and Resurrection already realized).

---

64   G.v.d. Borne, *Der Gral in Europa*.

CHAPTER 7
The Symbol of the Sword

"The sword will stay whole for one blow, but at the second it will fall apart. If you will then take it back it will be made whole again in that same stream, only you must take the water where it leaps from under the rock before the ray of dawn lights on it."
— Wolfram von Eschenbach, *Parzival* (B. V, 134)

A symbol is something that represents a different meaning: When one sees the object, one understands what it represents. Thus, for example, the dove represents peace and also the Holy Spirit; the cross represents the Church; the Star of David, the Jewish religion; the crescent moon on a green background, Islam; the picture of a skull means danger, and so on. It is in this way that we understand road signs, a company logo, and many other symbols. On his first visit to the Grail Castle, Parzival encountered three objects that were endowed with very special qualities. One can assume, therefore, that they were symbols. We will now examine them, starting with the symbol of the *sword*.

In general, the sword symbolizes authority, power, and justice. The pictorial or sculptural representations of Justice differ according to Greek or Roman tradition. The Greeks pictured Justice as a standing woman with open eyes (as Justice should not only hear but also see before making a declaration of rights), her left hand holding a sword and an off-balance scale in her right hand. Balance could only be restored when justice had been achieved. The sword symbolizes that Justice will always assert the declaration of rights, even if enforcement is required. In the Roman tradition, better known as Roman Law, Justice is represented by a woman often seated, blindfolded (she only listens) and holding a scale with the two pans in balance. Charles Kovacs stresses that one of the most important characteristics of a leader is the ability to make decisions; in this sense, the Greek image of Justice values the sword as the symbol of decision-making.[65]

In myths and sagas as well as in reality, some swords have their own names, such as King Arthur's *Excalibur*, and *Notung* and *Balmung* in Germanic mythology (see below). There are references to their origins, to those who forged them, and even to their "histories," since many of them went through a few owners because they were won in battle or given in acknowledgment of services rendered.

In the Middle Ages and even a little later, monarchs and noblemen were always portrayed carrying their swords. Kings basically believed that they were exercising a divine function: They felt they had been appointed by God to exercise power, and their swords represented this. It should be emphasized that in the Middle Ages the kings and noblemen were the ones who did, in fact, hold military and judicial power over their kingdoms or fiefdoms; therefore, nothing was fairer than for them to display swords to represent military might and the power of Justice. Usually, the outcome of combat was decided by a sword, and the outcome enabled Justice to prevail.

In the 13th-century Portuguese manuscript *The Quest for the Holy Grail*,[66] it is reported that Sir Galahad arrived at Arthur's court led by a hermit who was known as "the good man" and who made him sit on the so-called "dangerous seat"[67] without the young hero (who was to accomplish great deeds) suffering any harm. This meant that, besides being very pure, Galahad was under the protection of God. Then Arthur took him to the riverbank, where a block of marble had appeared, with

---

65 C. Kovacs, *Parzival and the Search for the Grail*.
66 H. Megale (ed.), *A Demanda do Santo Graal*.
67 According to Arthurian literature, on establishing the Round Table, King Arthur was advised by the wizard Merlin to keep the seat to his right vacant "in memory of Jesus Christ." In this seat only the elected one could sit, a pure being destined to find the Grail. If anyone else sat in it, the earth would swallow him up.

a sword stuck in it. The scabbard was floating above the block. None of Arthur's knights had dared remove the sword from the stone, all saying that this deed was beyond them. Galahad, however, who had no sword of his own, easily removed it from the stone, took the scabbard and girded it around his waist.

In his book *Merlin*, Robert de Boron tells how Arthur became King of the Britons. Arthur's very conception occurred through Merlin's magic, and the baby had been taken by the magician to be brought up by a knight of lesser rank. No one knew that this child was the son of King Utepandragun (Uther Pendragon). As this king had apparently left no descendants, a new king had to be chosen after his death. While Christmas Mass was being said, a rock with a sword stuck in it appeared in front of the cathedral. During the religious ceremony, the congregation had asked God for a sign showing them how to choose their new king. They now considered the sword in the stone as the sign, for it bore an inscription saying that "(the one) who is to own the sword—and is able to retrieve it—will be the king of the land, the one appointed by Jesus Christ."

None of the noblemen present could remove the sword from the stone, try as they might. The only one to accomplish the feat, actually with great ease, was Arthur, who was too young even to have been knighted. After the final decision was deferred to permit noblemen living in distant lands to attempt the feat, and also due to some other complications, Arthur proved capable of repeatedly drawing the sword from the stone. So he was finally crowned king of the Britons. Once again, God's will was evident. In Nordic mythology there is a similar story: Sigmund, father of Siegfried, was with a group of knights when a stranger entered the room, which was built around a large tree trunk. The stranger threw his sword at the tree so hard that only the handle protruded. He then proclaimed that the sword would belong to the one who had the strength to remove it from the trunk, and saying this, he disappeared. All tried, but only Sigmund managed to get it out, becoming, from then on, invincible in battle.

The name of this sword was *Notung*. Rudolf Meyer writes that, in this case, what really pulls the sword out of the tree is the strength of the Self.[68] Till then, the sword was linked to the "family tree." To free it from this tree would mean to win freedom of thought and autonomy in decision-making. Once, when Sigmund was quite old, he faced in combat a man who had only a spear. He recognized in him the stranger who had given him the sword long ago. In reality he was the god Odin, who had decided that the time had come for the knight to die. In the ensuing combat, the sword broke on hitting the shaft of the lance. Sigmund asked only that the parts of the sword be preserved so that in future they could be joined again. The person who then accomplished this was his son Sigurd (or Siegfried, in German mythology). From then on, the sword had a name, *Balmung*.

According to Julius Evola, drawing a sword out of a stone (or tree) could mean to free oneself of the power (sword) of anything material (stone).[69] Therefore, we can conclude that to be able to achieve this, the hero in question must have attained a certain degree of evolution, standing above the others around him. In all three examples the heroes had very special missions.

In the New Testament there are some strange references to the sword, different from those mentioned above, although the connotations of power and justice remain applicable. For example, in the first chapter of the Book of Revelation, a being is described as "bearing seven stars in his right hand, and from his mouth comes a sharp double-edged sword" (Rev. 1:16). Later, John describes another being:

> Then I saw heaven open and, behold, there appeared a white horse, whose rider is called "Faithful" and "Truthful," who *judges* and fights for *justice*. His eyes are a flame of fire; over his head there are many diadems, and a name written that no one knows, except himself. He is covered in a *robe soaked*

---

68 R. Meyer, *Der Gral und seine Hüter*.
69 J. Evola, *The Mystery of the Grail*.

in blood, and his name is the Word of God. [...] Out of his mouth protrudes a sharp sword to strike the nations [...]. (Rev. 19:11–15)[70]

This is therefore a spiritual being whose name is *Word* of God, from whose mouth comes a *sword*, with which he *fights* and *delivers justice!*[71]

In his letter to the Ephesians, Saint Paul says: "And take the *helmet of salvation* and the sword of the Spirit, which is the word of God" (Eph. 6:17). In the first two quotes there are spiritual beings from whose mouths extend swords instead of tongues, and Paul refers to the *sword of the Spirit* as *God's word*. It is interesting to note that the tongue, the muscular organ of the mouth, is one of the tools human beings use to articulate words and speech. We call languages "tongues," demonstrating this relationship. (In several Romance languages, the same word is used to denote both the language and the organ.) Does the word possess strength and power equal to the sword? Besides doing justice with the sword, can we also do it with the word?

Both answers are affirmative. Just remember the biblical account of Creation; the world is created by the power of the word. "God *said*, 'Let there be light'; and there was light" (Gen. 1:3). That is, God created the world through the word. The Gospel of John begins with the following verses: "In the beginning was the *Word*, and the *Word* was with God, and the *Word* was God. He was in the beginning with God. All things came into being through Him, and without Him not one thing came into being" (John 1: 1–3, our italics). And the power of words can also be observed in everyday life: There are words that can unsettle and even devastate another person; others can comfort and console, and still others can encourage and enlighten. Both positive and negative thoughts are expressed through words; words are used to make judgments. Therefore it is not so strange to relate the sword to the word.

---

70   Italics in the original.
71   Italics ours.

In Wolfram's *Parzival* we read the following about the Sword of the Grail in the section where King Anfortas offers it to Parzival: "Alas that he asked no question then." When Anfortas put his sword into Parzival's hands, the king wanted to encourage him to ask the question. (B. V, 157)

Later, during the second encounter with Sigune, seeing Parzival girded with the Grail Sword, she says the following:

> "You are wearing his sword at your waist [Anfortas]. If you know its secret magic you will be able to fight without fear. Its edges run true. [...] The sword will stay whole for one blow, but at the second it will fall apart. If you will then take it back, it will be made whole again in the same stream, only you must take the water where it leaps from under the rock before the ray of dawn lights on it. The name of that spring is 'Lac.' If the fragments of that sword are not scattered beyond recovery and someone pieces them together again, as soon as they are wetted by this water, the weld and the edges will be made one again, and far stronger than ever before, and its pattern will not have lost its sheen." (B. V, 13)

How may this section be understood, where it says that the sword will support the first blow but break under the second? At first glance this would not seem a very useful sword in combat, although upon offering it, Anfortas had said to Parzival:

> "I took this into the thick of battle on many a field before God crippled my body. Let it make amends for any lack of hospitality you have suffered here. You will wear it to good effect always. Whenever you put it to the test in battle it will stand you in good stead." (B. V, 127)

In fact, it must be a very special sword with miraculous power. What kind of combat could Anfortas be referring to? Why should Parzival always keep it with him? The mystery of the sword can only be unraveled by applying the image described in the Bible, namely, that the sword must be understood as the word. As stated above, the word has great power and, when properly applied, can win battles. The fact that it breaks at the second blow might mean that a word repeated too often wears out, loses strength, loses its value.

In Sigune's image, if it breaks, the word can regain power if it is taken back to its source; that is, when it returns to its origin, when one is fully convinced and aware of its power. However, this must occur "before dawn," before returning to waking consciousness—which means that this process is still beyond the reach of ordinary daytime consciousness, occurring during a state of unconsciousness or perhaps semiconsciousness. The fact that the sword needs to be immersed in water also refers to the word being revived, since water has a deep relationship with all that is living. Indeed, without water there is no life. So, to immerse the sword/word in water is like turning a dead word, without power, into a powerful living word.

In the introduction to the book mentioned above, Walter Johannes Stein reports on Rudolf Steiner's visit to his class.[72] On this question, Steiner says: "The old must be renewed at the living fountain. There, at the spiritual source, the sword becomes whole again." In Wolfram's narrative, a little further on, one reads as follows:

> To one side of the King's ring above a brook which took its
> rise there, yet on level ground, stood Cunneware's pavilion,
> and, above it, it seemed as though a Dragon were holding half
> of the entire button in its claws! (B. V, 146)

According to Rudolf Steiner, the dragon represented the barbarity of humanity in those days, and Parzival had to overcome this savagery, present in the forces of the blood. Note also that Parzival sent all defeated knights to serve Lady Cunneware, the guardian of this fountain, and his

---

72 W.J. Stein, *The Ninth Century and the Holy Grail*.

own tent was nearby, too. Early in Book IX, whose content is the central part of the story, i.e., the encounter with Trevrizent, Wolfram says, even before Parzival meets Sigune for the third time:

> The sword which Anfortas gave Parzival when he was with the Gral was shattered in a duel. But the virtues of the well near Karnant and known by the name of Lac made it whole again.
> (B. IX, 223)

It is worth remembering that by that time Parzival had been through his inner education: He had made great strides in his self-development and had grown inwardly, due to the very hard trials he had had to face. He had actually managed to reach the fountain. Incidentally, Steiner ended his talk with the students by saying that, like Parzival, everyone should always return to his or her origin, maintaining a connection with the spiritual source.

In the narrative one can observe that the knights of the Grail used their swords only to defend the Grail lands against intruders. However, several of the characters of the Grail (including women) were excellent wielders of words. For example, Herzeloyde taught her son everything she considered important for him to know. In their conversations, Sigune either gave Parzival directions or avoided talking to him entirely, remaining silent, leaving him lost and without guidance in the forest. Cundrie, the messenger of the Grail, cursed the hero in words, devastating him and almost destroying his life. At their second encounter, it was also in words that she called him to become the new King of the Grail. Trevrizent also made use of words to instruct Parzival and awaken his consciousness, causing him to repent and change his attitude. Finally he took on himself his nephew's guilt:

> "Give me your sins," said Trevrizent with all solemnity. "I shall vouch for your penitence before God. And do as I have instructed you: Let nothing daunt you in this endeavor."
> (B. IX, 255)

Bearing all this in mind, it can be concluded that while Arthur's knights were indeed knights of the sword, all the personalities somehow related to the Grail can be considered knights of the word.

When Parzival first arrived at the Grail Castle, he had been expected to ask a question, to make use of the word. Until then he knew only how to wield a metal sword. He did not know how to make proper use of the word, in the sense of the sword of the Spirit. To encourage him to ask the question, Anfortas offered him the Sword of the Grail, i.e., the gift of the word, the sword of the Spirit itself. But not knowing how to use it, Parzival remained silent, therefore not releasing the King from his suffering. It is of no avail to receive the appropriate instrument without having learned how to use it. Only after Parzival had been deeply hurt by Cundrie's words, and later purified by Trevrizent's words, was he able to cure Anfortas through the use of the word.

Therefore, the Grail sword represents the Divine Word, the Spiritual Word, the Cosmic Word, and the knights of the Grail were in the service of Christ, the Word, as set forth in the Gospel of Saint John (John 1:1).[73]

---

73 It is worth noting that in English "sword" and "word" are nearly identical; and there is also a certain similarity in German between *Schwert* (sword) and *Wort* (word).

CHAPTER 8

Differences in the Communities of Arthur and the Grail

> But Arthur warned him: "[...] We are approaching Anfortas's men, who are based on Munsalvaesche and defend the Forest by force of arms."
> – Wolfram von Eschenbach, *Parzival* (B. VI, 150)

Considering that in Wolfram's *Parzival* two communities are mentioned that seem to be confused in other works of medieval literature, we will now explore some essential differences that distinguish Arthur's court from the Grail Community. Various aspects spring to mind if we consider only what has been covered so far.

King Arthur's court was always located in a plain, by the side of a river or by the sea, at a lower altitude than the Grail Castle, which was perched high on a mountain, surrounded by dense forests. This may be an image indicating a level closer to the earth and including the conquest of land and properties—an occupation typical of the knights of the Round Table. On the other hand, the Community of the Grail was more inclined toward the achievements of the soul and was thus on a higher level, closer to heaven—thereby creating a spiritual knighthood.

As already mentioned, Arthur's court and the Round Table were part of Celtic culture. King Arthur was the king of the Britons, and Celtic civilization spread outward from Brittany. Famous characters such as Queen Arnive and even Gawain had some deep knowledge of nature, medicinal herbs, and the preparation of regenerative drinks and medicines, which reminds one of the wisdom of the Druids.

We also saw that the image of the king himself, surrounded by his twelve knights, pointed to a microcosmic imitation of what appears in the sky, and is the humanized representation of the zodiac surrounding the sun. Christianity appears mostly in the court's celebration of Christian festivals, while in the Community of the Grail basic Christian precepts were developed, particularly those found in communities that kept alive the prevailing spirit among Christians of the first centuries after Christ (see chapter "Historical Currents Related to the Grail").

Both Arthur's court and the Grail Community featured communal life. Wolfgang Greiner[74] states that the Round Table—founded by Merlin, the great representative of Celtic initiation focused on events of the world—reminds one of the community of the disciples of Christ at Pentecost.[75] The Community of the Grail—isolated and of difficult access—was a place where people who wished to cultivate the Pentecostal community spirit, i.e., spiritual Christianity, could join together.

Both communities had a leader who dictated the rules and whom all served. In the case of the Round Table, King Arthur exerted leadership in this typical medieval society, in which the sovereign acted as his subjects' legal–military leader and made final decisions on all matters. In the Grail Community, leadership was exercised by the Grail itself. It determined who would be called to serve, who would be king, and so on. During King Anfortas' illness he was totally unfit as a leader, and his community was led by the Grail stone, on which were inscribed the names of those called to serve and other important messages for the group.

Descriptions of Arthur's court always include scenes of the Round Table community gathered in feasting and merrymaking; then messengers would arrive, reporting certain challenging events, and one

---

74 W. Greiner, *Grals-Geheimnisse*.
75 These are the Twelve Apostles. After many prayers, Matthias was chosen by divine appointment to join the group of eleven (Acts 1).

or more knights would receive permission from the sovereign to leave and take care of the problem. Life at court is clearly illustrated by these passages. Arthur's court was based more on social norms, tournaments and events in the outer world, its most important mission being to bring order into a still-disordered society.

In the essay "The Polarity between Parzival and Gawain," Walter Johannes Stein explains[76]—by giving the example of the knight Orilus, whose heraldic symbol was the dragon—that this animal symbolized the forces of the blood and passions, called by the author the forces of the South, as opposed to the Northern forces represented by King Arthur, whose symbol was the constellation Ursa Major, the Great Bear or Big Dipper. Therefore, the fact that Orilus was one of Arthur's knights meant the subservience of the dragon to the bear: that is, the tamed dragon in the bear's service fought the wild dragon raging in the world.

The Grail Community, on the other hand, was also related to the forces of the blood; however, it had been transformed, cleansed. It was exempt from passions and carnal impulses because it was the blood of Christ. The community gathered for the celebration of rituals, and its members were more focused on an inner world, both individually and within the community itself. The Grail Castle was situated in a secluded place, isolated and inaccessible to those who had not been summoned. Some of its members (Herzeloyde, Sigune, Trevrizent) even isolated themselves from the society of their peers, forgoing community life and helping others.

Both communities had as a goal the fight against evil—which was actually a predominant impulse in the Middle Ages. However, Arthur's knights fought against evil in the outer world. They established order and justice when called or sent for this purpose. This outer evil even had a center, Schastel Marveile, the Enchanted Castle built by Clinschor the magician, and later liberated by Gawain, Arthur's nephew. The Grail

---

76 In *The Death of Merlin: Arthurian Myth and Alchemy*.

knights only went out to fight to defend the Grail Castle or help someone in trouble, as in, for example, the case of Lohengrin. Moreover, people connected to the Grail were continuously fighting against inner evil, fostering awareness in themselves or in others of errors, faults, and sins, and encouraging penance and self-development in everyone.

In this context, the primary weapons used were also different. Arthur's knights used lances and swords cast in iron or steel, and such weapons were also used by knights of the Grail to defend their kingdom against intruders, namely those not called to serve. These weapons, however, were useless for fighting evil inside human beings. The most important weapon of the people of the Grail was the word. As already mentioned, a word can destroy as much as a metal weapon, but can also comfort and soothe, edify, instruct, and raise consciousness, enabling transformation in each person. One could say that Arthur's knights were knights of the sword while the Grail knights were knights of the word.

The forms of admission into these two communities also differed considerably. To become a knight in Arthur's court, an applicant had to present himself and prove that he had developed the required virtues that guided the education of Arthurian knights. Three were the virtues to be achieved: dignity, which manifested itself in a high sense of *honor*; *courage* to face challenges, even risking one's life; and the ennobling of the forces of love, sublimated in *courtly love*. The knights that gathered around Arthur did so from their common origin and culture, jointly seeking to solve the problems of the world. To serve the Grail, these attributes were not worth much. The young man or maiden was called by the Grail itself, which took into account their purity of soul. They were recruited from many countries, bringing a universal aspect to this community. On the other hand, there were some (Herzeloyde, Trevrizent, Sigune) who walked away from this spiritual community to follow their own ways in search of a more personal path. In other words, in the Round Table community a sense of the group prevailed, and in the Grail Community, individuality. Thus, to belong to the Round

Table, knights needed to demonstrate a certain degree of improvement according to the requirements of horsemanship, but once admitted to Arthur's court, they hardly needed to demonstrate any further personal development. Their goal was to maintain the values and honor of the Round Table. Their deeds were not for self-promotion or personal glory, but mostly to further ennoble the court of Arthur.

However, there is another, more subtle aspect: It seems that these gentlemen did have specific missions in life and even underwent individual transformations and development, although they were not so evident. Wolfram describes this magnificently, as will be seen in the chapter "The Journey of Gawain." But in general, there was not much difference among the knights of the Round Table, for all were courageous, fearless, noble, honorable, etc. Only their names varied. It is worth recalling here the words of Cundrie, who said that Arthur's court was dishonored when Parzival was accepted among the knights. Arthur then released all the knights from the vows of allegiance they had made upon joining, and Parzival, leaving their circle, returned its lost honor.

On the other hand, the personalities connected with the Grail went through evolutionary stages. Each had his or her own biography, distinct from that of any other community member. They erred, sinned, redeemed themselves; they went through great difficulties, sought to recover their lost values, and helped one another in life. Again, Arthur's court still lived under tribal conditions in which each member acted on behalf of the group to maintain its integrity and community values, always obeying their leader's orders. In the Grail Community, each member's unique individual aspect was preeminent. Each of them had already reached self-consciousness as an individual, not by blindly obeying a leader, but by obeying their own moral conscience. This meant that each one felt responsible for his or her own acts, and, upon helping others to evolve, they developed selfless love. In reality, this small group had already developed the characteristics that present-day humanity needs to acquire.

In Arthur's court, woman had a secondary role. Her most important function was to be a companion to her knight at feasts and banquets, and to be his inspiration. She rarely acted on her own volition, and when she did, she was most often manipulating men. In the Community of the Grail, women were active and therefore suffered the consequences of their actions and took their destinies in hand just as men did; the big difference was they did not ride out to combat, but defended the Grail using the sword of the Spirit, the word, which they also used to address internal conflicts. In Wolfram's *Parzival*, the knights typical of these communities are Gawain in Arthur's court, and Parzival in the Community of the Grail.

However, there are also other aspects to consider besides the ones we have described, which only address basic meanings. In the chapter "General Considerations about *Parzival*," reference was made to the fact that the Celtic and Christian cultures had two quite different paths of inner development, i.e., of initiation.

The Celtic people (Westerners) represented the so-called path of the North, while official Christianity in the Middle Ages, represented by the Church of Rome, had its origin in the Eastern mysteries. The people from the West and North sought the spiritual world in nature. They were turned toward the outer world, while the Eastern path of initiation was directed more toward the inner Self of the human being; that was how humanity came into contact with the spiritual world. Still, in pre-Christian times, both paths of initiation accompanied the gradual approach toward Earth of a sun being, a solar deity: the Christ entity. Each people experienced this in its own way. When this entity incarnated in Jesus of Nazareth in Palestine, there were some people who were able to be with Him, hear His words, witness His deeds.[77]

Some became His disciples, as they had already achieved the necessary preparation. The Western initiates, on the other hand, though they had not had direct contact with Christ incarnated in a

---

77 Regarding the Incarnation, see R. Steiner, *The Gospel of St. John*, GA 103.

human body, experienced the events in Palestine during their initiation process. When these two streams—Christian and Celtic—met, the Celts accepted Christianity without difficulty. However, because there was such a different path of initiation, the Christianity they practiced was different. Later on, with the official establishment of the Roman Church—when the initiatory, esoteric aspect began to fade and make way for rationalism and the Church itself became more of a legal-administrative institution—other forms of Christianity appeared (see chapter "Historical Currents Related to the Grail").

These two communities, though so different, adopted the same outward characteristics in their exoteric life. If the early knights were illiterate and saw no use for reading and writing (which only the monks could do) in their battles, by the 12th century many were already literate. As will be further discussed in the chapter "Historical Currents Related to the Grail," in that same century a monastic military order was founded whose members were simultaneously monks and knights.

In his abovementioned book, Greiner describes how in the 9th century Arthur's chivalry gradually began to resemble the Grail Community and the behavior of the Grail knights.[78] The Round Table knights began to assimilate a spiritual cosmic Christianity: What had previously been a spiritual aspect of their process of education and self-development, more related to the soul, now became a more spiritual practice of esoteric Christianity. Therefore, the three ideals of Arthur's chivalry underwent a change: The ideal of HONOR was raised to the greatest possible RESPONSIBILITY toward the spirit; COURAGE to face death turned into DARING to enter suprasensory realms; the ability to practice COURTLY LOVE turned into complete SURRENDER TO CHRIST. Interestingly, these same ideals, modified, characterize the Order of the Knights Templar (see chapter "Historical Currents Related to the Grail").

---

78 W. Greiner, *Grals-Geheimnisse*.

In his lecture of May 16, 1920, Rudolf Steiner analyzed the Round Table in its relationship with Parzival.[79] He pointed to the fact that the last echoes of the twelve knights around King Arthur resounded simultaneously with the rise of the Parzival legends. Parzival "faced individually the twelve knights" and developed within himself the twelve qualities inherent in each of them. So, if in the Round Table there were twelve distinct forces converging in a center (King Arthur), in the figure of Parzival there are twelve forces radiating out from his own center. In this context, the people of the Middle Ages who strove to understand Parzival had to develop their inner Self, seek their own essence. A little further on, in the same lecture, Steiner said that people in the Middle Ages still had the awareness that, to be able to reach the figure of Christ, they first needed to understand the "representative of humanity, Parzival."

---

[79] R. Steiner, *Mystery of the Universe: The Human Being, Image of Creation*, GA 201.

CHAPTER 9

Differences between Gawain and Parzival

> This story will now rest for a while ... with Gawain.
> For this tale takes friendly note of many beside or beyond its hero Parzival.
> – Wolfram von Eschenbach, *Parzival* (B. VII, 176)

Most of this chapter is based on an article by Frank Teichmann,[80] although it also contains observations by other authors, in addition to my own. Comparing the stories of Gawain and Parzival, one can observe a clear polarity between them. The heroes' experiences in various situations, as well as their inner dispositions, are diametrically opposed.

While Gawain always rode through meadows and open spaces with good visibility, Parzival was, most of the time, lost in dense, dark forests,[81] always trying to find his way. This is already a very important statement, for one who is lost in the forest cannot see any distance or find his way. The outer world is not a safe parameter, hence his consciousness is not turned outward: It is drawn inward. Parzival was actually seeking an inner path.

Riding over hills and across open fields, in contrast, means to be awake, in full consciousness, totally focused on the outer world where the sun shines and it is easier to see one's surroundings and orient oneself. Thus, the situation in the forest corresponds to the night, when, as a rule, we are in a state of semiconsciousness (dreams)

---
80 F. Teichmann, "The Polarity of Parzival and Gawain in Eschenbach's *Parzival*," *The Golden Blade*, 47: The Quest for the Grail.
81 In many tales and legends, the hero's journey through the forest represents a path from a state of relative unconsciousness to another, higher level of consciousness.

or unconsciousness (deep sleep). Interestingly, several times Parzival came to a clearing, where forests are less dense and dark, and at those times his consciousness turned more toward the outer world. Relevant moments along his path always took place in clearings.

At the end of their adventures, both knights became rulers of kingdoms. Gawain won Terre Marveile after succeeding at all the trials of Schastel Marveile, the Enchanted Castle. This magnificent castle with its innumerable towers and palaces was clearly visible—one could almost fall over it. Yet it kept many women imprisoned, and many noble knights met death within its walls.

Parzival became King of the Grail, but only at the end of the story. When approaching the castle for the first time, Parzival asked the fisherman on the lake for a place to spend the night and was told that within a thirty-mile radius there was no dwelling except for a practically inaccessible castle. In contrast, Gawain, after defeating Lischoys Gwellius, was invited by the boatman to spend the night at his house. Thus both knights met persons with activities related to water. The fisherman indicated to Parzival the way to the practically inaccessible castle, warning him that many apparent (but false) shortcuts would present themselves.

Nevertheless, the young knight managed to reach Munsalvaesche: The Grail Castle suddenly appeared before him. This castle also had many towers and highly fortified palaces, but inside it was something like a source of life. In short, no effort was required to reach the Enchanted Castle; it was accessible to whoever came near, yet the hard part was trying to leave it, for inside one met death. On the other hand, the Grail Castle was so well hidden that, even following directions, one could not be sure of arriving; yet inside was the source that nourished and enlivened the community.

The knights' arrival times at their respective castles are also polar opposites. Gawain always arrived during the day when one is awake, fully conscious and turned toward the sense world, while Parzival always arrived at dusk, when one is normally tending toward semiconsciousness and then to deep sleep or unconsciousness. Once again, the author makes reference to the knights' respective states of consciousness during their journeys.

The second time Parzival arrived at the Grail Castle, however, although it was night, he was neither fully conscious nor dreaming nor asleep, like the first time. He had reached the state of "conscious perfection." In modern language, this means he had become an initiate, someone who enters the night realm (the suprasensory) in full consciousness. It can therefore be assumed that the Grail Castle, so difficult to reach, could be found not in the physical world at all, but in the suprasensory world.

With regard to the two castles' inhabitants, four hundred women were imprisoned in the Enchanted Castle and kept looking out its many windows. Wolfram tells us that four hundred knights took part in the Grail ritual. They stood facing the center, toward the Grail. Again, turning toward or away from the center underscores the characteristics typical of the communities of Arthur (Gawain) and the Grail (Parzival).

After these more general aspects, let us analyze how each hero was received at his first arrival at the castle. Gawain, leaving his horse in the care of the merchant at the gate, entered and did not encounter a single person. He went through several empty rooms—there seemed to be not a soul in that castle. Parzival, on the other hand, was warmly received by the knights, and many pages rendered him services.

Following the boatman's advice, Gawain entered the Enchanted Castle fully armed. He held his shield and gripped his sword, for he knew what was coming: He would be undergoing several trials. When a person is expecting a trial s/he will go prepared, armed to face the situation in the best possible way. Interestingly, Gawain had received a new shield from the boatman, as his own had been rendered useless by so much fighting the previous day. This "weapon," however, is only for defense; in fact, Gawain had to fend off constant attacks in Schastel Marveile.

Parzival, on the contrary, was promptly disarmed and bathed, according to the customs of the time, and received a precious coat of Arabic silk, offered by the queen. Thus he was unarmed inside the castle, with no notion that he was being tested, so he didn't prepare himself. Just like Gawain, Parzival also received an appropriate weapon—in this case, the Sword of the Grail; however, he did not know what it was for, or that he was already on trial.

In sum: Gawain received a defensive weapon of which he made good use, while Parzival received a weapon used not only for defense, but mainly for attack. The hoped-for "attack," however, was his question to the king. It would have been an attack of liberation and not of destruction.

Why was Gawain so well prepared? He never stopped asking his host questions about the Castle, its inhabitants, and who had been there previously, even when the boatman tried his best to avoid answering. The boatman had to tell Gawain what had happened to the ladies imprisoned in Schastel Marveile, and about the trials he would face. The boatman ended up not only giving the knight valuable advice, but also offering him a new shield.

When Parzival reached Munsalvaesche, only one question was expected of him in order to relieve Anfortas of his distressing situation. However, rigorously following Gurnemanz's instruction not to ask unnecessary questions, he kept silent. Parzival did not yet know how to distinguish between what was essential and irrelevant, necessary and unnecessary.

It is interesting to stress that Gawain's first trial was that of the Lit Marveile or Enchanted Bed. On a bed on which one would normally sleep, the knight had to stay awake, alert, and fully conscious. To make matters worse, this bed whirled around at breakneck speed. If a person spins around for a long time s/he will become dizzy, and if the spinning continues, may even lose consciousness. Gawain, however, managed to stay awake and conscious, emerging victorious from this and the other trials. Parzival, as mentioned above, did not even notice that he was being tested. It was as if he were "sleeping standing up," which is the reason he failed.

After undergoing their various trials, both knights fell asleep. Gawain slept deeply, regenerated by an infusion of herbs he had been given so as to achieve speedy recovery. Parzival, on the other hand, suffered through nightmares and forebodings of what he would have to encounter in battles and conflicts to come. On awakening, Gawain found himself surrounded by numerous maidens who served him courteously, while Parzival found himself alone and abandoned: the reverse situation of their arrival at the castles! Parzival had been received with great cordiality and had failed his trial, and when he awoke, he was alone. Gawain had not had any reception; he had had to find the way by himself, had passed his tests, and, when he woke up, was surrounded by people. When he went out to look around the castle he had won, he discovered a "magic" column in which he could see everything happening within a six-mile radius. Parzival, on the other hand, had to leave the Grail Castle as he was unworthy to remain there. Soon afterward he met Sigune, who left him lost in a dense forest where he could see almost nothing.

In their respective castles, both heroes encountered family members they did not expect. In the case of Gawain these were his grandmother Arnive, his mother Sangive, and his sisters Cundrie (not the Grail messenger) and Itonje, all of the feminine gender. In the Grail Community, on the other hand, Parzival met his mother's brothers; in the Grail Castle he met Anfortas and Repanse de Schoye, and in the chapel nearby he met Trevrizent. The two men, Anfortas and Trevrizent, had the greatest significance in the young knight's life. Note that the feminine side represents the forces of the soul, while the male aspect is related to the forces of the spirit. Rudolf Meyer points out that people's souls often seem trapped and isolated from one another, in an almost vegetative state. He writes that this occurs mainly because they succumb to the magic of sensuality, that is, they are trapped in their bodies.[82] Whoever breaks through this spell can open for many other souls the path toward freedom. It is a soul-awakening process. With this wonderful image, Wolfram revealed an important truth appropriate to the humanity of his time.

It is also interesting to examine the two knights' biographies and trajectories. About Gawain's childhood and youth, nothing is reported in Wolfram's writings: Indeed, information about that period in the hero's life has little bearing on the sequence of events. In the case of Parzival, however, the author begins his account with his ancestry and draws out the description of his childhood and youth, as these are all of fundamental importance for future events. Those early stages in Parzival's life determine the rest of the story. This again underscores the individual biographical aspect of the personalities in the Community of the Grail, and the less individual, more group character inherent in Arthur's court.

Both knights faced many different circumstances during their journeys, and their actions had consequences. Once again, there is a polarity of opposites. Gawain was already a knight of Arthur's court and as such was noble, fearless, courageous—in short, perfect. He invariably faced complicated situations which he sorted out masterfully, solving problems and creating harmony where there had been discord. Parzival, because of his inexperience and because he followed to the letter what he had been taught, left desolation in his wake until his first visit to the Grail Castle. Thanks to his interference, situations which had been harmonious became troubled or problematic. This happened because he was interested primarily in himself and naturally accepted any good done to him by others. However, every time he did become aware of his mistakes, he spared no effort to rectify them. It is interesting to note that in the first episode, after both heroes left Arthur's court to follow their respective destinies, the author reports that, without knowing it,

---

82 R. Meyer, *Der Gral und seine Hüter*.

Differences between Gawain and Parzival 171

they fought in opposing armies before Bearoche: Gawain fought for Lyppaut, Parzival for Melianz. According to Eileen Hutchins,[83] Gawain's destiny was to protect those who were innocently attacked (the outer version of what happened to him), while Parzival had to be on the side of those who had acted improperly, in order to redeem them. He himself had also acted wrongly and was trying to redeem his faults. It was for this reason that Parzival negotiated the release of Melianz.

The women both men encountered were very different. Gawain, as a rule, met complicated, proud, arrogant, challenging women, while Parzival met women who were humble and often in difficulties, although not necessarily always because of him (Herzeloyde, Sigune, Condwiramurs). Gawain did not have an apparent pre-established goal in life (or it may have been a hidden objective): He was simply carried by circumstances, accepted all challenges, and was always attentive to what was going on around him. He wanted nothing for himself—he was an instrument of Divine Providence. He received information and advice from many people, the majority of whom tried to dissuade him from his intentions. What stands out most in his story is his environment: In his own way, he always managed to change for the better whatever surrounded him.

At the beginning of the story, Parzival, too, had no objective beyond letting his horse carry him forward. Once he became aware of his mistakes, however, he established a plan and set himself a goal. He was searching for redemption and acted of his own free will.

Along the way, he was given indications and advice, mainly by Sigune. He is the central point in his story, with his mistakes, his achievements, and his struggle for self-improvement. When he was accepted into Arthur's court, he had already perfected some aspects of his character, but the curse of Cundrie revealed his inner imperfections.

He knew he could only help others once he had also reached this second form of perfection. In the course of his journey, therefore,

---

83 E. Hutchins, *Parzival, an Introduction*.

everything was drawn inward for his inner transformation and development, whereas Gawain, as a typical knight of Arthur's court, was fully turned toward the outer world and transformed by it. Parzival had to learn to transfer into himself what he experienced outside: He experienced what was in his soul as something external to himself. After all, the obvious ugliness of Cundrie was nothing but the ugliness of his own soul. Gawain, in contrast, did not have to recognize his essence through external factors, but he had to learn how to deal with acts committed by others and imposed on him.

In the end, both heroes reached their objectives, but by very different means: Parzival through compassion, and Gawain through the sublimation of love. However, the latter arrived at Schastel Marveile after showing compassion toward the injured knight, and Parzival reached the Grail Castle after receiving the love of Condwiramurs.

A curious aspect of Wolfram's work is that the episodes related to Gawain take place during the period in which Parzival was as if in a state of dependency on his friend. As mentioned above, when Gawain, by covering up the three drops of blood in the snow, freed Parzival from the altered state of consciousness into which he had fallen while contemplating them, he exerted some power over the Red Knight, who was now in his debt. Only by defeating Gawain in combat without knowing his identity did Parzival manage to free himself from this spell.

Wolfram writes that, in this fight, both were mounted on Grail horses. Gawain rode a horse he had received from Orilus, whose brother had taken it from a Grail knight he had killed; Parzival rode a horse he had won by defeating a Grail knight. No longer dependent on his friend, Parzival was once again the main hero of the narrative, ready for his last fight with Feirefiz. In all the episodes related to Gawain, Parzival's dependent state emerges, either explicitly or indirectly. (It should be emphasized that the narration of these episodes is interrupted by the encounter between Parzival and Trevrizent. This meeting, though, took place during Parzival's phase of introspection and maturation. Everything concerning Gawain happens in the outer world.)

It is very interesting that the destinies of Parzival and Gawain have many similarities, but are also very divergent. The spiritual stream Parzival came from originated in the East and spread to Spain (it is mentioned in the book found by Kyot in Toledo). Gawain belonged to Arthur's court; he came from the North and won his castle in Sicily. Together, these paths create an intra-European cross. Parzival, who walked the path of knowledge, experienced terrible doubts while searching for truth; Gawain followed the path of the heart—which is why he was not doubt-stricken. On the contrary, others doubted him, falsely accused him and defamed him. In reality, Gawain and Parzival are two aspects of human nature as a whole. It is impossible to walk only one of these paths. To get to the Grail Castle, one cannot unilaterally follow the path of knowledge. The path of the heart must also be followed; in other words, one must succeed at the trials of the Enchanted Castle. Parzival was able to get to the Grail Castle only after Schastel Marveile had been freed.

Bernd Lampe points to some other interesting polarities between the knights, examining events that occurred at different moments during their respective journeys. He subdivides these into seven stages for each hero. He follows Parzival's story only as far as Cundrie's curse. Soon after leaving his mother's house, Parzival *disgraced* an unknown woman (Jeschute) while Gawain *helped* a strange woman (Obie).[84]

In a second stage, Parzival encountered Sigune, who did not want to bury her beloved; Antikonie, King Vergulacht's sister, had the same name as a brave Greek woman (Antigone) who, against the laws of the state, dared to bury her brother.

In the third stage, both met their future wives for the first time. Parzival married Condwiramurs, but would abandon her; they could not, as yet, walk a path together. Gawain would still have to fight hard to win Orgeluse. In the fourth stage they both found their castles: Parzival saw the Grail and the suffering of Anfortas, but could not cure

---

84   B. Lampe, *Gawain*.

it. Gawain re-encountered the wounded knight, whom he had cured and who subsequently betrayed him.

In the fifth stage, Parzival again encountered Sigune, who would not release the embalmed corpse of her bridegroom. Gawain, in turn, freed the women who had been imprisoned in the Enchanted Castle.

In the sixth stage, Parzival reconciled Jeschute and Orilus, but to achieve this he had to defeat the knight in combat. Gawain became interested in the fate of Gramoflanz and his own sister Itonje, but the fight originally planned between them did not take place because Gawain managed to resolve the situation through dialogue—which is the true element of healing, rather than victory or defeat in combat.

In the final stage, Parzival left Arthur's court to seek the Castle of the Grail alone, and Gawain finally united himself with Orgeluse and her kingdom, connecting himself with the women in the Enchanted Castle.

In reality, these two knights represent isolated, unilateral aspects of the human being. The human body is commonly divided into three parts: head, trunk, and limbs. Each of them can be associated with a physiological system. The spherical structure of the head and the skull's flat bones form several cavities in which very sensitive organs lie protected: those of the senses and the central nervous system. The head is the center of the nerve-sense system. In opposition to this are the limbs, in which radially structured, generally cylindrical bones are at the center, surrounded by the muscle mass responsible for the body's movements.

According to Steiner, the limb system also includes the abdominal cavity, containing the organs mostly responsible for the transformation of the food we take in. There is great mobility in the digestive tract, though what happens in this region is generally unconscious. This system is thus called the metabolic-limb system and consists of the organs of metabolism and locomotion. Between the two is the rhythmic system, which has certain characteristics of the other two, in the sense that on the one hand it forms a protective shell (though not as tight as that of the skull) around the heart and lungs, the organs of the rhythmic functions of breathing and circulation. Furthermore, the ribs are both radial bones (like those of the limbs) and flattened (like the bones of the skull).

For this analysis of the roles of Parzival and Gawain, only the nerve-sense system and the metabolic-limb system are of interest. Examining the head in more detail, one can see that the whole world is *internalized* in it, in the form of sense perceptions—not only those originating with the sense organs in the head, but all of them, as nerves from the entire body converge in the central nervous system, bringing input from the senses of touch, warmth, proprioception, etc.[85] Air also enters the body through the head, as does food. It is true that air is also eliminated the same way; this polarity between internalizing and externalizing is characteristic of the middle system, which always presents aspects of both extremes. As for the metabolic-limb system, not only the transformation of food takes place there, as does the elimination of everything the body cannot use: Human beings use their limbs to move and go places where, through the activities of their limbs, they effect changes in the world; this is therefore an *externalizing* gesture. Relating these concepts to Parzival and Gawain, it can be concluded that the former represents the forces of internalization, those of the nerve-sense system, while Gawain, who acts in the world, transforming it, represents the externalizing gesture of the metabolic-limb system. That is, they reveal the two poles of the unitary human being: the nerve-sense system, the seat of thinking that leads to wisdom, and the metabolic-limb system, in which substances are modified and transformed. As both systems are like two sides of the same coin, in all the situations that Gawain experienced, Parzival, in a way, accompanied him. Chrétien de Troyes in his work *Perceval* recounted the episodes featuring Gawain, but never mentioned the simultaneous presence of Parzival.

---

85 See R. Steiner, "The Twelve Senses and the Seven Life Processes" in *The Riddle of Humanity*, GA 170, Aug. 12, 1916.

CHAPTER 10

The Journey of Gawain

> Gawain had these troubles to contend with—you may care to hear what was oppressing him? [...] In addition, his wounds were giving him much ado. And Love was giving him very much more.
> – Wolfram von Eschenbach, *Parzival* (B. XII, 299)

Although we have said that in a knight of Arthur's court there was apparently no room for improvement—because to be part of the Round Table already implied possession of all the requirements of knighthood, namely courage, honor, and dignity—Bernd Lampe shows magnificently in his work *Gawain* that Gawain was actually following an evolutionary path: the path of Christian initiation,[86] a sensory initiation since, in fact, this noble knight had not yet succeeded in sublimating sensual love into true courtly love.

As mentioned earlier, Parzival and Gawain represent different aspects of the human being, and therefore their adventures differ. It must be pointed out that, in all the episodes about Gawain, Parzival remains out of sight, or else present in a way not immediately recognizable. Actually, some parts of the Gawain stories remind one of events relating to Parzival. Comparing the two, one realizes that the story of Gawain moves very quickly, while Parzival's develops more slowly. Another aspect is the fact that Gawain did not seek out fights to boast about them afterward; he was always at the service of whoever needed help. Because of this friendly quality, however, he was often misunderstood. Gawain did not take up the path to the spiritual realm (as did Parzival),

---

86 The subject of initiation will be addressed in more detail in chapter 14, "The Trajectory of *Parzival*."

for his was the path of the soul: He had to purify and sublimate his soul. This path is important to the impulse of the Grail, although it does not lead to conscious knowledge.

The driving force in Parzival's trajectory was the desire to re-encounter the Grail Castle and be of service to Anfortas. The driving force in Gawain, however, was the feeling of love that pushed him into dangerous situations, in addition to causing him humiliation; but this feeling filled him equally with invincible courage, allowing him to face any trial or even endanger his life. It is thus that courtly love became his aim. He underwent a "life initiation" process because, through extreme suffering caused by external situations, he managed to sublimate the forces of the heart. Gawain, Arthur's knight, proud and accustomed to honor, had to learn the hard way to be humble. With Lampe, we will analyze the various steps of his journey.

Shortly after setting out for Ascalun to engage in the duel to prove his innocence, Arthur's nephew encountered the huge army assembled by King Melianz to confront Lyppaut, his foster father and servant. Wolfram reports that among other shady warriors in this army was Meliakanz, a knight mentioned early in Parzival's story. At that time he had kidnapped a maiden, and the knights the naïve boy met in the forest, thinking they were gods, had been tracking down this very ruffian.

It so happens, though, that Gawain was faced with a strange situation, because this army had been assembled by a king to fight the very person who had brought him up. In this army were knights who disrespected women; i.e., noble manners like those known in Arthur's court did not prevail. This might already have indicated the proximity of Schastel Marveile (the Enchanted Castle), a place that could be considered the visible representation of evil in the outer world. So Gawain decided to help the harassed nobleman; after all, his destiny was to help those who were unjustly attacked, which had happened to him already and would happen again.

In Lyppaut's castle good moral values might still have prevailed, but it was not to be. Lyppaut's daughter Obie insulted Gawain, calling him a merchant and dealer in counterfeit coins. He heard all these humiliations after having left Arthur's court, where he had also been humiliated. Only little Obilot, a pure child, gave him some credit, recognizing in him the knight and savior of her father's army. As the pledged knight of little Obilot—in other words, in the service of a child—he left for combat.

In the enemy army there was a brave and invincible hero. Only much later do we discover that it was Parzival. It could be considered a miracle that the two friends did not cross swords in battle; to recognize each other on the battlefield would have been impossible. The knight in red armor was actually fighting on the side of the evildoers; in the previous chapter we noted that Parzival's destiny was to stay on the side of those who were in the wrong (because he had also done wrong) so he could redeem them. As Parzival's horse was rather weak as a result of much fighting, Parzival asked the squires for another horse in reward for his deeds. They offered him a horse that had escaped its owner in battle. It was one of Gawain's horses. (Gawain had, in fact, another mount, once offered to him by Duke Orilus. It was a Grail horse, which Lähelin, Orilus's brother, had taken from a Grail knight killed in combat.)

It is important to stress that from this moment on, Parzival had one of Gawain's horses. However, Gawain had left Bearoche castle with everything resolved. The question remains: Had Gawain fought on the side of the right, and Parzival on the side of the evildoers? Walter Johannes Stein says that here the knights' two distinct paths can be seen:[87] Gawain opposed evil and fought it; Parzival joined evil in an attempt to transform it. As will be further explained (in "Historical Currents Related to the Grail"), this last path is the Manichaean one. Because Gawain had released Parzival from his contemplative trance before the three drops of blood in the snow, it can be considered that, in a way, he exercised a certain mastery over his friend; Parzival felt in his

---

87 W.J. Stein, *The Ninth Century and the Holy Grail*.

debt and therefore followed, somewhat unconsciously, in the footsteps of his rescuer.

In Ascalun reigned Vergulacht. Wolfram, always very thorough, describes the ancestry of this king, and we conclude that he was a cousin of Parzival, for Vergulacht's mother was Gahmuret's sister. When Gawain met this king going hunting and he suggested that Gawain go to the city, where he would be well received by his sister, one can well imagine that this was in fact a trial. And so it was, when Gawain and the king's sister Antikonie were alone in the castle and he fell in love with her. Although nothing really extraordinary happened between them, Gawain was again accused, this time by the old knight, of something he had not done. The strange thing is that when Gawain was being attacked by the mob, the person who came to his rescue was exactly the same knight sent to Arthur's court to accuse him of something he had in fact not done. And again Parzival appears on the scene, this time only mentioned by King Vergulacht.

As Gawain took on the task imposed on the king by the Red Knight, a potential fight was transformed into something else: the search for the Grail. The curious relationship established from then on between the two knights is this: Parzival rode the horse that once belonged to Gawain, while Gawain took on Parzival's task, the search for the Grail. Rudolf Meyer points out that in this episode it becomes evident that the strict law of guilt and atonement may be attenuated when someone decides to walk the path toward the spiritual world[88]—in this case, when Gawain assumes the search for the Grail. Thus, there are initiatives that can free people of the human entanglements caused through wrongdoing. When someone begins to tread a spiritual path, old relationships shift and destinies are reordered. In the following passage, Gawain has experiences that remind us of those that happened to Parzival. One must keep in mind, however, that Parzival's goal is the Grail Castle, and Gawain's is Schastel Marveile.

---

88 R. Meyer, *Der Gral und seine Hüter*.

Just as Parzival met Sigune holding her dead bridegroom on her lap, Gawain met a lady with a wounded knight on her lap. Gawain was able to cure him, but this knight did not possess very noble traits: He treacherously seized his benefactor's horse. Once again Gawain suffered humiliation and insults, but mainly had to endure Orgeluse's contempt. Even her squire, Malcreatiure, Cundrie's brother, mocked him (paralleling Cundrie's curse). It is interesting that many people (including the wounded knight, an elderly knight and Malcreatiure) warned Gawain about the falseness of Orgeluse, who reveled in all situations in which her suitor suffered some misfortune (his stolen horse, his hands injured in the squire's hair, etc.), besides calling him a witch doctor and a merchant. But Gawain did not let slander, defamation, and lies irritate him. The power of his love enabled him to grasp people's essence immediately, realizing that they only appeared to be wicked.

Another setback occurred when, after Gawain's defeat of Lischoys Gwellius, who had been invincible until that moment, Gawain regained his horse only to have it immediately requested by the boatman. It is important to remember that Gawain's horse was a Grail horse, given to him by Orilus. Twice he had almost lost it. This shows that he still needed to improve his attention and presence of mind. There is another parallel with the story of Parzival: Before reaching the Grail Castle, where he stayed overnight, he met the Fisher King; and near Schastel Marveile Gawain met the boatman, in whose house he spent the night. Both characters, the fisherman and the boatman, live by the water. The following day, the boatman would tell Gawain that, shortly before the fight with Lischoys, he had ferried across another knight who, according to his description, must have been Parzival. The next episode recounts the trials in Schastel Marveile.

It was mentioned earlier that, had Gawain not interrogated the boatman, he would not have committed himself to saving the women imprisoned in that castle. He was warned that he would face certain death, but that did not scare him either. By asking numerous questions, he prepared himself to face the challenges and even received a new shield from his host.

From the boatman's story, Gawain discovered that Parzival had been there the previous day; that is, he was also in the vicinity of Schastel Marveile, albeit with his identity hidden. This Terre Marveile of Clinschor represents the world of desires, and in fact Gawain deeply desired Orgeluse, who rejected him. When the Queen of Logroys met Parzival, who had already learned to master his impulses and desires, she tried to seduce him but did not succeed. In a way, he had already learned what was to be learned on earth. For this reason, Parzival is only marginally mentioned in this episode.

When one enters the world of desires, represented by Schastel Marveile, one penetrates into the dynamic world of the processes that take place in the organs and normally remain hidden to consciousness. Maybe that is why Gawain was warned to leave his horse outside the castle: The horse symbolizes thinking and intelligence, so having to leave it outside may mean that in this context Gawain could not enter with his intelligence connected to daytime consciousness. To undergo the experience of lying on the Lit Marveile, one must be fearless and utterly courageous. What Wolfram describes in this trial corresponds to the initiation process that Steiner called the "way in" into the body, the microcosm, unlike the "way out" to the macrocosm (see chapter "The Trajectory of *Parzival*"). Walter Johannes Stein explains that one must learn to tolerate the movements of the Lit Marveile. The fact that the bed suddenly stopped moving was no sign that the trials were over with, because stones and arrows were then hurled at Gawain. According to initiates, the experience of one's own mirrored thoughts and feelings being thrown back at one upon first entering the spiritual world may be considered an experience of self-knowledge.

Then there is the encounter with the lion, the archetypal representative of the rhythmic system. This beast was meant to be overcome, not killed; in the Middle Ages this was represented by a human being mounted on a lion's back. In *Parzival*, Gawain killed the lion, showing that he was not totally successful in this trial. He fainted beside the animal as if he too were dead, and was then rescued by the inhabitants of the castle. The fact that Gawain still did not have total control over his desires explains his partial failure. In all these events, the sphere of feelings is stressed.

Since he had not been able to control the lion but killed it instead, Gawain still had to undergo another trial. Overwhelmed by his passion for Orgeluse and still not completely recovered, he launched himself into new adventures. The (unconscious) aim of his trajectory was the total purification of his feelings; to achieve that, he had to search for a branch of Gramoflanz's tree. He was almost able to jump unscathed across the ravine, but not quite. Like Parzival in his fight with the Grail Knight, Gawain managed to cling to the branch of a tree. His horse fell into the turbulent river, but the hero managed to bring it back to shore.

After getting the requested branch, finding Gramoflanz, discovering that the latter loved his sister—one of the prisoners of Schastel Marveile—and accepting the king's challenge to combat, Gawain managed easily enough to return to Orgeluse, who had now completely changed her attitude, accepting and returning his love. Until then she had been as if under a spell, in the service of evil, diverting many knights from their paths and destroying them. Gawain served her patiently, and finally managed to rid himself of her seductive power. He expressed this in the following words:

> "By your dazzling looks, you must never again offer a knight such insults! If I am to be the butt of your mockery I would rather be without love." (B. XII, 307)

Thus, he managed to break the spell and liberate her, for he had turned his passion into true love. This transformation caused him to be successful in his trials and readied him to receive Orgeluse as his wife.

Orgeluse told Gawain about her encounter with Parzival, the only knight who had not been defeated by the Knights of Clinschor and who had refused her own offers. This shows that Parzival had already mastered, in a different way, his feelings and desires; he did not have to pass the tests of Clinschor's kingdom, the land of desires. Though he did have to pass through these lands, he did so without becoming entangled in the temptations of the senses: Another ideal lived in his soul.

Rudolf Meyer explains the method by which Clinschor obtained what he wanted: He terrorized people, and thus was able to paralyze the forces of resistance in their souls. He disarmed them through fear. The only way to overcome this situation was through courage. As Gawain's courage was fully present and developed, he managed to succeed and broke the curse of the magician.

Back in his castle, Gawain, whose identity was still unknown to all, took several other measures to help others: He freed the knights he had defeated; after verifying that his sister loved Gramoflanz and consequently hated Orgeluse, he promised to intervene on behalf of the lovers, promoting their meeting; he organized a banquet with music and dancing, gathering, for the first time, the ladies and knights who had been imprisoned by Clinschor, i.e., by their desires, and who, despite living under one roof, had never met. The celebration proceeded without overindulgence: In other words, Gawain had learned to ennoble the forces of the heart, and the world of desires was under control.

Ever since the fight between Gawain and Parzival (though Gawain thought he was facing Gramoflanz), the Red Knight no longer remained hidden, but took up his central position even though events were still happening in the vicinity of Schastel Marveile. Parzival, having defeated his opponent, was now freed of Gawain's power over him, which he had felt ever since the event of the drops of blood in the snow. As for Gawain, he was no longer important to the story. His wedding to Orgeluse marked the culmination of his journey, in which he had achieved control over his feelings; therefore his mission was at an end.

In several lectures[89] Rudolf Steiner described Christian initiation as an initiation through *feelings*. Whoever wished to take this initiatory path often needed the help of an instructor. This initiation was conceived as an "imitation of the Passion of Christ," i.e., a passage through everything Christ had experienced and felt deeply. During the process of initiation, a person underwent not only physical experiences, but spiritual ones as well. It consisted of seven steps, which will be summarized briefly:

- In the first step, the disciple learned how human beings came to be what they are today, a development made possible by the emergence of the other kingdoms: Without the existence of minerals, plants, and animals, human existence would not have been possible. This raised in the soul a deep sense of gratitude and devotion toward the lower realms. Having achieved humility, the disciple could spiritually experience the meaning of the ritual of the "WASHING OF THE FEET," when Christ, such a high being, knelt before His disciples and washed their feet.

- In the second step, the disciple was taught to learn to bear pain and suffering without complaining, accepting them as something necessary for the sake of development, and thus being able to contemplate the scene of the "FLAGELLATION" of Christ through spiritual eyes.

- The third step was not only to endure pain and suffering, but also to tolerate the contempt of others. This required from the initiate an attitude of firm strength so as to withstand the ensuing sense of annihilation and, at the same time, to recognize the existence of something extremely sublime and sacred within, to be defended at

---

[89] Among them, some delivered in 1906 and published in the cycle *An Esoteric Cosmology*, GA 94; in the cycle *The Gospel of St. John*, GA 94; in the lecture *From Jesus to Christ*, GA 131, Oct. 10, 1911.

all costs, even when abandoned and lonely, depending exclusively on him- or herself. Then the scene of the "CROWNING WITH THORNS" was revealed to the spiritual eye.

- In the fourth step the disciple experienced his or her body as a foreign object—for example, a piece of wood—and would then no longer identify the Self with the body. Spiritually, this experience was "CARRYING THE CROSS."

- The fifth step was called "MYSTICAL DEATH"; at this point the physical world appeared shrouded in a veil and everything lost its value. The person was surrounded by darkness. Suddenly the darkness was ripped open, allowing the person a glimpse into the spiritual world behind the physical world. Besides recognizing the essence of the human soul, the person also recognized the true configuration of evil and all the suffering in the sense world. This experience corresponds to the "DESCENT INTO HELL."

- In the sixth step, disciples experienced everything around them, including the suffering of others, as something as relevant to them as their own bodies. They related themselves to everything living on Earth. This meant "being confined to earth," equivalent to "BURIAL." Having thus lost their individuality, they assumed a higher life, that is, "RESURRECTION."

- Finally, the seventh step, named "ASCENSION," allowed the experience of returning to the spiritual world, of being fully absorbed by it. It is difficult to express in human words this highest degree of Christian initiation.

Bernd Lampe describes the seven episodes in the story of Gawain, relating them to Christian initiation. One can rediscover the WASHING OF THE FEET, essentially consisting of an act of humility, in the episode involving Gawain and Obilot, in which he proved capable of putting himself at the service of a child. In the episode involving Vergulacht, Antikonie and Kingrimursel, Gawain was the victim of several false accusations; only later was his innocence proved. This would correspond to the FLAGELLATION. Even the wounded knight whom he had assisted deceived him, and the woman he loved despised and hurt him; this is the CROWNING WITH THORNS. The CRUCIFIXION means going through death for love, and is exactly what happened in the combat between Gawain and Lischoys Gwellius. The trials in Schastel Marveile, the kingdom of evil, correspond to the MYSTICAL DEATH and DESCENT INTO DELL.

With the RESURRECTION after the BURIAL, a person is increasingly bound to the fate of others (and of humanity): This is what happened when Gawain made a crown from the branch of Gramoflanz's tree and not only bound the latter's destiny to Orgeluse, but even managed to reconcile them. As mentioned above, the mystery of the ASCENSION cannot be expressed in words. It is so sublime that it eludes earthly conditions. In the case of Gawain, it was represented by the state of *saelde*, usually translated as "bliss," but Wolfram also gives it the meaning of realizing destiny.

WASHING OF THE FEET	Bearoche (Obilot)
FLAGELLATION	Ascalun (Kingrimursel, Vergulacht, Antikonie)
CROWNING WITH THORNS	Logroys (Injured Knight, Orgeluse)
CRUCIFIXION	Fight with Lischoys Gwellius
MYSTICAL DEATH and DESCENT INTO HELL	Trials in Schastel Marveile
BURIAL and RESURRECTION	After going through the kingdom of Gramoflanz
ASCENSION	Bliss (marriage to Orgeluse)

CHAPTER 11

The Symbol of the Lance

> A page ran in at the door, bearing—this rite was to evoke grief —a Lance from whose keen steel blood issued and then ran down the shaft to his hand and all but reached his sleeve.
> – Wolfram von Eschenbach, *Parzival* (B. V, 123)

The scene described above is so unusual that it deserves some attention to help us unravel the symbolism of the spear. Toward this end we will initially mention some facts, legends, and curiosities and then seek a thread that will unite them all and explain the scene. Many people, when reading or listening to this passage, will immediately establish an association with the scene described in the Gospel of John, in which, after the crucifixion, a Roman soldier pierced the side of Jesus's body to make sure of his death, and blood and water[90] poured from the wound (John 19:32–34).

---

90 Although not directly related to the present subject, an understanding of this sentence may be interesting. Saint Augustine (354–430) interpreted these words by saying that blood was shed to redeem sins, and that water is a healing drink and is also used for bathing (which would mean purification). Some time later, Cyril of Alexandria (c. 375–444) a theologian and bishop sanctified by the Church, related blood and water to two sacraments: the Eucharist and Baptism.

It is possible, however, to consider these two substances from a different point of view. According to Rudolf Steiner, water is the representative element of the life or etheric body (see next chapter), which leaves the physical body at the moment of death. In several of his lectures Steiner said that in the human organism, the bearer of the "Self," the divine spark of individuality of every human being, is the blood.

In his lectures on Christ he also said, based on his spiritual research, that one may consider Christ as the "Cosmic Self" that incarnated in Jesus of Nazareth during his baptism by John the Baptist in the River Jordan. If one considers the

Among the curiosities about the lance is the fact that in the Middle Ages European noblemen brought back relics from their trips to the Holy Land. These sacred objects were stored in richly ornate reliquaries, and were often offered to people to whom one wished to show great esteem and affection. Among these relics were thorns from Christ's crown of thorns, chips of the wood of the Cross, bones and teeth of saints, pieces of clothing, etc. One of the most coveted and appreciated relics was a piece of the Holy Lance, the same used by the Roman centurion to pierce the side of Jesus.

It is said that during the First Crusade (1095–1099), the Christians were besieging Antioch when they were surprised and surrounded by the Muslim army. They were desperate, without food, almost defeated, when a poor priest from Provence told them of a dream in which it was revealed to him that a specific relic would bring victory to the Crusaders. It was the lance that had pierced the side of Jesus on the cross. It was also revealed that it was buried under the church. They dug all day, and in the evening they found the Holy Lance. Armed with it, the Crusaders charged, defeated the pagans and seized the city of Antioch.

The fact that the body of Christ had been pierced with a lance was considered very special by the Church Father John Chrysostom (c. 345–407), who lived in Antioch and introduced the sacred liturgy. He preached something quite different from the ancient initiated priests.

---

earth an organism equivalent to the human organism, possessing a physical, mineral aspect; a partially liquid or vital aspect; an airy aspect linked to the movement of feelings and emotions; and consisting of an individuality—the Self was still missing.

According to Rudolf Steiner, when the blood of Christ flowed from the cross, impregnating the earth, this very high cosmic entity, the Cosmic Self, became the Self or "I" of the earth. Therefore, it is possible that in describing this scene, John the Evangelist (the only one to do so) intended to refer to that fact and suggest that the "Self" of Christ (His blood) had separated from the body together with His life (water). For the various bodies constituting the human being, see chapter 12, "The Symbol of the Grail."

While these still preached of a macrocosmic Christ to be found in the universe, the cult founded by Chrysostom revered the Christ incarnated in a man, who died and rose from the dead and was therefore bound to the earthly sphere. According to some researchers,[91] the Byzantine liturgy, known as the Divine Liturgy of Saint John Chrysostom, was introduced later, and in its ritual, the wafer, representing the body of Christ, was pierced with a small silver spear, repeating the act of the Roman centurion. As this is a very realistic procedure, one understands the relation between this act and Chrysostom's realistic preaching. While he pierced the wafer, the priest uttered the following words: "Immortality is given to the human being through the lance." Therefore, there was somehow a relationship between the lance and immortality.

According to a medieval legend, the Roman centurion mentioned above was called Longinus and was blind. When he pierced the side of Christ with his lance, a few drops of the Savior's blood fell onto his eyes, and he was immediately able to see. At such a miracle, the soldier converted to Christianity and was later canonized by the Church. To us he is known as Saint Longinus, invoked whenever one is looking for something lost which is right before our eyes; he is also invoked to stop bleeding.

This legend should be examined more carefully. It is unthinkable that the Romans would have blind soldiers in their legions. This blindness of Longinus, therefore, cannot be physical; it is a spiritual blindness. When the legend says that he began to see when drops of blood fell onto his eyes, it means that at that moment, the centurion became clairvoyant: He saw the divine entity of Christ, recognized His greatness, and became one of His followers.

There are two sculptures that adorn the portals of various Gothic cathedrals, which should be analyzed in connection with this spiritual blindness. They are two very beautiful female figures. In the case of

---

91 Such as K. Burdach in *Der Gral*.

those in Strasbourg Cathedral, France, one of them is blindfolded, so she cannot see; she faces downward, and with one arm she supports herself on a broken lance that originally pointed upward. In her other hand, turned downward, she holds something that cannot be immediately recognized; only closer observation reveals the Tablets of the Law on which the Ten Commandments are inscribed, revealed by God to Moses on Mount Sinai. The second figure has her eyes wide open, looking to the horizon; in one of her hands she holds a vertical lance, which, instead of a spearhead, has a cross on top. In the other hand she holds a chalice. The first figure represents the Synagogue, the second one the Church. We must remember that in the Judeo-Christian tradition, before the coming of Christ, the Synagogue, the place of prayer of the Jewish religion, represented wisdom and the link with the spiritual world. After the advent of Christ, the Church took over this role. One can understand why the sculpture of the Synagogue is blindfolded; it highlights the fact that the ancient wisdom does not recognize [see] Christ.

In the days when knights roamed the world battling evil, thousands of churches, chapels, and small shrines dedicated to Saint Michael the Archangel appeared all over Europe. At that time (the 9th to 11th centuries), his importance exceeded even that of Christ and the Virgin Mary; the latter began to be worshiped mainly in the 12th and 13th centuries, inspiring artists of many disciplines. Many cathedrals and churches of that time are dedicated to Mary. But Saint Michael also inspired many artists, who represented him either mounted on a horse or not, holding a dragon at bay at his feet with his spear. In some paintings and sculptures he also appears holding a scale in one hand. The figure of Saint George, a knight subduing a dragon at his feet with a spear, is the earthly counterpart of Archangel Michael, a celestial being. The dragon, usually depicted with an animal's facial features and located in the lower part of the picture, represents human instincts, desires, and greed—in short, the evil in us, which rises within us and must be mastered by human consciousness. Otherwise, a person dominated by instincts and passions presents inhuman, animalistic behavior. Human beings can only act freely when they are not influenced by their lower nature. On the other hand, this lower nature is part of our organism and essential to our survival; it must be present, but within certain limits. Thus, it cannot be eliminated (killed), but must be controlled, dominated, conquered.

In the pre-Christian era, when human beings had not yet been given their inner Self, or rather when their self acted more from the outside, they could not dictate their own behavior; therefore, there were rules or external laws such as the commandments of Judaism, the Code of Hammurabi, and the like. Only since the advent of Christ and the subsequent internalization of the Self in each individual—that is, since human beings have truly become able to be individuals—is each of us able, little by little, more and more, to control our impulses through inner effort. Only then can we attain freedom. For this reason, life before the event of Christ still had a group or tribal character. The group leader dictated the rules; in other words, he was the Self of the group. True self-consciousness only dawned in about the 15th century, when, for example, artists began to sign their works of art.

With this information in hand, it is possible to sketch a symbolic meaning for the lance: It represents the Self, the human spirit. Pointing downward (Saint Michael), it represents the Self that dominates the instincts and animal forces of the human organism; pointing upward, as in the sculpture representing the Church, it symbolizes the Self in search of spirituality—as we are intuitively used to placing the spiritual world above the sense world. The Synagogue, however, is represented leaning on a broken lance; this means that, after the coming of the Christ, the ancient wisdom no longer served as a connection with the spiritual world.

We should remember the words of the priest during the Chrysostom Mass: "Immortality is brought to human beings by the lance." Here we can also see the relationship of the immortal element of the human being, the Self, to the lance. In this ritual one can even notice a reference to the meeting of the human Self with the entity of Christ, wonderfully described by Sergei Prokofieff in his work *What Is Anthroposophy?* There is another object, not exactly a spear, although one can imagine it as a kind of miniature spear, used by kings as a symbol of self-control; this object represents the Self which is able to control its own lower impulses, an essential prerequisite for a sovereign to rule over his people: the scepter.

In eurythmy,[92] the gesture for the phoneme "I" ("ee" in English) illustrates this very well. The person, standing upright, extends an arm upward toward the light, in search of the spiritual realm, while the other arm is extended downward and slightly backward, pointing to a dark region; this keeps the dragon in its proper place. Thus the whole body becomes the lance. It is not a coincidence that in many languages the term for the individuality contains the phoneme "I" or a sound similar to "ee": *I* (English), *ich* (German), *ik* (Dutch), *io* (Italian), *ia* (Russian; pronounced "eeah"), *yo* (Spanish), *jaz* (Slovenian, pronounced "eeahee"), *Jeg* (Norwegian; the "j" sounds like "ee"), *jag* (Swedish; the "j" sounds like "ee"), *ani* (Hebrew), *watashi* (Japanese); and so on.

According to Rudolf Meyer, a lance that bleeds would be an image of the active instinctive forces in the blood.[93] The lance could poison the noblest aspirations. But the same force that causes destruction when applied egotistically can manifest itself as creative power of the Self when used in freedom. A little later in his work, Meyer refers to the lance

---

92   Eurythmy is the art of movement introduced by Rudolf Steiner, in which gestures performed by the artist mainly represent musical intervals and phonemes. In the words of Steiner, eurythmy makes music and speech visible. Therefore it can be performed with music or poetry. It is not an expression of the body, as it follows laws determined by the movement of air passing through the vocal tract when a given phoneme is pronounced, or determined by the relationship between musical intervals. Besides artistic eurythmy there is also pedagogical eurythmy, which is part of the curriculum in Waldorf schools, and therapeutic eurythmy, used as a therapeutic resource in anthroposophical medicine.

93   R. Meyer, *Der Gral und seine Hüter*.

in Wagner's opera *Parsifal*. Clinschor was unable to strike Parsifal when he threw the lance at the hero, because Parsifal had already mastered all his instincts. Furthermore, by inserting this spear (which previously belonged to Clinschor) in Anfortas' wound, Parsifal healed him. Meyer says that the "holy lance," before which the natural, instinctive world falls apart to make way for the spiritual world, is the real Self.

Applying the above considerations to the scene described by Wolfram in *Parzival*, one will not only understand it better, but also find out why the whole community, and especially King Anfortas, suffered so much when they saw the lance being carried by the squire. In Wolfram's own words: "This rite was to evoke grief!" (B. V, 123)

This immediately leads us to imagine destruction. What grief is that? The lance reminded them that King Anfortas had not yet sufficiently developed the strength of his Self; he was not able to control his instincts. As King of the Grail, he should have consciously abstained from any frivolity. Falling prey to the seduction of a woman, he became vulnerable, he was wounded and became incapable. And not only Anfortas, but the whole Grail suffered the consequences of this act.

Curiously, the lance is not mentioned when Parzival returns to the Grail the second time. Walter Johannes Stein explains that the lance being carried around the four walls of the hall during the first visit is precisely a sign that the true goal has not yet been reached;[94] Parzival was still, in a sense, unconscious. It should also be noted that while the lance was in view the knights lamented and cried out in pain. When it disappeared, their lamentations ceased. The second time, the desired goal was fully achieved: That is, Parzival, fully conscious and in freedom, healed Anfortas, so there was no longer any reason for sorrow and lamentations, which is why the lance is no longer mentioned.

---

94 W.J. Stein, *The Ninth Century and the Holy Grail*.

CHAPTER 12

The Symbol of the Grail

> To everyone who conquers I will give some of the hidden manna, and I will give a white stone, and on the white stone is written a new name that no one knows except the one who receives it.
> – Revelation 2:17

First, let us verify the descriptions of the Grail by the principal authors who write about it.

1. CHRÉTIEN DE TROYES mentions, during Perceval's first visit to the castle of the Fisher King, the entry of two squires bearing chandeliers, followed by a beautiful maiden who held a Grail in her hands.[95] Its splendor was such that the chandeliers lost their brilliance, in the same way as the sun dims the stars' brightness. The Grail was of fine gold, adorned with precious stones. (The author does not mention its shape.) Behind this maiden was another one carrying a silver salver. All moved past the king and Perceval, and went to another room. Then a meal was served.

Before each course, the Grail was carried past the diners. In this narrative, it was anticipated that Perceval would ask about the meaning of the spear which was carried past with its tip dripping blood, and also about whom the Grail would serve. When Perceval met the hermit, he found out that the father of the Fisher King had been in the next

---

95 Here is the correct translation of the Old French text of *Le Roman de Perceval ou Le Conte du Graal*, into modern French by S. Hannedouche, published by Triades, 1969: "Un Graal, entre ses deux mains, tenait une demoiselle belle gentille et bien parée, qui venait avec les valets. Quand elle fut entrée avec le Graal un si grand éclat illumina la salle (...). Le Graal qui allait devant était de fin or pur." (p. 58)

room, and that he was fed by a wafer deposited in the Grail; this was his only food.

2. ROBERT DE BORON, in his work *The Legend of the Holy Grail*, also known as *Joseph of Arimathea*,[96] gives a totally different account. He begins by mentioning the cup in which, during the Last Supper, Christ offered wine to His disciples, saying "This is my blood, the blood of the covenant, which is shed for many" (Mark 14:24). After the crucifixion, Joseph of Arimathea[97] obtained permission from Pontius Pilate (governor of Judea, 26–36 AD) to bury the body of Christ. The governor, to whom a Jew had given the cup, wanted to get rid of it, so he gave it to Joseph. When Joseph washed the Lord's body to prepare Him for burial, His wounds bled again. Then Joseph gathered the blood of Christ in the same vessel used during the Last Supper.

But it has been translated as: "A beautiful, slender damsel, well-dressed, entered with the squires carrying a *chalice* [my emphasis] in her hands. Upon entering the room, a dazzling light emanated from the Grail [...]. The Grail, entering the room, was made of pure gold." The replacement of the word "grail" with "chalice" when it is first mentioned seems an interpretation based on other works.

When people heard that on the Sunday the tomb was found empty, the Jews accused Joseph of Arimathea of having stolen Christ's body to simulate the Resurrection and, after a brief trial, they condemned him. He was thrown into a windowless tower and walled in to die of hunger. Suddenly the room was filled with a great light, and Christ appeared and handed him the same cup, which then provided Joseph with food and light. Nearly forty years later, the son of the Roman emperor, miraculously cured of leprosy by an object touched by Christ, went to Jerusalem to learn more about Him. Someone remembered that Joseph

---

96 R. Boron, *The Story of the Holy Grail*.
97 Little is known about Joseph of Arimathea. He was a member of the Sanhedrin, the assembly of magistrates in Jerusalem, and also a disciple of Christ, though he kept it secret for fear of the Jews. He was a rich man and offered a tomb he owned for Jesus Christ's burial.

of Arimathea had been thrown into the tower a long time ago and would certainly be dead. Even so, Vespasian (9–79 AD)[98] asked to enter the tower, where an old man was found, enjoying full health thanks to the forces provided by the vessel. Wondering at such a miracle, the emperor became a Christian.

After his release, Joseph of Arimathea joined his family and gathered some disciples to whom he preached the words of Christ. At one time there was a food shortage, interpreted by his followers as the result of moral decay. So Joseph of Arimathea prayed to Christ, and Christ revealed Himself to him through the cup which contained His blood, instructing him to celebrate a supper to remember the Last Supper. On the table he should place the cup and a fish caught by his brother-in-law, Bron. The whole community gathered, and those seated at the table (occupying all the seats except the one reserved for Judas) experienced an indescribable sweetness and plenitude. Those not seated at the table felt nothing. Thus it was revealed that the latter had not, in fact, established a true relationship with Christ. Realizing this, they left the community, ashamed. Only pure people who had accepted Christ into their souls could take part in this supper. However, those who had left wanted to know more about the vessel placed on the table. They were told that, through it, believers were separated from nonbelievers and that its name was Grail.

The reference to the fish deserves some explanation. Rudolf Meyer[99] says that, in terms of natural evolution, the fish is still at the stage where warm blood did not yet exist. This signifies that its soul life is pure, not filled with desires. It was believed that in His earthly existence, free of any guilt, Christ had some affinity with this evolutionary stage

---

98 Robert de Boron refers to Vespasian as the son of the Emperor Titus. Historically, however, the reverse is true: Titus was the son of Vespasian, who had succeeded Nero. It was Titus who, in 70 AD, destroyed Jerusalem and the Great Temple of Solomon, ending the Jewish insurgency and dispersing the Jewish people. Certainly Robert de Boron was confused about the names.
99 R. Meyer, *Der Gral und seine Hüter*.

of the fishes. However, in order to save humanity, He had to inhabit a body in which warm blood flowed. Therefore He connected Himself with humanity's guilt out of pure love and purified the blood from the guilt and selfish impulses accumulated by humankind for generations and generations.

After the baptism in the Jordan, Christ gathered His disciples, all of whom were fishermen. According to the above author, the figure of the fisherman represents someone whose consciousness is on the threshold between the sense world and the higher spiritual world (see chapter "The Trajectory of *Parzival*"). Furthermore, it is known that the first Christians living in Rome were persecuted and hid in the catacombs. In order to identify themselves, they painted on the doors of their residences or meeting places a sign consisting of two fishes. These symbolized Christ himself. In ancient Greek, the word for "fish" is *ichthus*; the Greek initials of the words "Jesus Christ, Son of God, Savior"— Ιησούς Χριστός Θεού Υιός Σωτηρ (Iesous Christos Theou Uios Soter)—form the word *ICHTHUS*.

The fish is also a symbol of ancient initiation. After a neophyte had prepared and purified his soul for a long time and was deemed ready, he was taken by a hierophant to an isolated enclosure that was shut tight, and placed in a kind of sarcophagus.

Then the hierophant induced the adept into a deeper sleep than usual, a lethargic state similar to death, lasting three days. After being awakened from this initiatory sleep, the initiate was a changed person. He had been through experiences in the spiritual world that he could remember, and from then on he was sure of the existence of a suprasensory world. The book of Jonah in the Old Testament symbolically describes exactly this process. Having disobeyed God, Jonah boarded a ship that was hit by a terrible storm. Dice were tossed and "the lot fell to Jonah." He was thrown overboard and the storm ceased immediately, but Jonah was swallowed by a big fish and spent three days inside it, to be regurgitated on land. After that, Jonah was a changed person and became a God-fearing servant.

A fish on the supper table of Joseph of Arimathea may point to the fact that only pure people, initiated ones such as those in this special community, could partake of the meal. In fact, being in the presence of the Holy Grail meant belonging to the Community of Christ founded by Joseph. Between his seat and the one occupied by Bron there was an empty chair to remember the one occupied by Judas, the Traitor. If someone impure came and sat in that one vacant seat, the earth would open, swallowing that person; this actually happened. In fact, only after this episode was the cup called Grail. The Grail was only visible to those who were permitted to see it, since evil could not remain in the presence of the Grail. All those present felt honored and graced by the Grail.[100] According to Konrad Sandkühler, the original translator of Robert's text into German, this corresponded to the standing of the Cathars in their communities of *bonshommes*[101] ("good men"), for those who sinned had to leave them, forfeiting all spiritual privileges.

In his *Perceval*, Chrétien de Troyes called the King of the Grail only *Roi Pêcheur* ("Fisher King"). Now in French, a simple accent is the difference between *pêcheur* (fisherman) and *pécheur* (sinner), of identical pronunciation. One must remember that in the initial phase these stories were transmitted only orally. Interestingly, both forms of the word correspond to characteristics of Anfortas. Having reached the level of Grail King, he certainly had higher knowledge than his subjects (i.e., he had reached a certain degree of initiation). However, he had failed to master his instincts, which was a precondition for someone in his position; consequently, he was a *sinner*. Moreover, he only managed to gain some relief from his excruciating pain when he went fishing in the lake near his castle, which made him a *fisherman*.

---

100 The translator from French into German makes the statement that in the Middle Ages it was common to make a kind of play on words: "Grail" resembled "grace," or "to be graced."

101 In the Cathar communities (see chapter "Historical Currents Related to the Grail"), the *bonshommes* were the most evolved among them.

Returning to the narrative: In a later revelation, Christ asked Joseph of Arimathea, who was considered the first keeper of the Grail, to send his nephew Alanus to the Far West to Christianize the people of those lands (the Celts). Bron, Joseph's brother-in-law, who was also called the Rich Fisherman, was appointed by Christ to be Joseph's successor as guardian of the Grail; he was asked to take the Holy Grail, too, to the West. That is how the Grail reached Avalon, one of the sites of Arthur's court. In fact, it is customary to connect the monastery of Glastonbury with Alanus. This correlation illustrates the meeting of primitive Christianity, originating in Palestine and represented by Joseph of Arimathea, with the ancient Celtic line, represented by King Arthur. Gerhard von dem Borne mentions in his work that the writer Holmes says that in Glastonbury the ancient Celtic priests looked to the west, where the sun went down and gave way to darkness.[102] In their understanding, this was the region where the souls of the dead went to be cleansed and, like the sun, be reborn after the deep darkness of the night. They were absolutely sure that the sun would shine again after the long wintry nights, and plants would grow green again.

Similarly, human souls would return after a period of invisibility. For them, the earth itself corresponded to the "magic cauldron" of death and resurrection, of darkness and light, of suffering and joy. The researcher Geoffrey Ashe considers Glastonbury a site of worship related to the cosmos, the zodiac.[103] According to Rudolf Steiner's spiritual research, the Celts in their rituals were able to follow on the spiritual plane the events in preparation of the coming of the Christ, the descent of the Sun Being into life on earth, the Mystery of Death and Resurrection. Therefore, they did not have difficulty accepting Christianity when they encountered it on earth; it was just a confirmation of what they knew from their initiation.

---

102 Gerhard v. d. Borne, *Der Gral in Europa*.
103 G. Ashe, *The Landscape of King Arthur*.

3. WOLFRAM VON ESCHENBACH describes the following in the scene where Parzival visited the Grail Castle for the first time:

> Upon a green *achmardi*[104] she bore the consummation of heart's desire, its roots and its blossoming—a thing called 'The Gral', paradisal, transcending all earthly perfection! (B. V, 125) (After the tables had been set and all present had washed their hands), a hundred pages were bidden to receive loaves into white napkins held with due respect before the Gral. They came on all together, then fanned out on arriving at the tables. Now I have been told [...] that whatever one stretched out one's hand for in the presence of the Gral, it was waiting, one found it all ready and to hand.[...] The noble company partook of the Gral's hospitality. (B. V, 126–127)

Only much later, in the encounter between Parzival and Trevrizent in Book IX, does the latter offer more information about the Grail, after warning the youth about the folly of wishing to win it; service to the Grail could only be performed by people predestined for this mission. Here are some text excerpts (B. IX, 469–471), not in the order in which they appear, but grouped according to some of their features. Further on we will discuss them.

> They [the inhabitants of the Grail Castle] live from a Stone whose essence is most pure [...]. It is called Lapsit Exilis.

> The stone is also called 'the Gral.'
> Further: However ill a mortal may be, from the day on which he sees the Stone he cannot die for that week, nor does he lose his color. [...] Such power does the Stone confer on mortal men that their flesh and bones are soon made young again.

> Every Good Friday [...] the dove brings it (wafer) to the Stone, from which the Stone receives all that is good on earth of food and drink, of paradisal excellence.

---

104 Arabian green silk brocaded with gold thread.

By virtue of the Stone the Phoenix is burned to ashes, in which he is reborn. [...] Which done it shines dazzling bright and lovely as before!

As to those who are appointed to the Gral, hear how they are made known. Under the top edge of the Stone an Inscription announces the name and lineage of the one summoned to make the glad journey. Whether it concern girls or boys, there is no need to erase their names, for as soon as a name has been read it vanishes from sight.

When Lucifer and the Trinity began to war with each other, those who did not take sides, worthy, noble angels, had to descend to earth to that Stone which is forever incorruptible.

Since that time the Stone has been in the care of those whom God appointed to it and to whom He sent his angel.

4. ALBRECHT VON SCHARFENBERG[105] was the author of the last medieval work which deals primarily with the Grail, written around 1270. Its title is *Der jüngere Titurel* [The Most Recent Titurel] as there are fragments of a *Titurel* written by Wolfram in 1215, considered unfinished. As it is an earlier work, it would be the "Oldest."

Comparing Wolfram's fragments with Albrecht's completed work, it can be concluded that the latter based his book on the former, completing it. According to Albrecht's narrative, Titurel lived five hundred years, which would have been impossible in the same physical body. Therefore one must consider a suprasensory dimension, in which case Titurel's age would correspond to the entire period during which content related to the Grail had been available to human beings. (It is worth remembering that the first reference to the Grail, the *Grand Saint Graal*, dates back to the 8th century, and Albrecht was writing in the

---

105 As finding this work is rather difficult, information was collected from several works that refer to him, with the awareness that this summary is quite incomplete.

second half of the 13th century—five centuries later.) It can be noted that, in a way, this work is a condensation of all that was written about the Grail between 1180 and 1270.

Many characters mentioned in the previous poems reappear, making possible the full attainment of their destinies. Thus Titurel remained alive even though he had already bestowed the reign of the Grail to his son Frimurtel, who was succeeded by Anfortas and then Parzival. Chrétien describes Titurel as the elder nourished by the consecrated wafer brought by the Grail. In Wolfram's work, he is the old man of resplendent appearance glimpsed by Parzival in an adjoining room through the half-open door. Whenever necessary, he advised the community. While in other works Titurel is a marginal character, Albrecht focuses mainly on his history.

According to a summary cited by Heinrich Teutschmann,[106] published in *Kürschners Deutsche Nationalliteratur* [Kürschner's German National Bibliography] by Paul Piper and complemented by other quotes from several works mentioned previously, Titurel would have been from Cappadocia (Turkey) and was much praised by Flegetanis (mentioned by Wolfram as the wise man who could read the stars).

The birth of Titurel did not occur in the ordinary manner. His parents, quite elderly, had no children. Advised to visit the Holy Sepulcher in Jerusalem, they made a rich offering there, and then an angel announced to them the birth of their child, Titurel. He was educated with great care, and besides becoming a knight, also learned Grammar. He became a valiant warrior and defeated many pagans, whom he caused to be baptized. He was beloved by all, extremely pure, and devoted to God. Three great virtues were attributed to him, and he is described in Albrecht's book as "Titurel, the pure, the strong and wise." Because of his purity, an angel appeared to him, summoning him to serve the Grail. Thus, the noble knight started to build a temple to

---

106 H. Teutschmann, *Der Gral, Weisheit und Liebe.*

house the Grail, which was held by invisible angelic hands above the construction site. Titurel provided all the necessary building materials as well as food for the workers (see chapter "Historical Currents Related to the Grail: The Grail Temple"). At the end of Albrecht's work, Titurel, accompanied by Parzival, took the Grail to the Indies to leave it in the care of Prester John. There, before leaving this world, the old man revealed the Grail's spiritual aspect, in answer to a question asked by Prester John.

The book also makes important references to Sigune and Schionatulander, allowing for a better understanding of the mission of these two personalities and the circumstances surrounding Schionatulander's death. Among other things, the book also reveals that Parzival was the Grail King for ten years. After this time he accompanied Titurel on his journey to the East where, since then, the Grail has remained.

Just like Chrétien, Wolfram does not describe any physical form of the Grail. Only Robert says that it is the Holy Vessel, and Albrecht reports that it was a bowl of green jasper, in which Christ washed the feet of His disciples. When Wolfram mentions it for the first time, he speaks of an "object called Grail" and later describes it as a stone. Nothing makes one think of a cup, bowl, or tray, nor is there any reference to gold or precious stones, aspects mentioned by Chrétien. In a way, Wolfram separates the Grail from the dogmatic sphere of the Church.

In fact, the only writer to mention a strong liturgical connotation is Robert de Boron, because the supper he describes closely resembles the Eucharist. Chrétien said that the sole food of the Fisher King's father was the consecrated wafer brought by the Grail. Wolfram mentions that every year on Good Friday a dove brought a small, white offering from heaven (a communion wafer?) to renew the power of the Grail. The four reports have in common a community of selected people, guardians of the Grail who were members of the same family. The most important aspect of the four writings is the power of the Grail *to feed and sustain life.*

Georg Kühlewind points out that Wolfram says that the Grail possesses the same characteristics as the primeval power of Paradise: immortality (or enormous longevity), the power to heal diseases, the power of facilitating resurrection (evoked by the phoenix image), and the capacity to nurture (providing food).[107] It should also be remembered that among the ancient Celts the "cauldron of fullness and rebirth" conferred a priestly dignity to the Druids. Only in a later, decadent period did the image of the "cauldron of the Druids" appear, in which were concocted magic potions providing healing powers or eternal youth.

By the way, it is worth mentioning the Old Testament episode in which the people of Israel, during the forty years they spent in the Sinai desert after leaving Egypt, also received food in a miraculous way: God "rained bread from heaven" to feed them during that time. This was manna, a food that to this day remains a mystery to scientists. According to the Bible, no one must reap more than he would consume in a day, as any leftovers would deteriorate; however, on the sixth day one should collect double, since on the seventh day, the day of rest, God did not send manna (Ex. 16). A curious aspect of this is the fact that the manna for the seventh day, harvested the day before, would not deteriorate. One cannot imagine normal food with such characteristics, and one has the impression that this was spiritual food.

Another aspect to stress is the number forty. For example, in the biblical account of the Flood it rained for forty days and forty nights. According to Rudolf Steiner, the Flood, which appears in almost all mythologies, is a reference to the sinking of Atlantis, located where the Atlantic Ocean is today. The great initiate Manu (the biblical Noah) led some of the Atlantean population—those who had reached the expected level of development for that evolutionary stage of humanity—to the East, specifically to India, where a new phase of human evolution

---

107 G. Kühlewind, *Der Gral oder Was die Liebe vermag.*

began. This transition from the Atlantean age to the post-Atlantean age is, in Steiner's terminology, accompanied by the number forty. And the spiritual being Christ, soon after entering the body of Jesus of Nazareth during the baptism in the Jordan, spent forty days in the wilderness (Matthew, Mark, and Luke), where He suffered the temptations. The Christ being, coming from the spiritual world, had to go through this period of transition to really reach the physical realm.

There are several explanations for the fact that the crossing of the Sinai desert took forty years. The Bible itself mentions Jehovah's punishment, preventing the generation that left Egypt from entering the Promised Land for not having believed Him. This period, on the other hand, could also be considered a phase of transition. The Hebrews, slaves in Egypt, became the Israelites with their own identity, characteristics and particular mission, which turned them into the "chosen people."[108]

It is worth pointing out that many names of sovereigns, founders of ancient cultures, or personalities connected to a new spiritual impulse in the evolution of humanity, contain the phonemes *M* and *N*, the consonants of "manna." For example: *Manu* himself (Noah, as already mentioned); *Menes* (c. 3000 BC), unifier of Egypt, founder of the capital city Memphis and first pharaoh of Egypt's first dynasty; *Minos* (c. 1500 BC), king of Crete, unifier of the Minoan people and founder of the Minoan civilization; *Manitou*, one of the deities of the North American Indians; and so on.

Other terms containing these phonemes also point to the spiritual realm. The Hindu word *manas*, according to Steiner, denotes the "spirit self" of the human being; the Sanskrit word *manishiu* means "human

---

[108] "You will be consecrated to me, for I, Jehovah, am holy, and I separated you from all people so that you should be mine." (Lev. 20: 26) "For you are a people consecrated to Jehovah, your God; it was Jehovah, your God who chose you to belong to Him as His own people, among all the people that are upon the face of the earth." (Deut. 7: 6)

being" and from it derive the words *Mensch* (German for "human being") and *man* (English). We may assume, therefore, that these designate the spiritual part of the human being, while the Romance-language words *homme, homem, hombre, uomo*, etc., derive from the Latin *humus* (which originally meant "earth" but now means a product of decomposition of plant debris in the forest, very important for the formation of soil and plant nutrition), therefore designating the material, bodily part of the human being.

Why does Wolfram make reference to the phoenix? The image of the bird that dies incinerated and rises from its ashes even more beautiful was already known to the mysteries of antiquity. It is a symbol of the mystery of voluntary death and the overcoming of death in resurrection.

Ancient pre-Christian cultures worshiped a deity directly related to the sun. In each land the god had a different name: For example Vishnu-Krishna in India, Apollo in Greece, Lug for the Celts. This deity's triumphant nature was always stressed because it overcame evil, the dragon. In the mystery centers, this deity was represented by the phoenix. According to Sigismund von Gleich, quoted by W.F. Veltman,[109] these mysteries had their origin in the Arabian region, more precisely in the country of Sheba. There were many branches, including one in Tyre, capital of Phoenicia, whose name derives from "phoenix." Its initiates were aware that in the future, the great sacrifice of the overcoming of death was to take place, for the salvation of humankind. This sacrifice was in fact accomplished by Christ, who, after dying on the cross on Golgotha, was resurrected on Easter Sunday. According to Steiner, the meaning of Christ's resurrection is that He overcame death. Death has existed since humanity was "expelled from Paradise," established itself on earth, and became bound to the dead, material world. On the other hand, the divine-spiritual being of Christ, in the three years He lived in the body of Jesus of Nazareth, gradually spiritualized this corporeality.

---

109 W.F. Veltman, *Tempel und Gral*.

As this is the future task of every human being, one can consider the resurrected Christ as the model to be attained by humanity at the end of its evolution. Due to this fact, Christ is considered the Savior of humankind, as He showed it the way back to the spiritual world. The intention of the higher worlds on sending this cosmic being to inhabit a human body was to prevent humankind from attaching itself exclusively to the physical world and losing itself in it, as was about to happen. Therefore, since the Resurrection of Christ, the possibility exists for the human being to return, in full freedom, to the spiritual world (see chapter "The Trajectory of *Parzival*").

Since human beings by themselves are not able to renew their power to rise to the higher worlds, it must be periodically renewed within them by the action of the Spirit, represented by the dove in the writings mentioned above.

Rudolf Meyer compares the incarnated human being to the phoenix: While the Self is incarnated in a human body, the blood (which is connected to heat) is its vehicle.[110] In order to develop, the Self needs this continuous combustion process, and in death it rises out of this heat process as if rejuvenated, rising from the ashes. In other words, each death represents a rising toward eternal life. On a microcosmic scale one can have a phoenix experience in everyday life, for every night a person lies down tired ("dead tired") to wake up the next morning reinvigorated, as if reborn ("resurrected"). In the vernacular we have expressions such as "sleep is death's little sister."

One should also consider the fact that the Grail was described by Wolfram as a stone. In the Middle Ages a legend told of the "rebellion of the angels." In the struggle against Lucifer (whose name means "bringer of light") and his army, the Archangel Michael expelled them from heaven and was also able to extract, with his sword of fire, the largest and most beautiful stone from Lucifer's crown. The legend ends by saying that from this stone was made the vessel to receive the blood of Christ, the Grail.

---

110 R. Meyer, *Der Gral und seine Hüter*.

In his lecture of August 23, 1909,[111] Steiner stated as follows, referring to this legend: The advent of darkness, to which Saint John refers at the beginning of his Gospel, was necessary for humankind. Into this darkness shone the Christ principle—because the radiant stone, this star lost by Lucifer, became part of the Christ principle. This star can shine for any one of us, provided we have the certainty of something spiritual in our soul. To explain the relationship between this stone (star) and the Grail, Steiner added that it represents the human Self in its full strength. Initially, the Self had to go through a preparatory phase in the realm of darkness and then, renewed, could receive with dignity the light of Christ. In the course of human evolution, the human Self, the eminently spiritual part of the human being, should increasingly become more and more perfect and become a vessel ready to receive the light which, in fact, exists where our present external human eyes and external intellect only experience darkness. As stated above, the Luciferic beings made the journey from the heights to the depths; according to Steiner, they were beings full of wisdom.

Another way to understand this legend is to consider the brilliant stone torn out of Lucifer's crown, that is, away from his followers, representing wisdom that would turn into a receptacle for love. Another legend says that this vessel was initially kept and guarded in the mystery center of Hercules in Phoenicia. Later, it came into the hands of the Queen of Sheba, a queen of star wisdom who offered it to the wise King Solomon. Finally, it arrived at the house where Christ celebrated the Last Supper. After Christ's arrest, a Jew took the vessel to Pontius Pilate, who gave it to Joseph of Arimathea when he came to ask permission to bury the body of Jesus Christ. One can see that the trajectory of the Grail represents the path of wisdom: It came from the heavenly heights to Earth, where it must turn into a receptacle of love.

---

111 R. Steiner, *The East in the Light of the West, The Children of Lucifer and the Brothers of Christ*, GA 113.

Interestingly, in Wolfram's account he says that before there was a legion of knights of the Grail responsible for its upkeep, the angels who had remained neutral in the struggle between Lucifer and the Holy Trinity were actually condemned to remain on earth in order to look after the stone.[112] It can be assumed, therefore, that there were three realms: the celestial realm, with the angels and other hierarchies faithful to God; the abyss, where Lucifer and his followers ended up; and, in the middle, the earthly realm, home to human beings and, temporarily, the angels in charge of the Grail—that is, those who had sided with neither the heavenly powers (Michael or the Holy Trinity) nor with Lucifer.

Walter Johannes Stein points out that the stone of light torn out of Lucifer's crown did not fall into the abyss with the other Luciferic beings, and represents a very special entity: an entity who decided to come down from the heights of heaven to earth in order to redeem human beings, who were at that point at the mercy of the Luciferic beings.[113] Therefore, this entity prepared, so to speak, the path for the Cosmic Word to follow the same path of the fallen spirits. Gerard Klockenbring[114] calls attention to the fact that a fall is always something passive, caused by the attraction of gravity. Now spiritual beings do not have a physical corporeality, so no gravitational force acts upon them. That would mean that this special entity descending from heaven to earth "fell actively," as was His intention.

In Wolfram's book, the character Trevrizent says that the stone was called *Lapsit Exilis*, or "exiled stone." Taking into account, however, that these stories were initially transmitted orally, one could easily spell what was heard as *Lapsit Exilis* in other ways. Indeed, several studies have examined this possibility, with one interpretation being *Lapsit ex Coelis*, which signifies "stone fallen from the sky." In any case, both these possibilities are consistent with the contents of the legends.

---

112   Wolfram von Eschenbach, *Parzival*, B. IX, 471.
113   W.J. Stein, *The Ninth Century and the Holy Grail*.
114   G. Klockenbring, *El Santo Grial y el hombre moderno*.

Quite mysterious is the account of how the Grail summons those whose mission is to serve it. Simply having the intention to serve is not enough. Many attributes are taken under consideration before one may be called, including chastity, purity, sobriety, obedience, truthfulness, humility. The very fact that the Grail calls, and the consequent appearance of an inscription on the border of the stone which disappears once it has been read, again reveals its "power to speak" to the community. Its language is, in fact, a primeval language, and one may consider that it has an affinity with the Word, the *Logos*; the Logos would manifest through the Grail. Moreover, in Spanish, Portuguese, and Italian the word *lápide*, meaning "tombstone," comes from the Latin *lapsit*, or "stone." Now, the name of a person who received the call to serve the Grail was "written in stone": This could mean that in order to reach the Grail it was necessary to die, or that one had to be in a state of consciousness like that of the ancient initiation processes, a state similar to death (see chapter "The Trajectory of *Parzival*").

In the end, it is absolutely irrelevant what physical form the Grail may have had. Heinrich Teutschmann's approach in the above-mentioned book[115] is very interesting: He specifies four stages in the evolution of Christianity, relating them respectively to each of the works discussed earlier in this chapter. He also establishes a relationship with the four members composing the human being, as described by Rudolf Steiner in his basic books *Theosophy* and *An Outline of Esoteric Science*, and in numerous lectures.

In the briefest of summaries, these four members of the human being can be characterized with reference to the four kingdoms of nature. The dead mineral kingdom consists of elements and substances that can be studied in inorganic chemistry. They comprise what we call the physical body, which can be measured, touched, and studied according to natural laws, and corresponds, in fact, to the corpse which

---

115 H. Teutschmann, *Der Gral, Weisheit und Liebe*.

is left over when life ceases. It immediately decays according to the laws of physics and chemistry.

Therefore, any living being must also contain something during its lifetime that opposes these physical-chemical laws and maintains the vital functions responsible for the life cycle. These include germination, budding, growth, ripening, and also withering and fading, namely the devitalization processes. Steiner called this second element, present in all living beings, the life body or etheric body; human beings and animals have it in common with plants. Animals and human beings, on the other hand, distinguish themselves from plants since they are able to move on their own; they also have internal organs and an inner life with feelings and awareness, because of a third member which is called the soul or astral body. In addition, only human beings are endowed with self-consciousness, upright posture, speech, and thought. These qualities are granted by a fourth element—the "I" or Self, the divine spark which makes each human being a unique, individualized entity with his or her own characteristics that transcend heredity and environmental influences.

Teutschmann explains that between the 1st and 4th centuries, people could still experience the echoes of Christ's physical presence as they received the teachings of the disciples of the Apostles, who had received them from Christ Himself. (In reality, what is known about Christianity in this period comes from documents written by its enemies.) The work of Robert de Boron fits perfectly into this context, because Joseph of Arimathea actually lived with Christ—it was he who took His body down from the cross and offered his own tomb for His burial. In Robert de Boron's narrative, Joseph of Arimathea received not only the Lord's holy vessel, but also guidance on how to proceed, and he transmitted these teachings to his own disciples. The vessel was the Grail itself.

In a second stage, covering the period between the 4th and 12th centuries, the Christ impulse was directly present in people's etheric bodies, according to Rudolf Steiner's explanations in his lecture of February 15, 1909.[116] People did not have to look for Him in legends or traditions, because He was within them. Interestingly, Chrétien, the writer who represents this second stage, has a strong relationship with the plant kingdom (plants have a life or etheric body). The author begins his work *Perceval* with the following words:

> Who sows little reaps little. Anyone who wants a beautiful harvest should sow the grain on such good ground that God will return two hundred times, as on land which is worth nothing, good seeds dry and wither.

According to Rudolf Meyer, Chrétien applies this parable as if it were an expansion of a Gospel. In fact, this seed germinated and proliferated rapidly, and soon many stories and poems about the Grail sprouted. In his book, the Grail has an unspecified shape but is made of pure gold and studded with precious stones, and contains a consecrated wafer or host. It is carried by a maiden to an adjoining room, where an old man takes his nourishment exclusively from this wafer brought to him in the Grail. Therefore, Chrétien adds to the physical vessel the wafer, which is food from the plant kingdom.

Wolfram is the representative of the third stage of Christianity, from the 12th to the 15th century, and is therefore the most contemporary of the authors, as he is writing about his own time. It was a phase characterized by an increasing intellectualization because of the influence of Arabism, whose tendency was to ignore the spiritual Self, giving importance only to a merely conceptual understanding of it. This put humankind's future spiritual development at risk. According to Steiner, the year 1250 represented humankind's furthest distance from the spiritual world; nevertheless, during this period people were able

---

116 R. Steiner, *Spiritual-Scientific Anthropology/ Knowledge of Man*, GA 107; *The Principle of Spiritual Economy and its Relation to Questions Concerning Reincarnation*, GA 109.

to experience the Christ impulse in their soul or astral body. Wolfram reports that the providing power of the Grail was brought down from heaven by a dove; that is, he included the animal kingdom, bearer of the astral body.

The fourth stage corresponds to our time and is characterized on one hand by an intense crisis of faith, manifesting in atheism, and on the other hand by a real search for spiritual content. It is a phase represented in the work *Titurel* by Albrecht von Scharfenberg, written after 1250. In this work, the atmosphere is no longer primarily earthly; one has the impression that it is more contemplative, suprasensory.

The following is a table of the characteristics of the Grail, slightly modified from Teutschmann's book.

AUTHOR	CHARACTERIZATION	ESSENCE	PERIOD
Robert de Boron (before 1200)	Vessel (Mineral)	Existence or being (Physical body)	1st–4th centuries
Chrétien de Troyes (before 1200)	Golden Vessel + Wafer	Life (Etheric or life body)	4th–12th centuries
Wolfram von Eschenbach (before 1200)	Stone + Wafer + Dove	Consciousness (Astral or soul body)	12th–15th centuries
Humanity's greatest distance from the spiritual world: 1250			
Albrecht von Scharfenberg (about 1270)	Stone Vessel, directed by Angels	Self-Consciousness ("I" or Self)	Points toward the present

Another important issue highlighted by Teutschmann is the subject of the question, which is an inherent part of the present human being, whose task it is to develop the consciousness soul (see chapter 2). All four poets link the Grail to a question: It is important to ask about the Grail. In Robert de Boron this question was formulated after the institution of the commemorative supper, and was actually asked by people who could not connect to the Christ. They failed to sense the greatness emanating from the Grail, and wanted to know "What is this chalice we have never seen before?" Two answers were given: one related to its essence and the other to its name. The vessel (object) separated the true followers of Christ from the others, and the name of the chalice was Grail.

In Chrétien's work, the question to be asked was, "Whom does the Grail serve?" meaning, who was the person that was fed by the wafer? In Wolfram the question was "Uncle, what ails you?" That is, after being separated from the Grail Community and suffering great pain, Parzival was able to develop true compassion and neighborly love (feelings). He was called (the act of speaking) by Cundrie to become the new king of the Grail. Cundrie displayed the emblem of the Grail, the dove, embroidered on her robes. It also was this bird that, every Good Friday, renewed the miraculous power of the stone. Albrecht tells how Prester John asked old Titurel, when the latter took the Grail to the East, about its essence, as the people of the West were no longer worthy of it. The answer was that in ancient times, angels had brought the Grail to earth. It was made of very valuable jasper stone, from which the basin Jesus Christ had used for the washing of the feet before the Last Supper was made. Joseph of Arimathea was the first to keep it; later, the angels took it to Titurel, who then kept it for five hundred years. In short, Titurel gave an account of the spiritual direction of humanity, the final aim of which is the union of the individual Self with the universe.

Since pre-Christian times an image has existed that can be considered a symbol of the Grail: the figure of the sun beside the moon, in which the lunar crescent, cup-shaped, holds a dark disk. This symbol is found on many Egyptian altars. Its origin, however, seems to be in the land of Sheba (Arabia). W.F. Veltman[117] proposes that the Grail has

---

117   W.F. Veltman, *Tempel und Gral*.

accompanied history: Step by step, the Sun Being came down to Earth from celestial heights. His coming had to be prepared and conceived, corresponding to the moon element. The Sun Spirit Christ became incarnate in the Lunar Vessel of Jesus of Nazareth.

This relationship between the sun and the moon is an important aspect in the Grail. On January 1, 1914, Steiner described how, during his spiritual studies to clarify how we can find the Grail today, the proximity of the figure of Kyot from Provence was decisive.[118] Inspired by the work of Flegetanis, Kyot had turned to "knowledge of the starry script," and in the stars he contemplated the object called Grail. Now in the Grail the name "Parzival" appeared, and spiritually, Steiner began to seek Parzival's name. Thus he was led to the Grail mystery by means of a symbol in starry writing. In a lecture on February 1, 1914, he said:

> Then I saw in the starry script what anyone can see, but without finding, at first, the secret of the matter, because one day when, in inner contemplation, I followed the lunar crescent with its golden glow, just as it appears in the sky, I realized the scintillation of the dark side of the moon, which appears subtly as a large disk, and from the outside, from the physical point of view, one can see the lunar crescent with its golden glow [...] and, inside it, the great wafer, the great disk, which cannot be seen when looking at the moon superficially, but it can be seen when one looks with more attention; then one contemplates the dark disk and in the rising moon, in the wonderful lettering of the writing of the occult... the name Parzival appears! My dear friends, the starry script was, initially, like this. Indeed, under proper light, this reading of the stellar writing provides something for our heart and our sense of the Parzival secret, the secret of the Holy Grail.[119]

---

[118] R. Steiner, *Christ and the Spiritual World: the Search for the Holy Grail*, GA 149.
[119] Ibid.

In a lecture the following day, Steiner added to the subject:

> I mentioned that this writing can really be found in the sky. It is not the Grail itself, nor is it the Grail that provides it. I pointed out expressly (and I ask you to take such insistence seriously) that through this writing the name of the Grail can be seen in the sky, not the Grail itself. I pointed out that any person can see what is in the sky through precise observation, in the dark part of the rest of the Moon, in the lunar crescent of golden glow, as if enclosed in this golden crescent; there is revealed, in occult writing, the name Parzival.

Steiner then explained that physically, the crescent moon is the part of the moon onto which the sun's rays fall, and the dark part is dark because the sun's rays do not reach it. From a spiritual point of view, however, things are different. Even if the rays are reflected by part of the lunar surface, casting a golden glow, something corresponding to the dark shadow crosses the physical lunar materiality: It is the spiritual element that lives in the rays of the sun. Therefore, we contemplate the spiritual strength of the sun in what lies in the lunar crescent, that is, the Spirit of the Sun rests on the chalice of the moon. This symbol is the physical evidence that the moon, forming a shining golden vessel, appears to us as the carrier of the Sun Spirit of Christ, who manifests in the form of a disk similar to a wafer. It is important to highlight, says Steiner, that Easter occurs on the first Sunday after the full moon following the spring equinox.[120] After the equinox, the power emanating from the sun (the symbol of Christ) becomes more intense. As the moon decreases, the chalice becomes more and more bright and golden, while the dark part, the strength of the Sun Spirit, increases. In ancient tradition, something of this Sun Spirit had to be at work at Easter, meaning that during the Easter time anyone could contemplate the image of the Holy Grail in the sky.

---

120 In the Northern Hemisphere. In the Southern Hemisphere, it is the autumn equinox.

A very important aspect is the fact that Wolfram's book was written at a time when alchemy was still seriously practiced. Anyone familiar with it will see many of its symbols in his book. Veltman states that the occult science of alchemy was carefully guarded by the Order of Santiago, whose center was located in the Spanish town of Compostela, but it also had great importance in various knightly orders in the 15th century, such as the Prince Arthur Order in England (a name chosen to honor the firstborn son of King Henry XII, who married a Spanish princess).

Incidentally, it was Thomas Malory, the author of *Le Morte D'Arthur* [The Death of Arthur], who established the statutes of that order. It can be deduced, therefore, that alchemy was related to the Northern esoteric stream (the Celtic and Germanic people), which is confirmed by their great interest in the phenomena of nature. Nor is it surprising that it is related to the impulse of chivalry. Alchemy was just an inner path of development, which sought the higher entity in the human being through a deepening into nature. It can be seen as a Christianized continuation of the wisdom of the mysteries of antiquity.

Like other forms of esoteric Christianity (see chapter "Historical Currents Related to the Grail"), alchemy, too, disagreed with the prevailing Christianity in Rome. The ancient alchemists made a profound study of nature, primarily of physical substances which they considered the material manifestation of an underlying spiritual reality. In this sense, they knew very well the four elements mentioned by Aristotle as he instructed the young Alexander; since ancient times these had been known as earth, water, air, and fire. The mission of the alchemists was to discover the fifth element or "quintessence": matter's spiritual element or underlying essence. To this end they worked mainly to purify and sublimate metals, believing that in this way they would approach this quintessence. Moreover, they knew that to progress in their work they had to purify and sublimate their souls, so that their own spiritual element could manifest; that is, to understand the spiritual core of each material substance, they first had to understand their own core. And only by purifying their souls would they be able to achieve what is spiritual in human beings—in other words, the divine aspect, the Higher Self.

In a lecture on June 11, 1924,[121] Steiner explained that carbon presents itself in several forms: coal, totally black and opaque; graphite, gray with very little luster; and diamond, fully translucent and brilliant. Next, he says:

> And when the old alchemists and other similar people spoke about the Philosopher's Stone, they were referring to carbon in its various occurrences, and just kept its name in secrecy because, otherwise, anyone could obtain the Philosopher's Stone.

Only after Christ—the Cosmic Self, in Steiner's words—inhabited a human body, could the human being become fully aware of that Self. Therefore, imbued with deep Christ-feeling, the alchemists had a double task: first, to act within each self, purifying themselves and making contact with the divine-spiritual essence, with the "Christ within," the Philosopher's Stone; and then to be able to act upon substances, sublimating them so they could reach the spiritual element or quintessence inherent in them. Here is how Walter Johannes Stein describes this:

> Alchemy is the doctrine of the transformation of the human being onto a higher level. In this higher level, he must learn to reconcile the clear awareness of his humanity with the pure chastity of the plant. What the latter achieves unconsciously he must realize consciously. Alchemy describes how this may be achieved gradually and what transformations the human being has to go through during this inner development. It teaches, at first, how to purify the very environment of the

---

121 R. Steiner, *Agriculture Course: The Birth of the Biodynamic Method*, GA 327.

soul through clear thinking. Then how to take the earthly human being, permeated by life, soul and spirit, to a state that does not express wakefulness or sleep, nor being alive or dead, but is a fifth stage. In this stage, the human being receives "enlightenment." If he learns to apply to everyday consciousness what he learned in this fifth stage, he will have completed the full path. Then he will have transformed the darkness of earthly life (coal) into a sparkling diamond. Through enlightenment he will have become someone acting from intuition.[122]

According to Rudolf Steiner, one may consider that the human being who is able to take control over his or her body and modify it entirely from the spirit (that is to say, the human being capable of developing his or her highest spiritual member, the "spirit man" or *Atma*[123]), carries this spiritualized body within him- or herself as a Philosopher's Stone, as he said in his lecture of March 14, 1907.[124] In this sense, this is something still to be realized in the distant future. In any case, the alchemists tried to achieve a higher degree of purification of their souls and so managed to develop healing activities in their communities.

There is also a strong link between alchemy and the Rosicrucian movement (see chapter "Historical Currents Related to the Grail"). The present-day image of alchemists trying to turn base metals into more noble ones, such as iron into gold, is based on a decadent phase of alchemy, when the original spiritual aspect had begun to fade and only the material aspect remained.[125] Referring in a lecture on September 16,

---

122 W.J. Stein, *The Ninth Century and the Holy Grail.*
123 See R. Steiner, *Theosophy* and *An Outline of Esoteric Science.*
124 R. Steiner, *Supersensible Knowledge,* GA 55.
125 In his anthroposophy, Rudolf Steiner presents a modern-day conception of the study of metals derived from alchemy, emphasizing their spiritual aspects along with ample practical applications such as in anthroposophic medicine, biodynamic agriculture, etc.

1907, to the seventh seal of the Apocalypse as the "Seal of the Grail,"[126] Steiner drew a transparent cube, which can be interpreted as the Philosopher's Stone, the end of human evolution.

According to the sacred language, the term "Philosopher's Stone" refers to "the Stone that bears the sign of the Sun." This "sun sign" was characterized by a red color which varied in intensity, as reported by Basil Valentine (Basilius Valentinus, a Benedictine monk and important 15th-century alchemist):

> Its color goes from red to crimson, or the color of the ruby to that of the garnet. In weight, it weighs much more than its quantity.

Surprisingly, in the Bible there are several passages about a stone related to Christ:

> Therefore thus saith the Lord Jehovah: Behold, I lay in Zion a stone for a foundation, a stone in good faith, a precious stone, a cornerstone that holds the foundation: He that believeth shall not make haste (Isa. 28: 16). Jesus spoke to them: Have you never read in the Scriptures: The stone the builders rejected, became that same cornerstone.[127] (Matt. 21:42)

---

126 R. Steiner, *Rosicrucianism Renewed: The Unity of Art, Science and Religion*, GA 284, lecture: "The Apocalyptic Seals."
127 In architecture, the cornerstone is the trapezoidal stone placed at the center of the Romanesque arch. Its wedge shape exerts pressure onto the surrounding stones and provides the arch with the stability to support a column which in turn can form part of another arch. There is a similar structure in the human skeleton: regarding the legs as pillars and the pelvis as the arch, the sacrum, of trapezoidal shape, corresponds to the cornerstone on which the vertebral column rests, allowing us our erect posture. Now the only being who effectively has an upright posture is the human being, because of the presence of the Self. (Some animals seem to have a vertical spinal column, but they lack its double curvature.) Why is this bone called "sacrum"? What is sacred about it? In our view, an unconscious intuition gave it this name. If Christ, the Cosmic Self, such a sacred entity, is considered the cornerstone, our small human Self, to manifest itself as something divine and sacred, needs this bone to be able to keep its upright posture.

Then Peter, filled with the Holy Spirit, said to them, [...] may it be known by all of you and all the people of Israel that in the name of Jesus Christ of Nazareth, whom ye crucified, and whom God raised from the dead, in his name is this sick person here before you. Jesus is the stone rejected by you the builders, he is the cornerstone. (Acts 4:8–11)

When you come near the living stone, rejected indeed by men but chosen by God and precious, you, too, are like living stones [...]. That is why it says in the Scripture: Behold, I lay in Zion the main cornerstone, selected and precious, and he who believeth in it shall not be ashamed. Therefore, for those who believe it is an honor, but for those who disbelieve, the stone the builders rejected became a cornerstone, a stumbling stone and a rock of scandal [...]. (1 Pet. 2:4–8)

He who has ears let him hear what the Spirit says to the churches. To the winner I will give the hidden manna, and I will also give him a white stone, and on this stone a new name will be written, which no one knows but he who receives it. (Rev. 2: 17)

There is clear evidence that the stone symbolizes Christ; already in the Old Testament Isaiah predicted the Christ event. Pierre Ponsoye, too, states that initiated Christians considered Christ to be both the "authentic Philosopher's Stone" and the "true cornerstone."[128]

As for the passage in the Book of Revelations, it seems to correspond directly to the Grail as described by Wolfram: a stone, white and pure, which provides spiritual food (manna) and on which a name is inscribed! Referring to the work *Grand Saint Graal*, Julius Evola says that the person who opens the Grail case will enter into direct contact with the Christ.[129]

---

128 P. Ponsoye, *El Islam y el Grial*.
129 J. Evola, *The Mystery of the Grail*.

It can be concluded, therefore, that the three symbols of the Grail —the spear, the sword and the Grail itself[130]—are related to Christ. This becomes evident in the words that He Himself spoke: "I am the way, the truth and the life" (John 14:6). As we have seen, the spear points the *way* forward; the sword—namely the Word, Christ Himself—relates to the formulation of spiritual *truth*; and finally, the Grail supports and sustains health and *life*.

---

130 It is worth recalling the Celtic sacred treasures: the "lance of overcoming," the "sword of light," the "cauldron of plenitude," and the "stone of destiny."

CHAPTER 13

Historical Currents Related to the Grail

> But of its nature the Godhead is translucent, it shines through the wall of darkness.
> – Wolfram von Eschenbach, *Parzival* (B. IX, 238)

From all we have seen so far, we may conclude that the Community of the Grail has a deep connection with Christianity, expressed in an interiorized way of life, in the search of perfection, in penitence, in the practice of selfless love, in forgiveness, and also in symbols and rituals. Although *Parzival* was written in the Middle Ages when the Church was powerful in Europe, the author makes no reference to the Pope, bishops, priests, or the dogmas which were to be believed and followed.

Quite the contrary: Some situations even contradict official religious dogma. For example, Trevrizent forgives Parzival, taking his sins on himself before God, something only a priest could do. But the hermit does not seem to be a priest, only a knight in search of perfection in an attempt to redeem the sins of his brother Anfortas.

Another interesting aspect is the isolation in which the Grail Community lives, totally separate from society. In actuality, the dominant Roman ecclesiastical organization was a hindrance for devout Christians because it tended to conduct spiritual matters in a legal and dogmatic way. The emergence of so many hermits at that time, people who wanted to live their faith simply and devoutly, can be considered an escape from the Roman Church.

During the evolution of humanity, there have always been groups of people who left the official religion, seeking a spirituality of their own. They became known as heretics; some of them will be addressed below. In addition, there were still other groups in which we can find points of contact with the Grail Community.

The Essenes

The Jewish historian Flavius Josephus (37 or 38–93 AD), who later became a Roman citizen, wrote about the war in which the Romans conquered Jerusalem. He mentions a Jewish colony of mystics who lived apart from society in the Judean desert, a place near the Dead Sea, and who practiced purification before all else because they foresaw the imminent coming of the Messiah. Pliny the Elder (Gaius Plinius Secundus, 23 or 24–79 AD) and Philo of Alexandria (c. 30 BC–40 AD) also made reference to the Essenes, without adding anything significant to what Josephus had reported. Nothing more would be known about this sect if a nearly intact library had not been found in the caves near the Dead Sea in 1947. These were the Dead Sea Scrolls. Research by historians, and especially by representatives of the three religions interested in the scrolls—Jewish, Roman Catholic and Orthodox—shed light on the way the Essenes lived and thought, and their spirituality. These men lived in a kind of monastery on the banks of the Dead Sea, whose ruins have also been discovered and studied.

The community appeared in the 2nd century BC. It consisted of men who were unhappy with the direction in which the priests of the Temple in Jerusalem were taking Judaism; they felt the priests were subverting their religion. In preparation for the imminent coming of the Messiah, these ascetics retired to the desert to purify themselves and prepare for this event. Purification became almost an obsession for them, and was also the reason they did not allow women in their midst, for according to the Scriptures, women were unclean during menstruation and needed to take ritual purifying baths thereafter. The Essenes lived communally, studied the Scriptures, strictly followed the divine commandments, took daily ritual baths (in precious rainwater and dew which they collected in large cisterns), and ate modest communal meals. Their rules were austere and rigid. To prepare themselves to practice spiritual exercises, they had to free themselves from three things: property, impulses (particularly sexual), and emotions such as anger, hatred, and jealousy. They lived on local fruits and roots, and raised a few crops. They had some knowledge of medicinal plants and consequently were able to treat illnesses. One branch whose very similar writings were found in Egypt was known as *therapeutae*.

It is believed that the Essenes' way of life was the origin of the later monastic life of the Middle Ages. To be admitted to the order, participants had to donate all their possessions to the order; they took a kind of vow of poverty and the order provided everything they needed: shelter, food, a white robe, and a small shovel for burying their excrement in the desert sand, as it was considered unclean and should not be exposed to the sun's rays. Before being definitively allowed to join the order, applicants went through a novitiate period. Any slip-up would lessen their purity, necessitating a new effort to regain and surpass it.

One of the most important doctrines of the Essenes related to the question of good and evil. According to their belief, God was omnipotent and all-powerful, and created two spirits, the "Prince or Angel of Truth" and the "Prince or Angel of Darkness" so that the human being could choose between the two. On Judgment Day, however, God would end this conflict (as He stood above the two spirits He had created). Followers of the "Prince of Truth" would be saved and avenged of all the evil the followers of the "Prince of Darkness" had caused them; the followers of the latter would be exterminated in hell. One of the manuscripts that was found has the title "The War of the Sons of Light against the Sons of Darkness." The initiated Essenes considered themselves "Children of Light."

They also believed in the coming of two Messiahs, one a Messiah-King and the other a Messiah-Priest, which has caused many unsolved problems for researchers.[131] In 1910, in his lectures on the *Gospel of St. Matthew* and in another lecture cycle named *The Fifth Gospel*, Rudolf

---

131 One group of researchers assumes that the Messiah-Priest was John the Baptist and the Messiah-King, Jesus Christ.

Steiner gave quite detailed descriptions of the Essenes, their life and mission—facts which were then fully confirmed almost forty years later by the content of the Dead Sea Scrolls. Steiner also solved the question of the two Messiahs mentioned above, but to address it here would be quite beyond the scope of this book. Those who are interested may consult Steiner's work on Christology.[132]

It is generally believed that John the Baptist, as well as the disciples of Christ and probably the first Christians, including, for example, Joseph of Arimathea, had been Essenes or had had some contact with this sect, because as a result of their preparation and expectations, they were able to recognize Christ when He incarnated into a human body. A mystery as yet unsolved is the disappearance of this sect. Perhaps its members had to leave that region temporarily, as it was a war zone because of the Roman conquests, believing they might return one day. Perhaps as early Christians they no longer wanted to live in isolation, but now wanted to proclaim the coming of Christ and travel to other lands. In any case, they concealed their manuscripts in ceramic pots hidden inside caves, and the desert climate preserved them fairly well for nearly two thousand years. Unfortunately, only parts of the Dead Sea Scrolls had been published by 1956, when the project was halted. It was only when historians the world over rebelled at not being granted access to the scrolls that the process began again in 1991; however, soon afterward, their guardians, mostly Jewish and Christian religious leaders, again made the scrolls unavailable. Why would religious authorities wish to hide this seemingly mysterious content from the public eye? In August 2008 it was reported that the scrolls would be scanned in order to make them available on the internet, and this is now the case.

---

[132] For those who want to go deeper into the subject, we recommend the following works by Rudolf Steiner: *Christianity as Mystical Fact, The Gospel of St. Luke, The Gospel of St. Matthew, The Gospel of St. Mark, The Gospel of John, From Jesus to Christ, The Fifth Gospel,* and *The Apocalypse of St. John.*

The Manichaeans

In the 3rd century in Persia lived an individual by the name of Mani or Manes (216–277 AD). He traveled throughout the known world, having been initiated in the mystery centers (secret initiation sites) of various peoples. He acknowledged in Christianity much that had been foretold in the mysteries, and considered himself an apostle of Jesus. After returning to Persia he founded a new religion that encompassed the hidden wisdom of the ancient religions he had encountered, from the standpoint of Christian gnosis—a procedure known as religious syncretism. The new religion was called Manichaeism.

According to the Manichaean doctrine, good and evil are opposite principles of equal power and value because they have the same origin. At the beginning of Creation there was a single, uniform principle; part of it condensed, giving rise to matter, and the remainder, more refined and subtle, gave rise to spirit. The polarities of spirit/matter, good/evil, and light/darkness, as we understand them today, were then not so different from one another. In a lecture dated May 22, 1920, Steiner said:

> ...[T]he terms "spirit" and "matter" do not make sense in Manichaeism because in what appears as matter to the senses, Manichaeism recognizes something spiritual, and when it refers to the spirit, it does not transcend what manifests itself to the senses.[133]

Moreover, because of their physical components, the earth and human beings would already be committed to the forces of darkness and evil.[134] However, any evil carries within itself the power to lead

---

133 R. Steiner, *The Philosophy of Thomas Aquinas*, GA 74.
134 According to the Manichaean doctrine, the primeval earth, as it was born out of God's hands, was called "the world of light"; it was the one that fell, together with rebellious beings, and in which we now live. It was then the "land of pestilence."

to a higher force of goodness, which needs only to be released from enchantment. Therefore, the Sun Being descended into darkness so that matter would be permeated with the spirit. A chaste and simple life and the development of selfless love can make human beings spiritualize and purify themselves and, by extension, the earth; this means releasing the power of goodness from its enchantment. The redemption of evil is the most important task of the human being; this redemption will only be achieved when the human being finds the primeval light within him- or herself. This means that the human being must be able to appeal to the divine spiritual light within the soul, without the need for new revelations or external authorities. This is, therefore, a task based on spiritual knowledge, possible only after true freedom is attained. Consequently, the end of time will depend on each person, as he or she will either succumb to matter or rise to the spiritual realm. Each person taking this path can also help others in the process of spiritualization.

The Manichaean motto was "Love evil well." At first these words are quite incomprehensible; however, if we familiarize ourselves with the ideas and behavior of the Manichaeans, it is possible to imagine their meaning. The motto can be interpreted as follows: Love evil, and then turn it into good. Here is a concept totally distinct from that of the Judeo-Christian tradition, according to which God Almighty created evil to tempt the human being; in His omnipotence, He rules over evil and can eliminate it whenever he wants to. According to Manichaeism, good and evil are forces of common origin and equal power, neither ruling over the other, and the human being is free to choose which will prevail.

Another aspect of the Judeo-Christian tradition also teaches that evil must be defeated or eliminated, while in Manichaeism, evil must be recognized in order to be redeemed, and it will then lose its power. To recognize something, one must first have an interest in it, and interest means approach, involvement. Here is the secret of the injunction to "love evil well," for only when we show an interest in evil to recognize it—and having an interest in something or someone can be considered a kind of incipient love—does it becomes harmless (turns into goodness). In other words, evil must be recognized and illuminated by light and love, thereby turning it into something good. The effect of a tiny light shining in darkness is well known: As it intensifies, it turns darkness into light. A Manichaean legend[135] illustrates this concept:

When, in the course of evolution, there was a separation between light and darkness, a dragon appeared from the depth, and began to dominate and destroy everything in his way. Then the King of the Paradise of Light created the human being and sent it down in order to combat the dragon. The primitive human being received five powers: breathing, air, light, water, and fire. But the dragon came to win the fight and devoured the human being. However, the latter recognized and loved the King of the Paradise of Light, and this love filled him with radiance. Slowly, the dragon began to shine from inside out and wished for light. Goodness overcame hatred, and the dragon was redeemed.

Nevertheless, the focus of Manichaeism is not always on external evil. Its primary goal is the redemption of the imperfections, the evil in the human soul. So the idea of mere control over our soul impulses is not enough; much more important is evil's transformation in the soul of every human being, for only then can one contribute to the redemption of external evil, and also of the earth itself. Nowadays Manichaeism is misunderstood or misinterpreted; it is described as preaching unyielding antagonism between good and evil.

The disciples of Mani were encouraged to criticize and question the ideals of their master, who wanted them to develop spiritual independence because he did not admit submissive followers who simply accepted his assertions. Among the Manichaeans were individuals of various degrees of development; those who had reached the highest degree were called *electi*, or "chosen." They formed a kind of apostolate, and soon Manichaeism spread throughout the Roman Empire and to Northern Africa and Asia as well, reaching as far as China.

---

135 E. Hutchins, *Parzival, an Introduction*.

The Persian King Shapur I (ruled 242–272 AD), whose ascension to the throne coincided with the beginning of Mani's external activities, was an adept of Mazdaism[136] and expelled Mani from his country. Mani returned thirty years later, after Shapur had died, invited by his son and successor, Hormizd I. However, two years later, another son of Shapur, Bahram I, rose to the throne (c. 274–277). The magi, followers of Zarathustra, fearing the loss of prestige of their own religion, managed to influence the king, who then started to persecute whoever did not follow the official religion. Mani was captured and later executed. This is all that is known about the reign of Bahram I.

Later on, the institutionalized Church of Rome fiercely persecuted Manichaeans, who were considered heretics. Their total annihilation in the West occurred in the 6th century. Because of its hatred of heretical sects, the Church virtually destroyed all their writings and documents. Most of what is known about them nowadays is in incriminating documents of the Church, which contain mostly prejudiced or distorted opinions of the accused.

Marco Polo (1254–1324) came upon Manichaean communities during one of his trips to China, in 1275. In 1907, manuscripts containing the teachings of Mani were found in the Gobi Desert in China, with annotations in Chinese characters. In 1930, Manichaean writings were discovered in southern Egypt.

In *Parzival*, Wolfram describes the beginning of Gawain's trajectory as the journey of someone who faced evil (Clinschor's realm) and fought it. Parzival had to join evil (or darkness, during his period of doubt, which lasted from his cursing by Cundrie to his redemption by Trevrizent) and transform evil into goodness. This is the *Manichaean* path, and the more difficult one. If Gawain fought the dragon outside himself, one could say that Parzival let himself be swallowed, so to

---

136 Mazdaism was a religion founded by Zarathustra in prehistoric times, also known as Zoroastrianism, Parseism or devotion to the Sacred Fire. The name "Mazdaism" derives from Ahura-Mazdao, or the Sun Aura.

speak, by the dragon, developing within himself the power to transform it. The episode in which this is most evident is the battle at Bearoche, when Gawain fought with Lyppaut's army against the attackers, while Parzival fought with the latter, among whom Wolfram identifies several unworthy knights, even criminals.

The Manichaean ideology was brought to the inhabitants of medieval castles by the minstrels, who presented it in grandiose and complex images. The common people of the villages, however, had no access to such information. Charles Kovacs points out that fairy tales, mainly those collected by the Brothers Grimm in the 19th century, originated among the Manichaeans and were intended for peasants and villagers.[137] In these tales, the same Manichaean ideas were presented in a simpler, more accessible form, and were transmitted orally from generation to generation for centuries. One tale that beautifully illustrates the question of the transforming power of good is *Beauty and the Beast*:

Walking through a garden, a man saw a beautiful rose and plucked it to offer to his daughter, Belle. The owner of this garden was a terrible beast, who caught the man but promised to spare his life, provided he would send him his daughter. Belle then went to live in the domain of the Beast, a magnificent residence, surrounded by servants. Still, she was miserable and refused the Beast's request to marry him. One day her desire to be released from this horrible creature was so intense that she wished for his death. With her thoughts set upon this, she went into the garden and saw the beast lying motionless on the ground. Faced with this situation, she felt ashamed of herself and felt sorry for the poor creature. She ran to a fountain and took some water to try to revive him. The Beast opened his eyes and said, "You wished for my death, and as you do not want to marry me, I want to die." At these words, the girl, moved by compassion, agreed to marry the Beast. At that moment the horrible Beast turned into a handsome prince. A

---

137 C. Kovacs, *Parzival and the Search for the Grail*.

wizard had transformed him into that monstrous being, and he could be freed from the spell only if a beautiful girl, out of her own free will, agreed to marry him.

This brings to mind the final episodes of the story of Gawain, who also came to an enchanted kingdom, and only after succeeding at all his trials—namely transforming into true love his sensual passion for Orgeluse—managed to release the duchess from the spell cast on her by Clinschor, the magician. Thus we can find the same theme in what nowadays is considered a children's story, and in the other, much more complex tale which recounts the adventures of a knight.

The Catholic Church

At the beginning of the 4th century, the Emperor Constantine (272–337) adopted the Christian religion, but only in 380 under Theodosius I (c. 346–395) did it actually became the official religion of the Roman Empire. After this emperor's death, the fall of the Empire began; thereafter, Rome was no longer considered the political reference point, but became instead the center of religious power, as the seat of the Roman Catholic Church. Saint Augustine (354–430) had been a Manichaean, but after living with the Manichaeans for about nine years he had not found the answers his restless soul yearned for, particularly to the question of evil. Besides, he was seeking pure spirit, and could not accept, even in the form of an image, the idea that the material world was permeated with spirit, and that the spirit could be seen from the material point of view.

On the other hand, he was also unable to attain higher levels of development, and eventually abandoned this religion, disillusioned and full of bitterness. He went to Milan, where he encountered more philosophical aspects of Christianity, and in 387 he was baptized. Ewald Koepke states[138] that, in his *Confessions*, Saint Augustine reports quite

---

138 E. Koepke, *Rudolf Steiner und das Gralsmysterium*.

openly the dark places his soul had to go through, "overcome by the craving for life" (B. IV, 2), chained to the "vices of the flesh," carrying his chains "drunk with pleasure till death" (B. VI, 12), until he finally managed to wake up to God, "and that was a contemplation that did not come from the flesh." (B. VII, 14) Still, doubts and despair, darkness and deceit continued to assail his soul.

In a lecture on April 11, 1909, Steiner pointed to the abyss in Saint Augustine's soul, to "his wrong judgment and the illusions in his Self."[139] However, when he succeeded in becoming permeated by Christ, Augustine became the personality that "could reveal a part of the great truths of the mysteries to the West."[140] Later he returned to Africa, where he became Bishop of Hippo. He fiercely fought various sects (Manichaeism, Donatism,[141] Pelagianism[142]) that had distanced themselves from the official Christianity accepted by Rome, and in these conflicts he matured his conception of what the Roman Catholic Church should be.

The Church had now started to function as an institution. The Christians, who formerly existed in small groups persecuted by the Romans, had now themselves become part of the establishment and began their own relentless persecution of all those who disagreed, the so-called heretics. By becoming a structured institution, the Catholic religion lost part of its spirituality, since its representatives also had to manage administrative and legal—therefore material—matters. Within this administrative structure the need to establish a hierarchy arose, which invariably leads to power struggles.

In 529 Benedict of Nursia (480–543) founded the first monastic order in Europe, the Benedictines. Life in this community was not based on blood ties. Rigid rules prevailed. Each monk had to take vows

---

139 R. Steiner, *The Principle of Spiritual Economy in Connection with Questions of Reincarnation*, GA 109.
140 Ibid.
141 Sect founded in the 4th century by Donato, Bishop of Carthage.
142 English sect founded in the 5th century by Pelagius.

of poverty, chastity, and obedience. Only at the end of the Middle Ages were so-called fraternities formed, in which people came together in community life as free individuals without the need for oaths or vows; one example was the Rosicrucian fraternity. Besides monks who followed orders from Rome, there were others who came from Ireland, totally independent of the clergy and the Pope. In the 6th century they began to preach in Europe. They were part of Celtic or Irish Christianity (see chapter "General Considerations about *Parzival*") and also formed monastic communities in which no vows were required. Their way of life was marked by rigid asceticism. These monks also founded monastic schools in which Greek wisdom and Christianity were harmoniously united with the teachings of the Druids and bards.

Among the exponents of this doctrine were two saints of Irish origin, Saint Columba and Saint Gallus ("Gallus" meant "Celtic" or "Welsh"). They worked mainly in areas inhabited by pagans, the lands known today as France, Italy, and Switzerland—which still has a city named St. Gallen (which began as a hermitage founded by Saint Gallus and whose world-famous library contains approximately 2,000 medieval manuscripts, including Wolfram's *Parzival*). Unlike the missionaries from Rome, who tried to completely eradicate the pagan customs and religious traditions of peoples they ruled, the Irish monks did not destroy pagan beliefs, but knew how to lead the pagans to Christianity by way of feelings. Unlike the early Christians, whose lives were totally focused on spiritual matters, ordinary Church members in those days could not have direct contact with the divinity: In the established hierarchical structure, the priests were the intermediaries between the faithful and God.

For the forgiveness of sins and such matters, the faithful had to resort to a priest. Dogmas of indisputable validity were instituted and had to be believed without questioning. To maintain its power over the people, the Church threatened them with hell if they did not obey the rules imposed by the Church; those who followed its precepts faithfully and blindly were promised the reward of heaven. No further analysis is required to realize that this attitude totally hinders the freedom of the human being, paralyzing and even nullifying the action of a free Self. A person could decide either to obey or not to obey the precepts of the Church, which shows that it was not a free choice involving any discernment or judgment. Christianity was a religion of redemption, but it feared the development of independent and responsible aspirations.

On the other hand, it is surprising that, despite the profoundly Christian character of the Grail and its legends, the Church always ignored them, making no explicit reference to the subject. However, as discussed above, the spiritual essence of the Grail and its quest are based on the human struggle for freedom, and this contradicted the principles of the Church. Certainly the clergy knew of this literature, but because it was profoundly esoteric and referred to primordial Christianity, they chose to let the population believe that it was merely fanciful and legendary.

One may say, though, that this attitude and conduct of the Church were *absolutely necessary* for most of the population, as they had not yet developed full self-awareness and the ability to judge. Therefore, the distancing of the individual from the spiritual world, which could now be reached only via the mediation of priests, was part of the spiritual direction foreseen for the evolution of humanity, because only after this distancing could humanity return to the spiritual world in complete freedom.

On the issue of good and evil, the Church adopted the ancient Jewish tradition, according to which Almighty God created evil to tempt the human being and could eliminate it whenever He chose to. Evil had to be fought at all costs. This contrasts completely with the Manichaean ideology, which encouraged its followers to criticize and question their doctrine, in addition to preaching the common origin and equal value of good and evil. Thus evil should not be combated, but redeemed through the power of love. These Manichaean ideas were most definitely too advanced for humanity at that time. Perhaps it is up to the present human being to fulfill what Mani preached prophetically.

Over time the Church became a powerful institution and a true state (the Vatican, with its own bank, its own guard, etc.) within another state (Italy), exerting tremendous influence, including political influence, in many countries. In the Middle Ages, serious power struggles between the Pope and the Emperor were not uncommon, proving that sometimes the Church turned more to terrestrial matters than to spiritual ones. Dante Alighieri (1265–1321) and later Martin Luther (1483–1546) accused the Church of having become worldly and indulging in political intrigue.

Konrad Burdach points out that, from about the 5th century on, there existed in Spain a type of Christianity not linked to Rome, which had its own liturgy.[143] Apparently it had roots in either Southern Gaul or Asia Minor. Between the 8th and 9th century, but mainly after the Council of Constantinople in 869, its representatives began to choose their own Primate. From the 10th century onward, the Church tried, initially with little success, to adapt its liturgy, the "Mozarabic Mass,"[144] to the Gregorian worship practiced by Rome. At the height of the conflict, the Spanish clergy and people denied the Primate of Rome and claimed that the Primate of Toledo was the true guardian of the ancient apostolic traditions. However, the Roman Church would not tolerate an additional Primate, as it intended to build a world empire. After many disputes, councils and laws, the Mozarabic liturgy was abolished in almost all Spanish churches in the 12th century.

In any case, the heresies, which in a way represented early esoteric Christianity and were related to the Grail, constituted a serious obstacle to the supremacy and domination of the Church, which is why they were opposed with such ferocity and cruelty.

Something very important was happening on the stage of history at the time of the events recounted by Wolfram, which took

---

[143] Konrad Burdach, *Der Gral*.
[144] This liturgy was introduced in Spain during the Moorish occupation, and the term "Mozarabic" indicates Arabic influences. The headquarters of this movement was in Toledo.

on an almost occult aspect. In the chapter "General Considerations about *Parzival*," we saw that the events reported by the troubadours occurred in the 9th century, and that their transcriptions date only to the end of the 12th and early 13th centuries. In 869 (therefore in the 9th century) the Council of Constantinople took place. As was seen in that chapter, until then, in the Church and in general, it was considered that the human being consisted of body, soul, and spirit. At the Council, however, the concept of the spirit was abolished, and the human being was henceforth to be regarded as consisting only of body and soul, with the latter possessing some spiritual qualities.

This fact was to greatly impact the future development of humanity, which now had to move completely away from the spiritual world. This situation was supposed to be temporary, however, so that humanity could later return to the higher world, this time through its own efforts and in complete freedom. Only a few initiates knew of the existence of the spiritual world. It cannot be a coincidence that— at the moment the Catholic Church was abolishing the spirit of the human being— a movement that cultivated and developed the spiritual element in each human being (to the maximum extent possible at that time) went unnoticed by history.

A key problem whispered about in the Church was doubt about the Holy Trinity. The Western Church stated that the Holy Spirit was more related to the Son, and considered each individual to be permeated by the spirit; the Eastern Church gave more importance to the Holy Spirit, present in the baptism in the Jordan in the form of a dove, related to the Father and announcing the Son. This led to the Church schism of 1054, and the need to find a "middle way" showing that there is only one truth, contemplated from different angles. In other words: The spirit emanates from both the Father and the Son. The message of the renewing strength of the spirit (remember that in *Parzival*, a dove descended from heaven every Good Friday to renew the Grail's nourishing power) was directed at people who doubted, unable to understand the Mystery of the Holy Trinity. In the case of Parzival, who had doubted God's omnipotence and benevolence since leaving Arthur's court and had refused to serve Him, Trevrizent's revelations helped him not only to want to serve God again, but also to recognize the Holy Trinity.

The Bogomils

In the 10th century, between the years 927 and 954, a new heresy appeared in the Balkan Peninsula, particularly in the region of Bulgaria. A priest who was dissatisfied with the direction dictated by the Church condensed and renewed the ideas of early, spiritual Christianity, adding quite a few aspects of Manichaeism. His name was Bogomil, and his followers were soon known as Bogomils, which in the Slavic languages signified "friends of God." One of the aspects of the doctrine preached by Bogomil was each individual's direct contact with God: without the mediation of an intermediary, without laws, without dogmas, but in complete freedom. He also urged his followers to awaken the "budding light within." The question of good and evil was seen in a way very similar to that of Manichaeism.

The Bogomils believed they must develop selfless love, because only in this way could they help the human being, the earth, and even evil to redeem themselves. Just like the Manichaeans, the Bogomils believed that events at the end of time would depend exclusively on the choices human beings made between practicing good or evil, and they were most certain that they could transform evil into good. While the Manichaeans were perhaps rather vaguely interested in evil, claiming not to fight it but to love it, the Bogomils welcomed wrongdoers and criminals, people considered "bad" by society, thinking they could turn them into good people.

There were three levels of followers: listeners, people interested in hearing what this doctrine had to say; believers, who accepted these ideas and sought to improve themselves thereby; and initiates, the most pure and evolved, who constituted the core and were also called *perfecti*.

The movement quickly grew and spread, considerably displeasing the Church, which began to persecute and massacre this heretical sect with the help of various emperors. The brave resistance of the heretics lasted for several centuries, and many, to save their lives, eventually fled to present-day Bosnia and then to Italy, while others went along the Danube, taking their spiritual doctrine to Central Europe, and still others went to Central Asia. Only when the Turks invaded the Balkans in the 14th and 15th centuries were they exterminated. To escape certain death, many preferred to embrace the Islamic religion rather than returning to Catholicism. It's possible that the serious ethnic and religious conflicts that still exist in the Balkan Peninsula have roots in those times.

The Cathars

In the 12th century, a new heretical sect appeared in northern Italy and in the Provence region in southern France. These people, dissatisfied with the way the Church was becoming increasingly focused on material issues and less and less inclined to spirituality, lived in communities, often far from the big cities so they could lead a pure and simple life dedicated to introspection and meditation. Only in the 19th century did they become known as Cathars, a Greek term meaning "pure ones" because of their striving for purification.[145]

At an earlier stage they were better known as Albigensians, because most inhabitants of the capital city of Albi in the Provence had adhered to this heretical doctrine. As happened with the other heresies, the Cathars soon had large numbers of supporters, among whom it is important to mention the Waldensians. These were followers of Peter Waldo (c.1140–1217), a wealthy merchant of the city of Lyon. Around 1170 he had an experience that made him turn to Christ and follow

---

145 Remember that the word "catharsis," common in psychology, means "purification."

the words of the Lord as written in the New Testament. He distributed his wealth among the poor and set out to lead a simple and pure life. Many of his friends did the same, and thus was formed the Waldensian community, which in 1180 was already quite important in the south of France.

There are some interesting similarities between the lives of Peter Waldo and Saint Francis of Assisi (1182–1226). The latter was the son of a wealthy cloth merchant and had an affinity for the literature of the minstrels, especially those from Provence. After having a vision of Christ and complying with the request of an inner voice, he sold the fabrics his father dealt in to finance the rebuilding of a ruined chapel. Furious, his father took him to the bishop's court, where young Francis gave away all his belongings and disowned his father. He renounced material possessions and lived in prayer, trying to follow as closely as possible in the footsteps of Christ, doing good deeds. Saint Francis founded a new order of mendicant monks—the Franciscans—and always remained close to the Catholic Church.

It is believed that the Cathars are the spiritual descendants of the Bogomils who had fled from persecution in the Balkan Peninsula, moving toward Italy and France. The doctrine of the first Cathars has much in common with Bogomilism, starting with the issue of good and evil or light and darkness, which, for them, were of equal strength, value and power. They were enjoined to do good, for light brightens darkness, thereby overcoming it. That is how they sought spiritual development, purifying themselves through isolation, meditation, and penance. In addition, the Cathars preached tolerance toward all other religions, and Jews and Muslims lived peacefully among them. For the Cathars, women had the same rights and duties as men, with no distinction between the sexes in the pursuit of perfection: Women could attain the same degree of purification as men. The most advanced members of the community were asked to give advice and help their companions in the process of perfecting themselves. Highly developed spiritual leaders were called *perfecti* (as among the Bogomils) or "good men" (in

French, *bonshommes*), and in fact took on the equivalent role of priests of the Church. Obviously they could not celebrate the official church sacraments, but there was a specific sacrament which they performed: the *consolamentum*, i.e., spiritual consolation.

Catharism was becoming very important, especially in southern France, and more and more people joined the sect, including many noblemen, which introduced a political aspect. Fearing the loss of its power in the region, the Church began to persecute these heretics. By way of various intrigues, it managed to remove the Cathar leaders and sympathizers, and organized a crusade against the Cathars which lasted for thirty years (1178–1209). Originally, the purpose of crusades was to expel pagans from the holy sites in Jerusalem; this time it was to persecute and annihilate Christians. The noble families of the north of France were urged to combat their southern brethren. In this terrible war the Cathars fought bravely and offered strong resistance to the papal forces, but lacked the necessary armaments and were outnumbered.

In the same period the Dominican Order was founded, and through it Pope Innocent III (1160–1216) instituted the Inquisition. Numerous heretics died in the fires of the Inquisition and in the courtyards of Cathar fortresses, which were collapsing one after the other. In these fortresses, hundreds of young and old men, women and children were sometimes burned together.

The last Cathar stronghold to fall was Montségur, in 1244. Trying to escape, many of its inhabitants took refuge in caves in the Pyrenees, and when discovered, they were killed or walled in: The cave entrance was sealed so that they died of starvation. Comparing the doctrine and lifestyle of the Cathars with the Grail Community as described by Wolfram (or with Joseph of Arimathea's community by Robert de Boron), the resemblance is striking. In both communities there is a profound Christianity, more like early Christianity than the ecclesiastical Christian doctrine. In both communities there is a withdrawal from society (almost an isolation in the Grail Community), the pursuit of the spiritual realm through introspection, the practice of penance for self-purification and for redemption of the sins of others (as, for example, in the case of Trevrizent), the active role of women (Herzeloyde, Sigune), and even aspects of the priesthood. (Trevrizent, besides offering the *consolamentum*, took on himself the sins of Parzival before God.) It is interesting to note that in the work of Chrétien de Troyes this hermit does not have a name; when referring to him, Chrétien simply calls him "good man" (*bonhomme* in French), the name given to the most highly developed Cathars. Moreover, the information about God that Parzival received from his mother and Trevrizent[146] clearly reflects the relationship between light and darkness, good and evil, that was described by the Cathars.

Interestingly, at exactly the same time as the struggle between dogmatic Christianity (Church of Rome) and cosmic Christianity (Catharism), i.e., in the period when the Cathars were being persecuted, the works concerning the Grail were written, although these are placed in the 9th century. To explain this, Rudolf Meyer draws an analogy with the plant kingdom.[147] Just as many plants contract in the form of seeds so as not to die out in winter, a high spiritual longing had to be transformed into metaphorical images. Only then was it possible to acquire the force of sprouting for a new spiritual life at the appropriate time, as happens with the seed. It is from this period that fairy tales and other legends come, which also contain important spiritual truths in the form of images.

---

146 Wolfram: "(...) His appearance (God's) is more brilliant than daylight. (...) Another is called Prince of Darkness. Besides being sinister, he is invariably disloyal. Beware of him and doubtful hesitation." (B. III, 119) "God is synonymous to the very truth and abhors falsehood." (B. IX, 462) But the divine nature, origin of all purity, wanton, radiant, barrier of Joseph of Arimathea in the work of Robert de Boron, when Joseph receives instructions on what to say to his brother-in-law Bron when he passes on the function of guardian of the Grail: "Show him how the Wicked Enemy deceives and deludes my friends and all who follow me, he should beware; this is what I ask of you."
147 R. Meyer, *Der Gral und seine Hüter*.

Some considerations must be made in light of the similarities between the doctrines and lifestyles of the communities of the Cathars and the Grail. Surely, Wolfram (and it is believed Robert de Boron, too) was quite familiar with the Cathars. This does not mean that he took part in this heresy; it can be assumed, however, that through his writings he wanted to bequeath to posterity this spiritual doctrine, this legacy of esoteric Christianity, which the Church was keeping hidden from its congregations. Reading his work in this light, it is striking how much profoundly esoteric content he managed to insert in disguise, making it accessible only to those familiar with it. To those unaware of it, his book merely describes the interesting adventures of the knights.

In this context, just as the Grail—experienced as the stone exiled from heaven—came to earth, so did the spiritual entity of Christ come to inhabit the body of Jesus of Nazareth, exiling Himself, so to speak, from His own heavenly "fatherland." The power of the Grail, however, had to be renewed every Good Friday by a gift from heaven brought by a white dove. The early Christians still felt the presence of Christ very near them, and Pentecost, which celebrates the coming of the Holy Spirit, made them aware of who the Christ Being actually was, as Rudolf Steiner states in his lecture of October 2, 1913.[148] Recalling that the heraldic symbol of the Grail was white doves, one can assume that all the communities that practiced primordial, esoteric Christianity would represent this "gift from heaven," in the sense of the renewal of Christ's power—a power which, over the centuries, had lost all of its spiritual aspect.

In the materialistic atmosphere of the present day, even modern theologians no longer understand the esoteric aspect of Christianity, and Christ is seen either as a great prophet or as a revolutionary, a rabble-rouser, and so forth. There are even people who deny His existence, and consequently His sacrifice to save humankind. According to Rudolf

---

148 R. Steiner, *The Fifth Gospel: From the Akashic Chronicle*, GA 148.

Steiner's spiritual research, the Mystery of Golgotha, which covers the Death and Resurrection of Christ, was the central event of all human evolution, and was the Mystery of the Grail guarded by all the heretical movements.

Another point to be understood is the figure of Kyot from Provence, whom Wolfram describes in more detail just before Trevrizent reveals the secrets of the Grail to Parzival. According to Wolfram, master Kyot found a book written in Arabic in the city of Toledo (which, as mentioned, was the center of a Christian stream that had moved away from Rome). He learned the language of the pagans and communicated the content of this book to Wolfram. The book had been written by Flegetanis, who was descended, through his mother, from the line of Solomon. His father, however, was a pagan. Flegetanis was considered a wise man, who could, "read in the stars without more ado"[149] (B. IX, 232), and this also hints at the esoteric side of the work. He had read in the stars about the existence of an object named Grail, brought to earth by a legion of angels who then returned to heaven.

On earth, the Grail had to be guarded by people with a pure heart, initiated through baptism and who had achieved a high level of purification. It can be inferred that Flegetanis, a pagan familiar with the old star wisdom, had contemplated the approach of the macrocosmic Christ. He pointed to the birth of a human being in whose body would reside Christ, the high Sun Being. Many centuries later, Kyot, a Christian, acknowledged that in fact the manuscript was referring to Christ, who had lived on earth, suffered death and been resurrected; that is, the old Jewish tradition, influenced by lunar forces, had given rise to a new period to be led by the forces of the sun.

---

149 According to Steiner, the initiates of the Chaldeans, Babylonians, Egyptians, and also the Celts, whose cultures had had their climax between 3000 and 800 BC, knew how to read the mysteries contained in the movements of the stars. That is the period when true astrology began. When Wolfram says that the pagan Flegetanis "could read the stars," he was referring to someone who came from the time of those cultures and was an initiate.

According to Wolfram, Kyot had also studied other Latin books and discovered the lineage selected to guard the Grail on earth, and therefore the names of Titurel, Frimurtel, and Anfortas. Another important characteristic of Kyot is the fact that he was from and/or had lived in Provence, because he was called "the Provençal." Provence is the region where Catharism was most widespread. The pagan book had been found in Spain, then under the influence of the Moors, which illustrates the good relationship between the Cathars and the Arabs.

Rudolf Meyer claims that Kyot permeated with the spiritual light of Christianity the ancient wisdom of the stars, which reached Spain with the Arab or Cabbalist traditions. He was able to renew these traditions, so to speak, according to the Christian spirit of the time. In this context, we must remember that Wolfram states that Chrétien was not very truthful when telling the story, while Kyot offered the authentic version of this narrative.

Pierre Ponsoye, referring to Kyot, says that the authority assigned to him by Wolfram does not necessarily apply to the man Kyot, but to the "true tradition" he revealed, a "Gnostic mystery."[150] One can even assume that Wolfram created this figure of Kyot to protect himself from possible investigation or prosecution by the Inquisition for revealing the Cathar doctrine, i.e., for helping to spread heresy. In this case, he could always blame Kyot and the pagans for the content of his work.

The Order of the Knights Templar and the Order of Christ

Having considered some important heretical movements, we should now examine other historical currents related to the Grail, like the Knights Templar, the Order of Christ, the Freemasons, and the Rosicrucian movement. One may consider that their practices contain

---

150 P. Ponsoye, *El Islam y el Grial*.

metamorphoses of the Grail impulse. Some have a historically familiar exterior aspect and simultaneously an esoteric spiritual one hidden from historians. Others are to this day shrouded in a cloak of mystery, and what is known of their true content is very little. Besides being movements of a spiritual nature, they have strong social connotations as well.

First the Order of the Templar Knights will be addressed. It started in the early 12th century, precisely when Catharism was flourishing. The order was founded in 1118 by Hugues de Payens (1070–1136), who became the first Grand Master, Godfrey of Saint-Omer, and another seven knights, and was conceived as a monastic military order—which means that its members were monks as well as knights.

This was something revolutionary at the time, because knighthood was a fully outward occupation, requiring a lot of action, while monastic life was lived in seclusion, with prayers every three hours to accompany the breathing of the earth.[151] Among the main objectives of this order were the protection of the holy places in Jerusalem which were being attacked by the Turks. It is important to stress that the members of this order did not fight Arabism, but Turkish Islam. In addition to this, another outward task was the protection of pilgrims traveling to the Holy Land, as they were easy prey for robbers who stole their belongings.

As the seat of this order of knights was located next to the ruins of the Great Temple in Jerusalem, it became known as the Order of the Knights of the Temple, and its members were the Knights Templar or Knights of the Temple. The regulations of this order were developed by Bernard of Clairvaux (1090–1153)[152] and accepted by the Church

---

151 An obvious phenomenon that follows this rhythm is that of the tides, which rise or fall about every six hours; in the three hours in the middle, a point of equilibrium is reached, corresponding to the origin or zero point in a coordinate system.
152 Bernard of Clairvaux was a mystic Cistercian monk, one of the most influential clerics of his time. He founded Clairvaux Abbey and was canonized in 1174.

during the Council of Troyes in 1128. W.F. Veltman calls attention to the fact that from the time of the order's foundation to its official recognition, only one other knight joined the group, and during that period there were no major battles.[153]

The author believes that during those ten years the knights went through a phase of esoteric preparation and initiation. Only after 1128 did the order begin to expand and act in the outer world. The fact that their first location was next to the ruins of the Temple of Solomon is also important, because this temple was highly significant from an esoteric point of view, as will be seen. But we may also expect that the order followed Solomon's impulse (to build a house for the Lord), infused with Christianity. The equipment of a knight consisted of armor, shield, sword, and spear, and the Templar monks would also need "spiritual armor" in accordance with the words of Saint Paul in the Epistle to the Ephesians (Eph. 6:14–17): the armor of righteousness, the shield of faith, the sword of the Spirit. Thus, these knight-monks acted both outwardly and inwardly. In addition to them, many other people participated in the life of the Knights Templar, but they had not taken vows or committed to a spiritual path, so they were not counted among the initiates. They included farmers, artists, and other supporters.

On their spiritual path, the Knights Templar led a life of meditation, self-sacrifice, and purification. António Quadros says that the Knights Templar were a society of initiation.[154] When a knight was initiated into the order, he had to be willing to face all manner of tribulations, including going without sleep, food, and any kind of luxury. In addition, he had to "swear that he was not married, had never been engaged, had no debts, did not belong to another order, was in good health, was not a priest, was of good lineage, and had not been excommunicated." If he was accepted, he would pledge full obedience to his superiors, take a vow of poverty and chastity, submit to the rules of the order, be faithful

---

153 W.F. Veltman, *Tempel und Gral*.
154 A. Quadros, *Portugal: Razão e mistério*, vol. 1.

to the religion, help conquer and protect the Holy Land, and protect and defend Christians and their property.

This ability to face both inward and outward is one of the strongest features of the Knights Templar. Julius Evola therefore concludes that they have quite a resemblance to the "spiritual knights of the Grail."[155] Other authors even claim that the Grail Castle must, in fact, have been a Templar castle, and that Wolfram must have been a knight of the order. Veltman points out that the Templars had to devote themselves fully to Christ and fill their souls with the meaning of the Mystery of Golgotha; this explains their statement that their bodies and blood were not theirs, but belonged to Christ. The Templars also considered the soil they worked agriculturally to be the body of Christ.

The double life of the Knights Templar was extremely revolutionary at the time and, therefore, misunderstood. It actually corresponds to the behavior that humanity must develop at the present time: to act on one's own initiative and weigh each issue on its own merits while, at the same time, renouncing one's own will and acting according to what is required in each situation. This means being responsive to the needs of the environment and acting in the world accordingly.

The Templars' path of inner development led through the seven steps of Christian initiation described in the chapter "The Journey of Gawain." The highest level was that of the Grand Master. Quite often there are illustrations of two Templar knights riding the same horse; the most common interpretation is that in their vow of poverty the monk-knights had to share a single mount. Because they were an order of initiation, however, the explanation could also be that the Templars always made sure they had a "helper" from the spiritual world, a spiritual entity who accompanied them wherever they went. This would be the figure sitting behind the Templar knight.

The Templars were highly respected for their courage and exemplary behavior. In a short time their numbers grew rapidly, and

---

155   J. Evola, *The Mystery of the Grail*.

soon there were hundreds of Templar castles throughout Europe. They helped pilgrims, mainly by managing their properties during their absences. They set up the modern banking system to protect travelers who needed to take large sums of money or goods to serve as currency during their long journeys: The pilgrims would deposit their goods at the Templar castle closest to their residences and, keeping the receipt, travel to the next Templar castle, taking only a small amount of money with them. On arrival at the new castle, they presented their receipt and received whatever they needed to reach the next castle. Consequently, robbers lost interest in assaulting them, as they would get next to nothing from these travelers.

There was never any proof of fraud or wrongdoing of the Templars; their transactions always seemed clean and transparent. In the long run, they eventually knew everything about the financial conditions of the nobles they helped. Yet another innovation was the fact that, as the Knights Templar were brave and fearless and no one dared confront them, documents and important commissions were entrusted to them to be transported to other locations.

Although the Order of the Knights of the Temple extended throughout the countries from Europe to the Holy Land, it was a very cohesive order; according to Steiner, this was due to the intense strengthening of their spiritual life. They were innovators in the development of the forces of the heart, of enthusiasm, and sacrifice. People were attracted by their demonstrated love and the enthusiasm they radiated.

Another important feature of the Knights Templar was their relationship with the soil: They considered the earth the body of Christ, and cared for it with the greatest possible respect. Furthermore, they had an amazing sense for administration, and the pilgrims' properties cared for by the knights during their absences prospered enormously. If a noble died during a pilgrimage and left no heirs, his property would automatically belong to the Knights Templar. Although the individual members of the order were poor, the order itself soon amassed great wealth, and because they were well liked and respected everywhere, the knights enjoyed privileges such as exemption from taxes, duties, and tithes on cultivated land, and the inviolability of their persons and of properties belonging to them and others. Later, they even lent money to the nobles to fund campaigns.

One of these noblemen, King Philip IV ("the Fair") of France (1268–1314), owed the Knights Templar a fortune. Contriving a way to avoid paying his debt, he tried to become a member of the order, but did not meet the requirements for membership. Having been denied entrance, he and his minister, Nogaret, hatched a diabolical plot to take over the treasures of the Templars. He knew there was only one way to end their power: slander, false accusations, and false witnesses. In 1307, he ordered that all the Templar castles in France be invaded on the same night, and all the knights imprisoned. A trial that would last seven years began. For the first time in history, false testimony, libel, and slander were used to accuse people and deceive the public, who had great respect and admiration for the Knights Templar. Under false pretenses[156] the knights were tortured, and when they were out of their minds with pain and suffering, they were required to sign documents in which they confessed to crimes they had never committed. When they returned to consciousness and their "confessions" were presented, it was no use denying the facts. Questions asked of them were related to their experiences during the initiation process, including temptations they had suffered.

Philip managed to convince all the royal houses of Europe of the "crimes" of the Knights Templar, and in all the lands where they operated their castles were closed, their property confiscated and the knights imprisoned in deference to the mighty king of France. However,

---

156 Some of the accusations against them were that they denied Christ, practiced idolatry, and worshiped an image of God called Baphomet, a figure which appears androgynous and double-faced, with a chiaroscuro aspect perhaps representing the original force, cited by Mani, in which the power of light and darkness were still united (E. Jung and M.-L. von Franz, *The Grail Legend*).

in no other country were their "heresies" confessed; the Vatican itself had great esteem for the Templar Order. Therefore, to get the Pope, too, to ban the order, Philip managed through various manipulations to have another Pope, "his own," elected: Clement V (1264–1314), a sick person with a weak personality, totally submissive to the king, who never occupied the papal throne in Rome but resided in Avignon instead.

At the Council of Vienne in 1312, after several postponements, Pope Clement abolished the Templar Order, although he had never declared it guilty. Finally, after the seven-year trial following the mass arrest of the French Templars, the Grand Master of the Order, Jacques de Molay (1244–1314), was condemned to be burned at the stake. The Order of the Knights Templar ceased to exist.

In 1319, King Denis of Portugal (1261–1325) founded a new order, which he named the Order of Christ. The royal family of Portugal had always sympathized with the Knights Templar; they shut down the order at the behest of Philip the Fair but did not confiscate the knights' property, saving it instead. This treasure was donated to the new order, whose rules were very similar to those of the Templars. There were again two paths to follow, an internal path and an external one, and the degrees of improvement and purification were the same as those of the Templars.

The order's most important Grand Master was Prince Henry (1394–1460), who founded the nautical school in Sagres, becoming known as Henry the Navigator. He is described as a very brave person, strong, logical, and also compassionate. Highly learned, he had his eyes on the future. According to Günter Kollert, he is considered the "father of the Age of Discovery."[157] The helmsmen trained at the Sagres School learned everything related to navigation and even went through an intense spiritual education of the esoteric Christian kind. Later on, when Portuguese ships sailed the oceans in search of a sea route to India, there were in fact two reasons for undertaking this journey.

---

157   G. Kollert, *Apocalipse Português*.

One was the outer reason, widely known and related to the spice trade: The intention was to break the Arabs' monopoly on trade, which in a sense also represented a fight against Islam. However, every captain that left Lisbon also carried documents and gifts to be offered to Prester John, should they meet him. In Portugal there was an awareness of a community existing in the East that followed esoteric Christian precepts, the Community of Prester John. It is worth remembering here the end of Wolfram's *Parzival* story, in which the author describes the departure of Feirefiz and Repanse of Schoye to the East, where the former would spread the Christian faith. Their son would become known as Prester John, a title also common to all his successors. This points to an irrefutable connection between the Order of Christ and the Grail movement.

Quoting the historian Jaime Cortesão (1884–1960), Kollert reports that already in 1481, there was news in Portugal of a mighty Christian king whose lands were located in present-day Ethiopia, also known as "African India." Some scientists attribute to the Genoan cartographer Giovanni da Carignano (c. 1250–1329) the location of the kingdom of Prester John in Africa, after his contact with the Abyssinian ambassador in 1306. In 1487, King John II of Portugal (1455–1495) sent an expedition to find the kingdom of Prester John, commanded by Pero de Covilhã (c. 1450–1530) and Afonso de Paiva (c. 1460–1490). They first went to Egypt by land and ship and, starting out from Cairo disguised as merchants, they traveled the Spice Route in reverse. They joined a caravan and traveled along the Red Sea from Saudi Arabia to the city of Aden.

There they learned that Ethiopia was actually governed by a Christian sovereign, but confused by the mission of going to India, they decided to continue by separate ways, agreeing to meet again in Egypt. Afonso de Paiva went to Ethiopia and Pero de Covilhã to India, where he arrived at the cities of Kannur and Calicut. He was the first Portuguese to see India and its surrounding seas, and also visited several locations on the East African coast (Malindi, Mozambique) before returning to

Egypt. Thus he concluded that, if it were possible to go around the so-called Cape of Storms, the sea route to India would be assured.

Back in Cairo, Pero de Covilhã found out that his companion had died. The king of Portugal had sent a message informing him that Bartolomeu Dias had sailed around the Cape of Storms (which was then renamed Cape of Good Hope), and reiterating the mission of searching for Prester John. Along with his answer, Pero de Covilhã sent an account of his travels. Shortly after, Vasco da Gama (1469–1520) would sail to India.

Following the king's orders, Covilhã continued his journey and arrived in Ethiopia, where he was welcomed by the sovereign, who, however, died a few days later. His successor invoked the custom of the country, that is, foreigners who had arrived there could no longer leave. Thus, Pero de Covilhã, the Portuguese ambassador, spent the rest of his life in Ethiopia, where he started a family and became counselor to the king. By way of other Portuguese travelers, he received and sent news to the court in Lisbon.

In short, Pero's major achievement was demonstrating that it was possible to travel by sea to the real India, located east of the Indian Ocean, while Ethiopia, the "African India," was situated west of the same ocean. The ruler of Ethiopia was also known as the Negus of Abyssinia (another name for Ethiopia), and his kingdom practiced a more spiritual, essentially Coptic, Christianity, introduced to the region in the 4th century and distinct from the Christianity of the West. However, this king was not as powerful as was thought: He was often at war with his Muslim neighbors so as not to be crushed by them.

It is worth adding that Albrecht von Scharfenberg reports at the end of his work, *Titurel*, that the question was frequently asked: What happened to the Grail after Parzival became King of the Grail? Wolfram mentions nothing about this. Albrecht reports that, having reigned for ten years as Grail King, Parzival accompanied Titurel, then five hundred years old, on his way to the East, where the Grail was entrusted to the care of Prester John, as the West was no longer worthy of it. This means that for the West, the Grail simply ceased to exist. Georg Kühlewind makes an analogy between this fact and the Ascension of Christ, remembering that at the Ascension the disciples felt abandoned for the second time (the first having been after the Crucifixion), since He had now definitely gone into the spiritual world.[158] They knew they would not meet Him again as He was after the Resurrection—recognizable in His external form, yet not experienced by way of the senses. In short, He was gone from their physical eyes and would only manifest Himself within each human being, as long as He were sought. The same could be said of the Grail. It disappeared from the earthly sphere, but nowadays any person can develop the means to search for it within the inner self.

Since during their travels to India the Portuguese navigators were seeking Prester John, guardian of the Grail, one can conclude that the discovery of Brazil in 1500 was indirectly linked with this impulse. The red crosses on the white sails of the Portuguese ships were the same as those that adorned the white robes of the Knights Templar.

Freemasonry

Freemasonry is another stream that represents a somewhat indirect spiritual search loosely connected with the Grail Community. Freemasonry dates back to the time of the construction of the Great Temple of Jerusalem by King Solomon, about 950 BC. In reality, Solomon's father, King David, had received from Jehovah the mission to build a "temple in honor of my name" (1 Kings 5:5–18). Now in Exodus 3:14, when Moses sees the burning bush in the desert and hears a voice speaking to him, he asks who is speaking. Jehovah's voice answers, "I am who I am," also translated as "I am the I-am." Therefore, this temple was to be the abode of the "I-am."

According to Rudolf Steiner's teachings, we should be aware that this is the "Cosmic Self" preparing the incarnation of Christ. For this,

---

158 G. Kühlewind, *Der Gral oder Was die Liebe vermag.*

a specific people was required in which each individual could develop self-awareness; this was the Jewish people, the first to be able to conceive an abstract god who would be worshiped not through images, but within each person. In fact, the temple should be a visible image of the complete human being, whose corporeality must be understood as the dwelling of God, the divine spark that every human being carries within, the individual Self. At that time, the spiritual element could not manifest and act on earth without having an appropriate "dwelling."

As David had sinned against Jehovah, he was punished and prevented from completing this work, and passed the task on to his son Solomon. This king became known for his wisdom, which could be considered the ripe fruit at the end of a thousand years of the Hebrews' evolution. His reign can be considered the only calm time in the history of the sons of Israel, because before and after Solomon they lived in continuous warfare. However, this king's religious wisdom—a gift obtained through divine inspiration—allowed only for the wise design of the temple by his power of thinking, which is usually related to the sphere of death; it was not enough to build the temple. He needed the help of someone who possessed practical knowledge, who was learned in the art of construction, who knew how to work with earthly materials. He would be the representative of the forces of will and action, very living forces of transformation.[159] Thus Solomon appealed to King Hiram of Tyre in Phoenicia. Two passages in the Old Testament (1 Kings 7:13–14 and 2 Chron. 2:12–14) refer to the personality who undertook the work: It was Hiram Abiff [note that the Phoenician king and the builder had the same name, but are not the same person], "son of a widow,"[160] whose father was Phoenician.

---

[159] The polarity between the forces of thinking and willing was briefly outlined in the chapter "Differences between Gawain and Parzival."

[160] In his lecture of Feb. 6, 1913 (*The Mysteries of the East and of Christianity*, GA 144), Rudolf Steiner mentions that in the ancient Egyptian mysteries an initiate was known as a "widow's son." It is noteworthy that Parzival was also the son of a widow.

Hiram Abiff was initiated into the mysteries of the Phoenicians, where the phoenix was venerated. In the chapter on the symbolism of the Grail it was mentioned that in pre-Christian times, the future event of death and resurrection (that is, the overcoming of death) was recognized in the Mysteries of the Phoenix.

In his cycle of lectures on the so-called "Temple Legend,"[161] Rudolf Steiner explained that the legend dates back to Christian Rosenkreuz (see below), was very important in the Rosicrucian fraternity from the 15th century onward, and later became the foundation of modern Freemasonry. According to the legend, Hiram Abiff descended from Cain and, following his initiation, became very knowledgeable about the Mysteries of the Earth and everything material. That is why he knew so well how to use the earthly resources available.

During the construction of the temple, the Queen of Sheba went to Jerusalem, as she had heard of Solomon's great wisdom. She became enchanted with his wisdom and beauty, and accepted his offer of marriage. But then she heard about the construction of the temple and wanted to meet Hiram. When she saw him, she was fascinated by him. Solomon became jealous, but could not get rid of the builder before the end of his work. The temple was almost finished; only the Brazen Sea, a large decorative bronze basin representing the ocean, was missing. Hiram had prepared everything for the casting of this masterpiece; however, three apprentices whom he had not considered suitable for the degree of Master decided to take revenge by sabotaging the casting of the Brazen Sea.

The plot was discovered in time by a friend of Hiram's, who informed Solomon so as to avert disaster. Because of his jealousy, however, the king ignored the warning, and Hiram had to watch as the incandescent bronze vaporized because of the addition of a contaminant. In his desperation the image of his ancestor Tubal-Cain

---

161 R. Steiner, *The Temple Legend*, GA 93.

appeared to him, telling him to throw himself into the fire, which would not hurt him. Thus Hiram reached the depths of the earth, where he was initiated into the secret of the generation of fire. Tubal-Cain also gave him a hammer and a golden triangle for Hiram to wear around his neck.

Then Hiram returned to the surface and succeeded in casting the Brazen Sea, thereby winning the hand of the Queen of Sheba; however, the three apprentices finally killed him. Before dying, Hiram still managed to throw the golden triangle into a well and was able to reveal that Tubal-Cain had predicted the birth of his son, who would, in turn, father many children. They would populate the earth and would finish his work: the construction of the temple. Hiram also revealed where he had thrown the golden triangle, which was rescued and kept, along with the Brazen Sea, in the Holy of Holies in the Temple.

Here we see once again the polarity between the thinking process, the wisdom of Solomon, and the doing process, the practical activity of Hiram Abiff; or the spiritual sphere on one hand and the dense material realm on the other. Thus two opposing, antagonistic streams are represented here, both not only necessary but essential for the development of humankind. W.F. Veltman says that they represent two streams of humanity: cautious wisdom, or religion without passion, vs. the stream related to fire, impulsive, and enthusiastic. With the advent of Christ, the old religion had to be impregnated by fire—not the fire of passion but the fire of love, to become a warm religiosity. After all, Christ is not only wisdom: He is Himself divine love incarnate. In the future, human beings will also have to reconcile these two principles, but out of free choice.

Therefore, in the course of its evolution, humankind had to become less religious and develop materialism, the knowledge of all that is material, and then, in freedom, to seek the union of both impulses. The continuation of the construction of the Temple, as planned by Hiram, was no longer the physical temple in Jerusalem; this was destroyed a few years after the advent of Christ, for its mission had been fulfilled. The Temple to be built after the coming of Christ is no longer a temple related to a certain people, but the "Temple of Humankind." Then the principle of the Self, as brought by Christ, would manifest in social forms based on fraternity and the feeling that all human beings are equal before the divine entity.

After having been forgotten for many centuries, Freemasonry appeared once more in the 12th and 13th centuries during the construction of the great Gothic cathedrals in Europe. The masons were stonemasons, men who worked with stone, the bricklayers of that time (*maçon* means "bricklayer" or "builder" in French); however, they were not just simple workers. During the construction of those huge churches, where it was easier to rise toward divinity, they formed groups who were also aware that they were contributing to the construction of a better society.

In his lecture of December 13, 1919,[162] Rudolf Steiner addressed the construction of temples during different periods of human evolution, even relating each building's form to the type of consciousness current at the time of its construction. Thus, for example, during the height of Hellenism (the first centuries of the fourth post-Atlantean cultural epoch) the Greek temple was the abode of a certain god or goddess; the statue of that deity (his or her representative) "resided" in that building, as the Greeks still felt that their gods actually "lived" among the people.

Nobody went inside the temple, as this would correspond to breaking into the home of that deity. Yet in the final centuries of the fourth post-Atlantean cultural epoch (approximately from the 8th century onward), the temple had another connotation. Human beings felt abandoned by God, for in this period there was no longer any perception of the immediate presence of divine-spiritual forces; they had become very distant. Human beings longed to find the path that would lead to the divinity, and this became possible in the great

---

162 R. Steiner, *Michael's Mission*, GA 194.

cathedrals, within which many people would gather. In other words, while the Greeks did not dare enter the deity's "abode," medieval people felt the need to enter the temple. God was not there, but they could address Him through the experience of being inwardly elevated. This did not occur individually, but happened in the form of the "group soul" of the community gathered there. Full awareness of the individual Self would only come in the 15th century.

Incidentally, in the cycle "The Temple Legend," Steiner said that within Freemasonry there were two totally different conceptions of the fraternity. One idea considered its origin to lie in the art of constructing material buildings; the other thought this naïve, stating that Freemasonry was an art of the soul, and that its symbols (square, plumb line, compass and trowel) had just been borrowed from the art of construction and referred to the work to be realized within each human being. Therefore, according to this second conception a better human being could be "built." Nowadays Freemasons accept the second idea, even denying the former. Steiner, however, confirmed the relationship of Freemasonry with the art of building, but stressed that it needed to be understood in a much more profound sense.

In the 12th century, to be a Mason meant to vehemently oppose official power, and therefore everything had to happen in secret. At the same time, Freemasonry developed a new aspect. Remembering that Cain offered the fruit of his own labor in sacrifice to God (Gen. 4:3), the masons began to assign great importance to the power resulting from their own sacrifice, especially on behalf of others. From this a strong sense of brotherhood was born, becoming the foundation for interpersonal harmony. That is why Masonic communities have this fraternal, intensely social aspect. The highest degrees of Freemasonry had their origin in the ancient mysteries.

On the other hand, everything constructed by human hands and all works of culture produced from dead raw materials, are related to Freemasonry. Already at the time of the ancient Chaldeans and Egyptians, people didn't just use simple reasoning to construct buildings; structures were imbued with high inspiration. It was felt that the ability to master and structure inorganic nature corresponded to a "royal art" (royal because the rulers, being initiates, were more spiritually developed than their subjects).

It is known that the construction of each medieval cathedral involved many master builders. Every year after the winter hiatus a new group of bricklayers arrived, each with his own yardstick and building technique, to join in the construction without any plan or blueprint to follow. More important than a blueprint were numerical relationships between length, width, and height, and also certain geometric shapes. Modern studies reveal "imperfections" in these constructions: slight angles in lines that should have been perfectly straight, and so forth. Differences in the proportions of walls, pillars, column details, etc.[163] can also be discerned. Contemplating these magnificent buildings while cognizant of the facts just described, one has the clear impression that they were the result of inspiration by higher powers, and not only of plans and calculations comparable to those of modern engineering.

With the end of the Gothic period, Freemasonry was relegated to oblivion.

At the end of the 18th century and the beginning of the 19th, Freemasonry returned, but no longer in the form of "royal art," the transformation of material substance. It continued as a secret society, with its own rules, initiation processes, and different degrees of improvement, but committed to the building of a better society, that is, transforming people's souls. As mentioned above, the Masonic symbols continued to be the tools needed for physical constructions: the compass, the square, the plumb line, and the trowel.

---

163   L. Charpentier, *Les mystères de la Cathédrale de Chartres*; J. James, *The Master Masons of Chartres*; Klug, S.U., *Catedral de Chartres, A geometria sagrada do Cosmos*.

In this third phase of Freemasonry, there was a change in human consciousness, which became more individualistic, developing knowledge of the world through scientific methods that denied the existence of a spiritual world, and believing that all the answers could be found in natural phenomena. Therefore, Freemasonry became a movement of social renewal to help improve humanity. At that time liberation movements were flourishing everywhere, the result of greater self-awareness. Today we know that most of these liberation movements were led by Freemasons. Thus, the American Declaration of Independence (1776) was initially formulated by Thomas Jefferson (1743–1826), John Adams (1735–1826), Benjamin Franklin (1706–1790), Roger Sherman (1721–1793) and Robert R. Livingston (1746–1813), apparently all Masons. The French Revolution (1792) was also led by Masons. Incidentally, the ideal "Liberty, Equality, and Fraternity" is the great Masonic ideal transposed into the social sphere and made public. The liberation movements in Latin America were led by Simon Bolivar (1783–1830) and José de San Martin (1778–1850), who were also Masons. Brazil, too, had a liberation movement inspired and led by Freemasons: the Minas Gerais Conspiracy.

What kind of relationship can be found between Freemasonry and the Community of the Grail? The latter did not consist of Knights Templar, nor was it made up of Masons. However, one can find in both communities a "secret" character, much more evident in Freemasonry, and both proclaimed that an inner path had to be developed to acquire a higher degree of perfection. The Grail Community also built a castle, the "temple" where the Grail was kept (which, as we have seen, symbolizes the Cosmic Self, the Christ, and which is reminiscent of the construction of the Temple of Jerusalem). Finally, both Freemasonry and the Grail Community were engaged in building a better world.

Chapter 13

The Grail Temple

Although the events related to the Grail are of a suprasensory nature, researchers have tried to find the physical location of the castle and the Grail Temple. The novel *Titurel*, written around 1270 by Albrecht von Scharfenberg, which ends the Grail cycle in Central Europe, contains a detailed account of the construction of the Grail Temple. The book is full of dense imagery behind which important spiritual truths are hidden. It tells the story of Titurel, a noble knight of pure heart, who was designated to build an appropriate site for the Grail. He was taken to a remote and inaccessible forest, full of shrubs and trees, on top of a mountain, *Munsalvaesche*,[164] where he thinned out the trees and polished the stone, "which was of onyx," making it as bright as moonlight. One morning, he found the blueprint for the temple miraculously set in the stone, and he found instructions for the details in a piece of writing originating with the Grail.

The narrative reports that during the thirty years it took to raise the building, worked on by builders from all over the world, the Grail, which at that time was floating in the air, provided all the required material as well as sustenance for all the knights called to work there. The temple was a tall, circular building with a large dome, surrounded by 22 chapels (according to Albrecht and other writers; still others mention 72), forming an octagon. The richness of materials was surprising: rare woods, gold, silver, precious stones, crystals. The plant and mineral kingdoms were represented in the decorations, and artificial birds and fish moved around under the crystal floor, driven by air from bellows and windmills. That is, to house the object representing what is spiritual in the human being, all the other kingdoms were included: mineral, plant, and animal. The dome was a replica of the sky, with the sun, moon, and stars moving mechanically in accordance with the heavenly configuration corresponding to each season. The construction of this

---

164   Concerning Munsalvaesche, see footnote 28 on p. 57.

Temple was the work of the whole community called to realize this task, the temple being an imitation of the whole universe. In the center of the building was a miniature version of it that housed the Grail, a microcosm within the macrocosm. In the annex, there was a palace with the dormitories and other rooms of the brotherhood, which was reached through a cloister.

In his abovementioned lecture about the Temple Legend, Steiner addressed the format of the Grail Temple. As did the cathedrals, this temple also expressed longing for the pursuit of something shrouded in deep mystery. To spiritually contemplate the object of the highest aspiration (the Christ), it was necessary to transcend what prevailed in the Gothic cathedrals; the community now needed to turn spiritually toward a mysterious central point. One could then imagine human souls arriving from every direction in space, converging at one point, like all of humankind gathering in a great cathedral. It is worth remembering the passage in which Trevrizent told Parzival that the members recruited in service of the Grail (B. IX, 471) came from many lands. In the Gospel of Luke (10:1–24), it is reported that Christ sent 72 disciples (or apostles) in all directions, who through their preaching should spread the spirit that would converge toward the Mystery of Christ.

Medieval people believed that the radiance of the souls of those who accepted the words of the disciples would converge at a central point. Walter Johannes Stein wrote that the number 72 was used when one wished to express that a large number of people was working individually toward a common cause.[165] In the abovementioned lecture, Steiner suggested that 72 columns could be situated so as to form a circle, from which rays would emanate in all directions, representing humankind moving toward the Mystery of Christ. If a wall were built surrounding these columns, it would become a cathedral, as it were, to embrace humanity. Unlike the Gothic cathedrals, whose main axes run in an east-west direction, the floor plan of this circular building would

---

165 W.J. Stein, *The Ninth Century and the Holy Grail*.

have two main axes (east-west and north-south), forming a cross. Where these axes crossed would be the "Temple of the Temple," a concentrated, reduced form of the whole. This form is the representation of an ideal: a cathedral at whose center converges all humanity, turned toward the Christ.

This type of construction can be found in the East, in the regions of Persia, Azerbaijan, and Armenia, where there are ruins with architecture similar to the ones described, the "temples of fire." The most impressive is perhaps the *Takht-i-Suleiman*, the Throne of Solomon.[166] It is very similar to the temple described by Albrecht: Under certain conditions, mineral deposits in the soil (mainly limestone) may give the impression of onyx. The building is circular, with arches (chapels), traces of an artificial garden and of the star map of the dome, and so on. These ruins are on an arid plateau on which a shrine had been built, dedicated to Zarathustra, the great sun initiate who lived around 2800 BC, when fire was worshiped.

Zarathustra was the inspirer of the Proto-Persian people. He taught humankind the cultivation of grains and fruit trees and the domestication of animals, introducing agriculture and animal husbandry. As a religious leader, Zarathustra spoke of the great Sun Aura, the spiritual element of the sun, Ahura Mazdao, who was approaching the earth and opposed the spirit of evil or darkness, Ahriman.

These ruins, some of them dating back to 1000 BC, are on a low but wide, round mound, the crater of an extinct volcano, filled with mineral deposits. Nearby was another high, extinct volcanic cone with sulfurous springs next to it, the *Zindan-i-Suleiman*, "Solomon's Prison." There was also a sanctuary in which were found pottery shards, grain grinders, ovens, and the remains of a dagger, the symbol of the plow which cuts furrows into the earth and is evidence of humans' mastery over the soil.

---

166 John Matthews, in *At the Table of the Grail*, called it the *Takht-i-Taqdis* or Throne Arches; G.v.d. Borne, *Der Gral in Europa*; F. Teichmann, *Der Gral im Osten*.

The name of Solomon is related to both shrines, solar and earthly (light and darkness). According to Wolfram, besides being the builder of the Temple of Jerusalem, Solomon was also an ancestor of Flegetanis. However, despite many similarities, this does not mean that Solomon's Temple was the Grail Temple. Yet both Wolfram and Albrecht state that knowledge of the Grail came from the East. It is possible that this type of construction, described in a deeply symbolic way by Albrecht, was in reality the earthly representation of a spiritual impulse.

Also according to Albrecht, the Grail Castle was in Europe, in Galicia in northern Spain, a place he called Salvaterre and San Salvador (Wolfram's *Munsalvaesche*). But gradually, people unworthy of living in the proximity of the Grail began to inhabit the land surrounding the castle, after which its guardians decided to return the Grail to the East, to the kingdom of Prester John. There are authors who claim that the fortress of Montségur,[167] the last stronghold of the Cathars, was the Grail Castle. Perched high on a cliff 1200 meters above sea level, this fortress was the Cathars' main stronghold. However, since the fortress was small, it was not inhabited by the Cathars, who lived in houses on the mountainside or in a village at the foot of the mountain. Before the surrender of the fortress, the Cathars' treasure was moved to a safe place, never to be found. Perhaps it was not a material treasure but spiritual in nature, as the Cathars considered themselves "guardians of the Grail," i.e., of an esoteric Christianity.

As a curiosity, it is worth mentioning the castle of the Knights Templar in the city of Tomar, the headquarters of this movement in Portugal. Its construction began in 1160 (thus more than a century before Albrecht's work) and the first building completed was the temple. According to António Quadros,[168] its shape is unusual: It is octagonal, and in its center is a miniature replica, also octagonal, almost circular,

---

167 G. Sioen and H. Gougaud, *Vivre le Pays Cathare*.
168 A. Quadros, *Portugal: Razão e mistério*, vol. I.

with the altar, showing a similarity to Albrecht's description. During the service, the knights were arranged in a circle around the altar "in accordance with the archetype of the knights of the Round Table."

Indeed, this octagonal construction became typical of the temples built by the Knights Templar, as the circle is the ideal way to represent divine perfection. The octagon is the geometric figure that comes closest to the circle, at least compared to the square or rectangle, which were the shapes commonly used in the construction of European churches. Moreover, the Templar cross has four arms of equal length, each consisting of an almost rectangular shape with a curved tip; if we take into account the corners of each rectangle, it is actually a cross with eight points.

The Emperor Charles IV (1346–1378) built Karlstein Castle near Prague not to reside in it, but to create a place where human beings could follow a path of inner strengthening and higher knowledge through prayer and meditation. The author Michael Eschborn writes in his work on the castle[169] that this emperor was still imbued with the spiritual essence of the Grail in the 14th century, and wanted to create a community inspired by those elements.

Esoteric Christianity after the 13th Century

In the various heretical movements we have examined, there was always an attempt to cultivate Christianity's spiritual, esoteric aspect, which was not only stifled but also rigorously fought by the official Church. In the 14th and 15th centuries, an individual by the name of Christian Rosenkreuz (1378–1484) lived in Central Europe. His life was described by Johann Valentin Andreae (1586–1654) in his work *Fama Fraternitatis*, published in 1614. This author also wrote the most important work on the original Rosicrucian movement, *Chymische*

---

169 M. Eschborn, Karlstein, *Das Rätsel um die Burg Karls IV*.

Hochzeit des Christian Rosenkreuz [Chemical Wedding of Christian Rosenkreuz].

Fama Fraternitatis relates how Christian Rosenkreuz assimilated Eastern wisdom and, after going through a period of initiation, linked it with the Mystery of Christ. On returning to Central Europe, he gathered a group of twelve disciples to keep alive the flame of spiritual or esoteric Christianity. The beginning of the Rosicrucian fraternity dates back to 1459.

Based on his spiritual research, Rudolf Steiner reported (for example in his lecture of Sept. 27, 1911[170]) what had happened to this personality before that time. Around 1250 in central Europe lived twelve wise men whose mission was to renew the esoteric impulse of Christianity. They were deeply imbued with the Christian spirit, each one based on a specific mystery school, and were aware that external Christianity, represented by the Church, gave a distorted image of true Christianity. Their intention was to obtain an overview of all religious and ideological orientations. For this they needed a thirteenth person, and they found one who was still a child.

They gathered around the boy to become his teachers. Until his adolescence he had no contact with the outside world, receiving only instruction from his twelve masters. Then this young man went through an initiation that affected him deeply, and the twelve wise men now began to receive their wisdom back from him, in a renewed form.

All this happened in secret. Soon after, the young man died. About a century later he was born again as Christian Rosenkreuz, and lived over a hundred years. Initially he received an education similar to his 13th-century schooling, but not in such isolation from the world. At the age of 28 he traveled to the East, receiving his initiation near Damascus, in much the same way as that of Saint Paul (Acts 9).

It is important to stress the following statements by Steiner:

---

170 R. Steiner, *Esoteric Christianity and the Mission of Christian Rosenkreuz*, GA 130.

Around 1250, the era of humanity's most profound separation from the spiritual world ended. [...] Even those beings who had achieved high spiritual evolution in previous incarnations and reincarnated around 1250 had to endure, for some time, a complete disruption of their capacity to see into the spiritual world. Highly illuminated individualities had been as if separated from the spiritual world, and were able to know it only through their memory of previous incarnations.[171]

The first renewed initiation after this dark age was that of Christian Rosenkreuz. Until 1250, human beings assimilated the principle of Christ unconsciously. From the time of Christian Rosenkreuz onward, people began to consciously understand the Christ impulse, and it became a driving force for those who wanted to take up the path leading to knowledge of the higher worlds. However, this conscious process had to be prepared, and that is where the Rosicrucian movement came in, though in a rather restricted manner at first. It consisted of twelve disciples led by Christian Rosenkreuz. Although very small and intimate, this fraternity managed to survive the following centuries in secrecy, hidden away and unknown to the general public and the ecclesiastical institutions. From the beginning its mysteries, which included a method for achieving initiation, were transmitted only orally, and only to people who had sworn an oath to keep secret the revelations they received. However, they were required to make available to everyone the results, the fruits of their wisdom. In addition, they must not stand out among the people and culture they lived in, meaning that they had to set aside any sign of pride or selfishness.

Occasionally, in a phenomenon comparable to the betrayal of the ancient mysteries, isolated portions of the secrets were leaked and appeared in various publications; their content was highly enigmatic, difficult to understand, and often misinterpreted. This leaked content

---

171 R. Steiner, *The Spiritual Guidance of the Individual and Humanity*, GA 15.

may have been the origin of many of the Rosicrucian movements known today.

Only in the early 20th century were the esoteric contents of Christianity made public, in the form of lectures taken down in shorthand, and later published in books. It was Rudolf Steiner who, considering the humanity of his time mature enough to find out about these matters, publicized revelations based on his spiritual research. As early as 1909–1910 he made statements about the Essenes that were only confirmed after 1947, the year of the discovery of the Dead Sea Scrolls. Steiner, too, was harassed by the Church, and his work was listed in the Vatican's Index of Forbidden Books.[172]

Steiner also started researching the stream initiated by Christian Rosenkreuz. In various lectures and in his book *An Outline of Esoteric Science*, he states that in reality, the initiatory path followed by the true Rosicrucian had to remain secret until the present day, as humanity has only recently become able to follow it.[173] The Rosicrucian path is one of the current paths of initiation, and consists of seven steps, which will be covered in more depth in the next chapter.

1. Study.
2. Acquisition of imaginative knowledge.
3. Understanding the secret writing or occult script.
4. Cultivation of the rhythm of life, or also: preparation of the Philosopher's Stone.
5. Knowledge of the relationship between the microcosm and the macrocosm.
6. Integration in the macrocosm.
7. Beatitude.

---

172 The *Index Librorum Prohibitorum*, instituted in the 16th century by Pope Pius V, was a list of books that the Vatican forbade the faithful of the Church to read. It lasted until 1962, the year it was abolished by the Second Vatican Council, presided over by Pope John XXIII.
173 R. Steiner, *An Outline of Esoteric Science*, GA 13, "Cosmic and Human Evolution Now and in the Future."

Anthroposophy is a spiritual science founded by Rudolf Steiner, also named by him The Science of the Grail.[174] Besides providing expanded knowledge of the human being and our relationship with the universe, and providing a path of self-education, anthroposophy has as one of its central aspects the knowledge of Christ and its importance in the evolution of humanity, always from the esoteric point of view. We may note that Rudolf Steiner, therefore, also considered the Grail the equivalent of Christ.

---

174 R. Steiner, *An Outline of Esoteric Science*, GA 13, "Cosmic and Human Evolution Now and in the Future."

CHAPTER 14

The Trajectory of Parzival

> A brave man slowly wise—Thus I hail my hero
> – Wolfram von Eschenbach, *Parzival* (B. I, 5)

The analysis of Parzival's trajectory presupposes prior knowledge of the course of the evolution of humanity. Both the Bible and ancient myths have very descriptive symbolic images of this evolution. One legend refers to the rebellion of the angels, mentioned earlier in the chapter "The Symbol of the Grail," which resulted in the angels' fall; expelled from heaven, these angels were later active upon the earth when it was created. The biblical account of Creation describes how in its early days, humanity lived in Paradise, in harmony with nature and in the presence of divinity, but unconsciously. Having fallen to the temptation of the serpent (representing the fallen angels, or the Luciferic angels) and eaten the fruit of the tree of knowledge of good and evil,[175] the human beings (represented by Adam and Eve) became aware of the world and of themselves ("So their eyes were opened and they realized they were naked," Gen. 3:7).

This was, in fact, an awakening to the earthly world. Thereafter, the human being could no longer remain in the presence of God, i.e., in the suprasensory world, and was expelled from Paradise. One could say that it was only then that humankind began to inhabit the earth: the physical, material world. Having lost its natural perfection, humanity now had to make a living through hard labor and give birth to children in pain (Gen. 3:16–17). Suffering, disease, and death came

---

175 The fruit is supposed to have been an apple because the word *malum* in Latin means both "evil" and "apple." See R. Steiner, *The Lord's Prayer: an Esoteric Study*, GA 96, Jan. 28, 1907.

into the world. This expulsion from Paradise, however, was necessary for the evolution of humanity because, had it not occurred, humanity would have remained in God's presence, preventing the acquisition of freedom.

As a result of the Fall, human beings gradually lost their connection with the world of their spiritual origin, moving away from it. In contrast, little by little they began to acquire various attributes: consciousness; the intelligence needed to survive in this world, manifesting as creativity and inventiveness; individuality; self-awareness; free will; and, consequently, responsibility not only toward others, but also toward ideals. Before humanity's separation from the spiritual world, and even the denial of its existence, had reached their peak, a very high spiritual being assumed human form and lived among human beings to show them a future way back to the spiritual paradise, without, however, denying or repudiating all the attributes humans had achieved so far. During His stay within a human body, He demonstrated by His own life the attributes to be acquired by humankind: full freedom, compassion, altruistic love, and

GRAPH 1: *Development of Humanity*

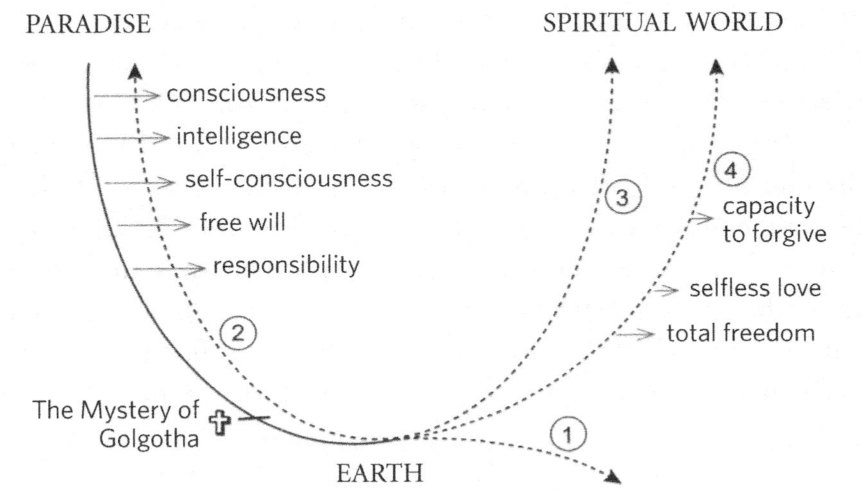

the ability to truly forgive. This event had to occur while there were still at least some human beings on earth capable of recognizing the spiritual being, Christ; otherwise, His coming would have been in vain. Therefore, as will be seen in Graph 1, modern humanity stands before four possible paths:

1. Continue on the downward path, which would lead to a definitive break with the spiritual realm. Those who opt for this path will remain chained to the material world.
2. Turn back to the past, nostalgically longing for the spirituality of the "good old days," thereby denying the values we have attained in the meantime during life on earth.
3. Seek immediate experiences of the suprasensory world by altering one's state of consciousness by any means available, without proper preparation and without having effectively acquired all the competencies to be developed on earth.
4. Return to the spiritual world equipped with all the attributes acquired on earth, as well as others yet to be developed, such as total freedom, compassion, and the practice of unconditional forgiveness—in short, selfless love.

In a lecture dated December 17, 1912,[176] Rudolf Steiner said the following:

> The only actions from which we have nothing in the future are those we perform out of true, genuine love. This truth may well be disquieting, and men are lucky in that they know nothing of it in their upper consciousness. But in their subconscious all of them know it, and that is why deeds of love are done so unwillingly, why there is so little love in the world. [...] But from occultism it is possible to gain powerful impulses to deeds of love.

---

176 R. Steiner, *Love and Its Meaning in the World*, GA 143.

He also states that spiritual beings depend on human development of all these attributes for their own further evolution. In short, the goal of earthly evolution is to develop (among other attributes) freedom and selfless love, which do not yet exist in the spiritual world. They can only be developed by beings inhabiting a solid, material physical body, which earthly human beings are the first to possess. Therefore, according to the cosmic plan, the objective of human development is to complete evolution in accordance with the path appointed by Christ. Rudolf Steiner spoke about this in several lecture cycles. By way of illustration, the following is an excerpt from his lecture of April 18, 1909:[177]

> The great mission of the human being is to bring freedom to the world, and with this freedom, something which can be called love in the true sense of the word. For, without freedom, there cannot be love. [...] Therefore Earth is the cosmos of love and freedom. [...] In the Universe there is no repetition, but with each new cycle something new is introduced into the cosmic evolution. The introduction of this novelty is always the mission of the corresponding hierarchy[178] at its human level.

As long as human evolution is not fully complete (path 4), there is always the possibility of deviations occurring, either leading toward the earth (path 1) or away from it (path 2), or attempts to reach the spiritual world prematurely, without being fully prepared (path 3), even in the final stages of the path. Human beings did not require any great effort during the first part of this trajectory; we were guided by the entities responsible for the spiritual direction of humanity. But the second part

---

[177] R. Steiner, *The Spiritual Hierarchies: Their Reflection in the Physical World*, GA 110.
[178] Steiner is referring to the nine celestial hierarchies as described by Dionysius the Areopagite (an Athenian converted by Saint Paul, see Acts 17:34). According to Steiner, when modern human beings have accomplished their mission, they will constitute the tenth hierarchy.

depends exclusively on us. Therefore, it still remains to be seen whether humanity will reach its goal.

During a lifetime, every human being repeats humanity's evolution. This recapitulation also happens in the Waldorf curriculum, where the student is gradually led from a more mythical-mystical consciousness in fairy tales, to fables and stories of saints, to the Old Testament and Norse mythology ("twilight of the gods"), to Greek mythology (where what distinguishes gods from humans is basically immortality, as they have otherwise similar qualities and attributes), up to the scientific thinking of modern times.

In each individual human biography there is a phase that corresponds (or at least should) to paradise, when the child is under the protection of parents, relatives and, later, teachers. During this period, children still radiate cosmic innocence and purity. The Fall or expulsion from Paradise occurs during puberty. According to Steiner, at that moment the adolescent achieves what he called "earth ripeness" or earthly maturity, i.e., really arrives on earth. Any learning that is still missing is provided by adults, at least until the end of formal education; after that, young people continue to develop on their own.

It is also from puberty onward that adolescents increasingly have to bear the consequences of their actions, although they only take full responsibility for them when they come of age. In the old days it was around the age of fourteen that young people left home to learn a profession, first as apprentices and then as helpers, before becoming masters. In the Middle Ages, sons of the nobility left home at seven, but always went to castles of other noblemen, friends of their parents, where they became pages. At fourteen the youth became a squire; that is, he went out into the world accompanying a knight, later to become an independent knight himself.

Nowadays, it is after puberty that abstract thinking really begins to develop. Young people keep more and more distance from their parents, which can be interpreted as rebellion, although we know it is necessary for them to develop their own personalities. They gain more and more knowledge about the world around them, so as to be able to act in it in the future, both professionally and socially. They become increasingly aware of the world and of themselves; they develop discernment and start to have their own opinions. After coming of age (it was wisely determined that this should occur at the age of 21) a person can no longer be educated by somebody else; all future learning will be achieved through self-education.[179] This is the phase in which the adult lives and acts in the outside world and, in overcoming the inevitable crises, undergoes an inner maturation.

Some adults are highly satisfied with the lives they lead, feel that their wishes are being met, and give themselves fully to their work and to consumerism, aspiring to nothing more. Others may not feel so well in this adult world, experiencing a deep nostalgia for childhood, when life was so good and carefree and devoid of worries and responsibilities, and others took care of everything. A third group wants to achieve their goals quickly at any cost, skipping intermediate stages when possible, stepping on others if necessary with no concern for their well-being, without realizing the damage they are causing themselves in their own development.

Finally, there is a fourth group of people who are well adapted to earthly social conditions, whose needs are met but who crave something higher, knowing that achieving it depends exclusively on them, on their personal striving. When these ideals arise in them they go through an inner struggle in an effort to realize their ideals. The desire of any person should be to reach old age having managed to achieve his or her goals, with a clear mind and good health, radiating wisdom and goodness and sharing life experience with the younger ones. Yet only those who have acquired knowledge and experience (both good and

---

[179] In the context of this book, "self-education" means the inner work by which adults can improve their moral qualities and also develop the stages of higher consciousness (imaginative, inspirational, and intuitive – see below).

bad) will have something to share or give; after all, one can only give away something one has.

In short, the ultimate goal is to develop wisdom (knowledge plus outer and inner experiences) and share it with others in an attitude of selfless love. It is a process similar to the one described by Steiner in his book *An Outline of Esoteric Science* on the evolution of the earth.[180] At each stage, very high spiritual entities donated something of themselves that they could spare, which then became part of humanity and the earth. For an old person to be able to radiate wisdom, light, and love, the physical body must be healthy; if one is ill, one's consciousness focuses only on the disease and not on the outer world, let alone the spiritual world. Unfortunately, nowadays many elderly people are in poor health, turned inward, adopting a self-centered attitude. Instead of being able to give to the world, they need to be cared for by others. Therefore, in each person's individual progress, the final phase of life is left open.

The evolutionary curve of Parzival's life showed that he, too, began in an idyllic situation of innocence and purity of soul, living with his mother and a few servants, secluded in the forest of Soltane. There he was perfectly adapted to nature, with no other knowledge at all, not even of the existence of another world beyond his own. His mother wanted to keep him in that "paradise" forever. In the chapter "Important Encounters and Events in the Life of Parzival" it was mentioned that this apparently selfish attitude may also have had some very positive aspects, allowing the child to retain certain forces that otherwise might have been used up prematurely, had he been in contact with the outside world. But then the "Tempter" came to the boy, in the form of the knights who told him about Arthur's court and the world of chivalry. As a result, he abandoned his paradise of his own accord. When he learned about an outside world, his whole being longed to

---

180 R. Steiner, *An Outline of Esoteric Science*, GA 13, "Cosmic Evolution and the Human Being."

live in it. However, because of the way he had been brought up by his mother, the young man was a stranger to his time and place. In several of his lectures, including one on May 26, 1922, Steiner said that destiny or individual karma begins at the age of fourteen; before that, karma is related to that of the parents.[181] It was at approximately this age that Parzival abandoned his mother and began to follow his personal destiny. Yet in this way he caused his mother's death, illustrating the completion of his previous stage of karmic interdependence.

Moving further and further away from his place of origin, Parzival gradually acquired all the attributes he needed to become a knight of King Arthur's court, which was his fervent wish upon leaving his maternal home. On his way he was assisted mostly by Gurnemanz and Condwiramurs. He acquired fame, won the hand of his wife, and, after many trials in which he behaved like a true knight of Arthur, was admitted to the Round Table. He had everything a knight could wish for.

But at that moment Cundrie appeared, accusing Parzival. Surprisingly, once he had reached his goal (which usually means the happy ending of the story, as in Gawain's case), a person appeared, delivering an accusation that revealed another path to him and provoked him to make a decision. No one actually advised him: He had to make his own decision in full freedom. No one would have taken it amiss if he had returned to his kingdom and his wife, but his decision became his new goal in life: to find the Grail Castle again and serve King Anfortas. Even without being aware of it, from that moment on he had become a knight of the Grail. The greatness of his personality became evident at the moment that he reached the highest outer perfection, recognizing his inner faults.

Because Parzival became aware of the fact that he had failed to cure the king through his own omission, he felt his responsibility for the

---

181 See, among other works: R. Steiner, *The Human Heart*, GA 212.

perpetuation of Anfortas' suffering, and he wanted to make up for his failure. This is the turning point in his life's curve. He left behind fame, his wife, and the Round Table to undertake a long and painful path of inner work. Having lost, or rather given up, everything he owned, from now on only what he won in full freedom and through his own efforts would have any value.

In the path corresponding to the ascending part of his life's curve, toward the Grail Castle (the spiritual world), Parzival went through his inner development in total isolation. He acquired new attributes (full freedom, compassion, altruistic love) that finally led to his being called to become the new King of the Grail. However, he could only receive advice and help from Trevrizent when he had matured sufficiently and was fully prepared. Still, only when he was facing death in his fight with Feirefiz was Parzival really ready to heal Anfortas. This means that he had reached the level of development necessary to "forgive" the king, just as Trevrizent, thanks to his own evolution, had been able to take on ("forgive") the faults of Parzival. In the end Parzival not only reached his goal but transcended it.

As mentioned above, on this upward stretch of the curve Parzival was already, even without knowing it, a knight of the Grail, seeking inner development and always wandering in the vicinity of the Grail Castle. At his meeting with Feirefiz he acted like a Grail knight, attempting to keep strangers away from his realm. Looking at Graph 2, it is clear that Parzival reached the goal of his life's evolutionary curve, and even surpassed it. The knights he met in the forest, along with Gurnemanz and Condwiramurs, helped him during his disengagement from the original (spiritual) world; Cundrie and Trevrizent assisted in bringing the spiritual realm nearer to him. Herzeloyde wanted to prevent him from ever leaving that spiritual sphere, and Sigune led him along the entire journey. Interestingly, the first three of these personalities are related to Arthur's court, and the rest belong to the Community of the Grail.

As a reminder, Trevrizent tells Parzival that Anfortas was still an adolescent when he was summoned to the Grail. "At that time we were still quite small [...] at which the first bristles begin to show [...]. (B. IX, 243) But this was not the case with Parzival. On his mother's side Parzival came from the Grail lineage, and one can assume that, from the beginning, his fate was to become King of the Grail; however, he was not called as an adolescent.

It seems that there was a need to renew the Mysteries of the Grail, as simple family succession was no longer adequate to maintain the tradition. The new Grail King would have to start on his mission after undergoing a different type of development from that of previous kings, which had happened within that protective community. Parzival

GRAPH 2: *Development of Parsival*

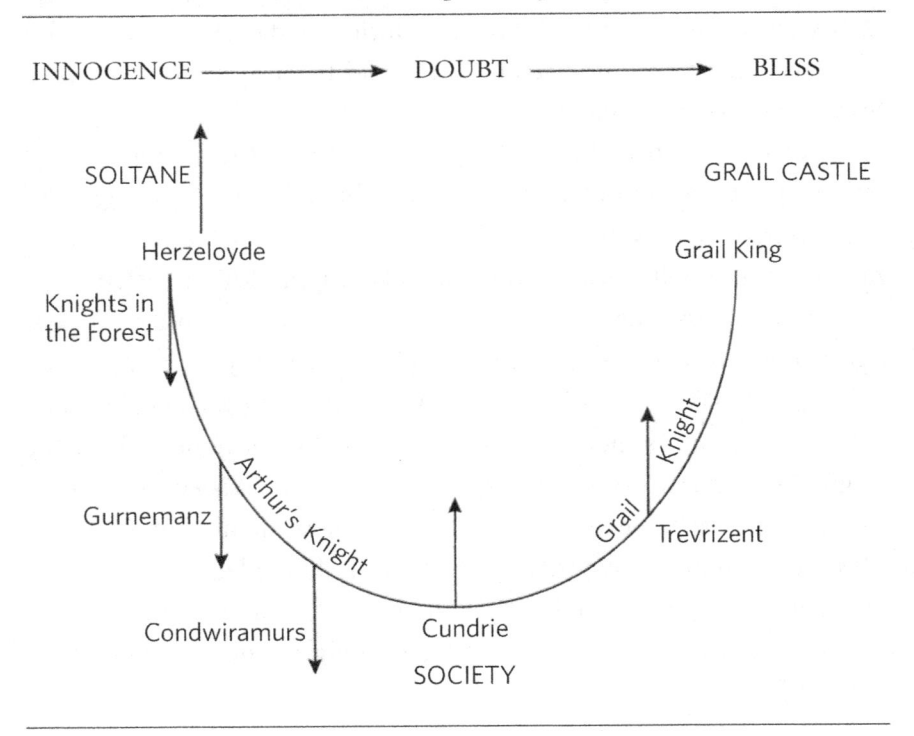

INNOCENCE ⟶ DOUBT ⟶ BLISS

SOLTANE · GRAIL CASTLE
Herzeloyde · Grail King
Knights in the Forest
Gurnemanz · Trevrizent
Arthur's Knight · Grail Knight
Condwiramurs · Cundrie
SOCIETY

achieved his evolution in complete solitude, depending solely on himself. Only after that could he definitely participate in the Grail Community, and so, instead of pursuing only his own individual goal, he trod the path of the goal of the humankind of the future. In ancient initiations, the masters determined the steps to be taken by the neophyte, from the outside in; Parzival's yearning acted within him, from his core outward. Pre-Christian initiations excluded questions, but questions are essential to Christian initiation, as they concern the secrets of the Holy Grail. (The subject of initiation will be addressed in more detail later.)

Another possible conclusion is that on his first visit to the Grail Castle, Parzival did not actually fail; the fact that he did not formulate the question actually made it possible for him to go through his subsequent development process. After all, at the time he was not prepared to stay in the presence of the Grail. In Robert de Boron's work, something similar occurred with the community gathered around Joseph of Arimathea, when famine was raging in the region. It was believed that the famine was caused by the presence of impure people. When Joseph asked Christ for advice, he was instructed to celebrate the Last Supper with the Sacred Chalice at the center of the table. But those who were impure could not perceive the greatness emanating from the Chalice. They just saw an object, and, realizing that they were impure, they left the community. Heinrich Teutschmann states that, because they left after seeing the Grail, they would be able to develop the necessary strength to be able to return in the future to reach the Grail and contemplate it from a higher level.[182] So their faults became the means for them to evolve, which also happened with Parzival. Incidentally, in his lecture of January 1, 1906, Steiner says that the way to freedom passes through guilt.[183]

All in all, there were three important phases in the life of Parzival. Wolfram employed the words *tumpheit, zwîfel,* and *saelde,* corresponding

---

182 H. Teutschmann, *Der Gral. Weisheit und Liebe.*
183 R. Steiner, *The Temple Legend,* GA 93.

to "dullness," "doubt" and "bliss." They refer to the phases of youthful, foolish elation (childishness), doubt as to the omnipotence of God, and certainty of the existence of the spiritual world.

In Graph 2, naïve innocence corresponds to the time Parzival spent with his mother and his first adventures after leaving her, ending when he left his wife to look for his mother. Doubt, the period corresponding to the greatest alienation from the spiritual world, accompanied him from the morning after his first visit to the Grail Castle, when he failed to understand the changed behavior of the castle's inhabitants. It culminated in Cundrie's damnation when she made him aware of his mistake in the Grail Castle. As a consequence Parzival stopped serving God until he heard Trevrizent's revelations about the divinity who had sacrificed Himself for humanity, as well as those about the events of his own life. Bliss is the culmination of his self-development and purification. This state began to emerge when Parzival's hermit uncle took the latter's failures on himself. Yet Parzival subsequently "acquired new life" when Feirefiz interrupted their fight, after Parzival's sword broke and Feirefiz declared Parzival the winner.

His highest achievement came when he was called to become the new King of the Grail. At that moment Cundrie said:

> "Your sorrow is doomed to pass away. [...] You raised a brood of cares in tender years: But the happiness which is on its way to you has dashed their expectations. You have won through to peace of soul and outlived cases." (B. XV, 388)

One can also say that Parzival started out from unconsciousness, went through a phase of conflicts, and reached full consciousness.

On March 29, 1906, Steiner described doubt as a very important aspect in the development of any human being.[184] This stage corresponds to a darkness in the soul. Anyone who wants to attain real knowledge

---

184 R. Steiner, *The Riddles of the World and Anthroposophy*, GA 54.

must go through the suffering caused by doubt, by unbelief, and only then will there be any certainty that the knowledge acquired will never be lost. In this sense, although doubt seems cruel, it has the character of purification or sublimation.

To doubt means being able to choose between two or more options. Until the Middle Ages, human beings did not know about doubt in relation to existential issues. Everything was determined by the recognized authorities, both politically and socially and also in religion. Both demanded obedience. Furthermore, God, represented by the Church, was omnipotent and omniscient, and people simply believed. Now belief, faith, and blind obedience do not admit doubt. It is very comfortable to live without doubt, believing in the wisdom of one's leaders, needing only to surrender; everything is predetermined, even punishments for noncompliance, and there is no need to make decisions. Only since the 15th and 16th centuries, with the advent of the modern era, did humankind as a whole begin to have doubts.

Ewald Koepke explains that this is the evolutionary process of the human being of the fifth post-Atlantean cultural epoch,[185] which, as we have seen, began in the 15th century. We must now go through the abyss of a world in which the divine entity can no longer be found, having moved away from it. Those who cannot cross the abyss, in which the focus is on the destruction of the world, cannot rise to the pinnacle of life. Only when there is doubt can the human being develop the ability to question, evaluate, discern, judge, and choose. This is the path toward one's own autonomy and freedom.

This highlights the importance of doubt in personal development. As already mentioned, the process is not pleasant and brings suffering with it. Wolfram himself revealed this in the first lines of his work: "If vacillation (doubt) dwell with the heart the soul will rue it." (B. I, 15) Now Parzival was written between 1203 and 1217, at the

---

185 E. Koepke, *Rudolf Steiner und das Gralsmysterium*.

beginning of the 13th century, when most people did not even know the meaning of doubt.

Wolfram then refers to the colors of the magpie, a bird of black and white plumage. He is pointing to a polarity, to opposing situations, light and darkness, glory and disgrace. He then says: "But such a man may yet make merry, for Heaven and Hell have equal part in him." (B. I, 15)

At first glance this seems very strange, but considering what has been said above, those who falter—that is, doubt—may be glad, as they have a chance to develop. Those who have no doubts settle down, stagnate, do not evolve. Wolfram thus introduces characteristics and values which were not yet of his time; they would develop in the future, in our present time.

Gerard Klockenbring outlines the main events in each phase of Parzival's life, taking into account these three steps.[186] During Parzival's phase of foolish innocence, he points out the destinies of the people the hero met:

1. His *mother* died when he abandoned her.
2. *Jeschute* was disgraced by her husband because of him.
3. *Sigune* lost her fiancé in combat, as he had assumed the task which, in fact, should have been executed by Parzival.
4. *Cunneware* was humiliated because of him.
5. He killed *Ither* treacherously.
6. *Gurnemanz* raised him, but was abandoned by him.
7. *Condwiramurs* welcomed him with all her love, but was also abandoned.

How much guilt Parzival accumulated with his naïveté! There are seven events during the second phase:

---

186 G. Klockenbring, *El Santo Grial y el hombre moderno*.

1. *Failure in the Grail Castle*, which Parzival left without clearly understanding what had happened.
2. The second encounter with Sigune, who left him *lost in the woods*.
3. *Awareness of the wrong done to Jeschute*, the subsequent fight with Orilus and their reconciliation.
4. *Redemption of the humiliation suffered by Cunneware* and the union of her destiny with that of Clamide.
5. *Admission to the Round Table*, the achievement of everything he had wished for. This was only possible because he had redeemed himself of all the sins he had become aware of.
6. However, this was only apparently so, for Cundrie permitted him to *perceive the impurity of his soul*.
7. *Self-imposed solitude*, refusing to serve God, doubting His benevolence and omnipotence.

This is the stage of the adult human being, full of doubts. After maturing, the following events led the knight to attain bliss:

1. Sigune encouraged him to *follow the horse tracks of Cundrie*, the messenger of the Grail.
2. In combat with the Grail knight, he won the *Grail horse*.
3. Kahenis made him *think of God* again.
4. Trevrizent made him *fully aware of his life and forgave* him for his guilt in relation to Herzeloyde and Anfortas.
5. Feirefiz "*forgave*" the death of Ither.
6. Cundrie *summoned* him to become the new King of the Grail.
7. Parzival *healed* Anfortas.

The table on the following page illustrates what is outlined above. (It is important to note that there is no relationship between the three items on each line. The importance lies in the columns.)

INNOCENCE	DOUBT	BLISS
1 Mother's death	Failure in the Grail Castle	Following Cundrie's tracks
2 Dishonor to Jeschute	Sigune leaves him lost	Winning the Grail horse
3 Sigune lost her fiancé	Redemption of Jeschute's dishonor	Return to thinking about God
4 Cunneware's humiliation	Redemption of Cunneware's humiliation	Total consciousness of his life; forgiveness granted by Trevrizent
5 Ither's death	Admission to the Round Table	Feirefiz's forgiveness
6 Gurnemanz is abandoned	Cundrie's accusation	Summoned to become the Grail King
7 Condwiramurs is abandoned	Self-imposed solitude	Healing of Anfortas

These three steps or degrees toward perfection point to the word *gradalis* (meaning gradually, step by step), considered by some the origin of the word "Grail."[187] Steiner, discussing Cardinal Nicholas Cusano (1401–1464), reported that the latter had said that there were three possible paths to reach what he himself had achieved.[188] The first one is a positive belief that reaches us from the outer world. The second is despair at finding oneself alone with one's burden, feeling one's existence shattered. The third is the development of the deepest

---

187   Other authors relate the term *gradalis* to the fact, mentioned earlier, that throughout the evolution of humanity the approach of the Sun Being Christ to Earth happened step by step, gradually, until he incarnated in the physical realm in Jesus of Nazareth.
188   R. Steiner, *Mysticism at the Dawn of the Modern Age*, GA 7.

strengths within us. Two guides are needed for such development: *trust* in the world, and *courage* to follow this trust, regardless of where it might lead. This is another way of describing these steps. One should remember that the name Perceval, in its French origin, means "through this valley" or "that which runs through the valley," and it becomes evident in the chart above that in fact the hero crossed the valley and moved across the abyss, reaching the opposite side, his goal.

Another way to follow this evolutionary path is the passage through the physical, etheric, and astral worlds to attain the spiritual world. This was described by Frank Teichmann, who draws attention to the fact that Parzival started out in the external natural world.[189] He then went through the world of vital forces, where Gurnemanz developed habits and skills in him. Next, together with Condwiramurs, he experienced the soul world, full of sorrows and joys, until he attained the spiritual world, represented by the Grail Castle, which lies beyond the sensory level. According to Steiner in a lecture of July 23, 1922,[190] this is where "the dead live," and where the Mysteries of the Grail originated. This route is marked by four castles: The first was Arthur's castle in Nantes, representing the external world; next, the castle of Gurnemanz; next, Condwiramurs' castle, and finally the Grail Castle, which would be his own castle in the end.

Comparing Anfortas' evolution with Parzival's, the former, according to Trevrizent, had to take up the role of Grail King very early due to his father's premature death, and he was still insufficiently prepared for it. He was presumptuous and proud and, contrary to the rules of the Grail, not having acquired mastery over his physical impulses and instincts, he courted a woman, Orgeluse, who had not been intended for him by the Grail. Now the name Orgeluse means "proud," and one can assume that this connection with pride, un-

---

189 F. Teichmann, "The Polarity of Parzival and Gawain in Eschenbach's *Parzival*," *The Golden Blade*, 47: The Quest for the Grail.
190 R. Steiner, *The Mystery of the Trinity*, GA 214.

acceptable for a King of the Grail, made him vulnerable. Incidentally, Trevrizent also reprimanded Parzival for his proud attitude of wanting to challenge God (B. IX, 463 and 472), and told him that in ancient times this had been the attitude of Lucifer. The consequence, the so-called "rebellion of the angels," was Lucifer's expulsion from the heavenly realm. Thereafter, Lucifer and his followers started to live in hell. Heinrich Teutschmann indicates that, to fill the vacuum left by these fallen angels, the divine entity created Adam and Eve and all humankind,[191] an image familiar to some writers, especially Robert de Boron and Albrecht von Scharfenberg. When Trevrizent and Parzival met a second time, after the latter had been called to become King of the Grail, his uncle told him: "Yet your affairs have taken another turn, and your prize is all the loftier! Now guide your thoughts toward humility." (B. XVI, 798)

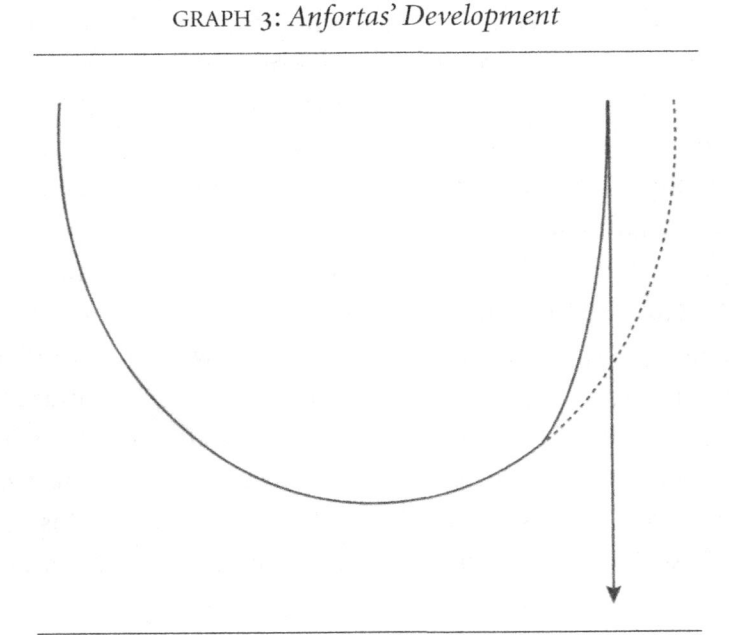

GRAPH 3: *Anfortas' Development*

---

191 H. Teutschmann, *Der Gral. Weisheit und Liebe.*

Graph 3 shows the trajectory of Anfortas, in which the goal (to become the King of the Grail) was reached ahead of time, without the proper training. Nowadays the desire to contact the spiritual worlds, to possess the faculty of clairvoyance, is very strong, but it happens most often without the preparation of the soul. Various means are employed for this purpose, such as natural or chemical substances, or certain practices and rituals. In most cases these are undertaken out of mere curiosity, for one's own satisfaction, or to exercise control over people who do not possess such clairvoyance. These are totally selfish goals.

The results are often disastrous for the individuals involved. They may include psychotic episodes, or dependency on their masters, as the individuals are no longer able to exercise free will or have their own opinions. In short, the Self weakens.

In his book *Knowledge of the Higher Worlds: How Is It Attained?*, Rudolf Steiner wrote in the first chapter:

> All cognition that one seeks for the sole purpose of enriching one's knowledge, only to accumulate one's own treasures, will divert from the path. All cognition, however, that one seeks to become more mature along the path of human ennoblement and cosmic evolution will make one advance one step. [Furthermore:] For each step on the road of self-development one should take three steps in moral development.

In fact, the path of self-education described by Steiner concentrates specifically on personal development. If on this path one happens to have clairvoyant experiences or something similar, that should be considered a special grace. But those experiences should not be the goal. The important thing is the process, the path.

Let us now examine Parzival's two fights with unknown knights, both of which were interrupted as he was winning. These were the fight with Gawain, who thought he was fighting Gramoflanz, and with Feirefiz, which was stopped when Parzival's sword broke. (Another fight interrupted while Parzival was winning was the one with Gramoflanz, but in this case Parzival knew beforehand who his opponent was, though Gramoflanz did not.) To help understand this situation, let us investigate the relationships of these three knights with the Grail.

Feirefiz, a pagan from distant lands, had never heard of the Grail, and therefore could not be looking for it. Even when he was already in the Grail Castle and witnessing the Grail ceremony, he could not see it; he only saw the queen bringing something invisible to him. After receiving baptism, however, he was able to see the Grail. It can be said that at first he was totally unaware of the Grail and, not knowing about it, was unable to search for it.

Gawain, Arthur's knight, knew about the Grail but did not care to find it. When King Vergulacht of Ascalun gave him the task of seeking the Grail, the king and his counselor were, in fact, almost certain that he would meet death in this venture. In this case, one could say that Gawain was semiconscious of the Grail; he knew about it, but did not think it his duty to seek it.

After his first visit to the Grail Castle, Parzival not only knew about the Grail, he had seen it; shortly after leaving the Castle, realizing that something strange had happened, he wanted to return there to serve the king. When, by way of Cundrie's accusation, he became aware of his failure, his only goal in life was to find the Grail again, which means he had reached full consciousness. He knew about the existence of the Grail and endeavored to seek it.

In his pedagogical work and elsewhere, Rudolf Steiner spoke of the threefold constitution of the human organism. As the context of this book is not intended for a detailed explanation of the subject, only the main ideas will be presented (see also chapter 9).

In the head is the center of the nerve-sense system, namely the central nervous system and the sense organs. Its main function is to allow us to have sense perceptions and make sense of them through *thinking*, and to perform this function, the human being must be fully conscious. In the chest region are the rhythmic organs (heart and lungs), therefore it is the center of the rhythmic system. The corresponding function is *feeling*, experienced semiconsciously, i.e., we are aware of our feelings but often cannot control them. The third system is the metabolic-limb system, in which ingested substances are transformed and which is also related to the movement of our limbs (by the way, the entire gastrointestinal tract is in continuous movement, we are just not aware of it). This system is related to *doing* or to *willing* (voluntary or involuntary movements), which are executed in total unconsciousness. When someone executes a voluntary movement there is awareness of the *intention* to move, but what actually happens in the muscles remains unconscious. It is well known that any movement is performed better the more automatically and unconsciously one performs it. If our movements remain stuck in our consciousness, this can cause inhibition or even paralysis.

Relating this to the three knights' degrees of awareness of the Grail, one can say that every human being contains these three heroes: Parzival in thinking, Gawain in feeling, and Feirefiz in willing; and the fact that Parzival did not really win in combat, but instead mastered these two opponents, could mean that thinking should not conquer or eliminate feeling and willing, but should dominate them. When Parzival was fighting with Gawain, he exclaimed: "To think that I have been attacking noble Gawain here. So doing, *I have vanquished myself and waited for misfortune*"[192] (B. XIV, 344), and after recognizing each other as brothers on their fathers' side, Feirefiz told Parzival: "On this field *you were fighting with yourself.*" (B. XV, 274) Had Parzival defeated them both, that would have meant the destruction of important parts of the human constitution. Every human being has to develop and make use of these three functions of the soul, but the light of thinking must guide feeling and willing.

---

192 Italics ours.

Parzival's third fight, interrupted when he was winning, differed from the other fights because he knew his opponent to be Gramoflanz, who, on the other hand, was unaware of the true identity of his opponent, thinking it to be Gawain. The reason Parzival was winning is that he had decided to fight in place of his friend, out of true friendship without expecting anything in return, while Gramoflanz was fighting to prove his worth and for the love of Itonje, selfishly expecting to win her.

It was mentioned above that when one has doubts, when one wants to choose a path out of free will, to evaluate possible consequences and make a conscious decision, one asks; one formulates questions. Now there are two types of questions: those asked out of curiosity, when one wants to obtain information or understand something experienced in the outer world, and those asked to solve intimate issues, those questions that spring up in the teenage mind and accompany the human being for life more or less consciously, such as: "Who am I?" "Where did I come from?" "Why am I in the world?" "What is my task?" "Where will I go?" "Does life have meaning?" and the like.

Questions of the first type can usually be answered by others, or by research; the answers are straightforward and can either satisfy our curiosity, or not. Questions of the second type have no obvious, ready-made answers. Those asking them must find the answers within themselves, and this can take a long time. Naturally, others can help in the process of finding solutions, but this differs from one person to another, as each person must find his or her own individual response. Furthermore, the answers are not final, and may change depending on the moment in the person's biography.

Therefore, to obtain answers to this second type of question, one must go through an inner struggle with oneself, in complete solitude. To lead a life without this second type of question would mean not to develop as a human being, to stagnate, merely to take advantage of whatever life brings, or else to obey established rules blindly for fear of punishment. This attitude would be retrograde, only valid in some ancient past. To be curious about the outer world, to want to understand it and appreciate it, is something very positive. However, there is also an inner world, and to become aware of it and understand it requires a different path, one based on existential or essential questions.

The central point of *Parzival* is precisely the question Parzival should have asked King Anfortas on his first visit to the Grail Castle. It has a very particular characteristics.

In general, when one asks a question, one expects an answer. Georg Kühlewind says that asking involves different points of view.[193] One needs to have some specific knowledge to know what to ask, but, at the same time, the question is asked because not enough is known yet. This means that one must have doubts.[194] So asking starts with a duality, and those who ask must keep a certain distance from the object of the question. The answer should come from a higher level and its aim should be to lead the duality to a unity, a certainty. Moreover, a question that does not originate within the person who asks it is not a true question (which is why Parzival could not be induced to ask the question). To ask also requires a certain maturity: the attainment of wisdom, love, and action out of one's own initiative. In other words, it is the act of someone who is beginning to act out of free will. To quote Kühlewind, "To ask a true question is an act of creation." Such a question can restrict neither the freedom of the person who asks nor that of the person who is asked. Rudolf Meyer states that in the spiritual realm, to ask is at the same time to recognize.[195] Looking more deeply at the question of questions, we see that there is no concrete answer.

We should point out that in pre-Christian initiations, questions were not permitted, but Christian initiation is based on questions.

---

193 G. Kühlewind, *Der Gral oder Was die Liebe vermag.*
194 The German term for "doubt" is *Zweifel*, which contains the word *zwei*, meaning "two." Surely it has something to do with "duality," as it allows for at least two possibilities, ways, or choices.
195 R. Meyer, *Der Gral und seine Hüter.*

In his lecture of April 16, 1921,[196] Steiner revealed that at the time of the ancient mysteries the priests went out into the world and chose new followers by contemplating people's auras. From the 9th century onward, however, to seek an initiatory path, each person had to have the urge to ask about secrets of the cosmos and of each human being's existence. In his following lecture,[197] Steiner added:

> [T]he esoteric secret revealed to the disciples [from the 9th century onward] was that people had not yet reached the time when they would realize in full consciousness how to meet again the spiritual world, [...] so far they could only have a glimpse inside the holy Grail Castle [spiritual world]. Yet, the time had come in the evolution of humanity when they should ask, and if a person would not ask, i.e., would not develop inwardly, would not seek the impulse of truth and instead remain passive, the experience of his own being would not be achieved.

In his lecture of March 29, 1906,[198] Steiner also addressed the subject of questions, saying that the Grail existed and anyone could look for it, but it does not impose its existence:

> The Grail does not come to us. We have to feel in our souls a yearning for this Holy Grail, the inner sanctum, the divine vital spark within the human soul. We must have the urge to ask about it. If the human soul rises toward God, then God will come toward the human soul. This is the secret of the Grail itself—the descent of God when the human being evolves, ascending toward the divine realm.

Nowadays, reason prevails, and the spiritual world must be rediscovered through the intellect and not through suppressing the

---

196 R. Steiner, *Materialism and the Task of Anthroposophy*, GA 204.
197 Ibid.
198 R. Steiner, *The Riddles of the World and Anthroposophy*, GA 54.

power of thought. This means that one must ask. In another lecture, delivered on January 1, 1914,[199] Steiner addressed the issue of Parzival's question, saying that the relationship established with the Christ impulse within the young knight's soul would have been disturbed if he had assimilated what other people taught about Christ. It did not matter what people did or said; what mattered was what the soul experienced when surrendering to the suprasensory through the impulse of Christ. External teachings always belong to the sense world. The Christ impulse, however, acted in the suprasensory realm, and that is how it penetrated the soul of Parzival. Deep within his soul he was permeated by the Christ impulse, although consciously he was rather ignorant. Thus, his soul should have felt the urge to ask the question exactly where the Christ impulse could be in front of him: that is, before the Holy Grail. He should not have asked stimulated by what the knights believed should be venerated in Christ. He should have asked what the Holy Grail might reveal— namely, what the Christ event was.

At their first encounter, Anfortas had already spoken of his incurable wound. Later, Trevrizent explained to Parzival in detail the reason for his brother's suffering and told him about all the attempts to cure him. If this question had no answer, it had, on the other hand, consequences. Even Cundrie said that Parzival had failed in not asking the question and that he had shown a lack of compassion: "You ought to have had compassion on his sufferings." (B. VI, 165)

However, in other situations Parzival clearly showed feelings of sympathy—he suffered, for example, when his mother ordered the killing of the birds, or when he met Sigune with her dead bridegroom in her arms, or when he saw the poor, hungry people of the besieged city of Pelrapeire. That he may have failed because he was blindly obeying Gurnemanz's instructions is also incorrect, according to Kühlewind. This author draws attention to the fact that Parzival did remember not

---

199 R. Steiner, *The Fifth Gospel: From the Akashic Chronicle*, GA 148.

to ask inconvenient questions when he saw the ritual of the Grail, but the same was not the case when he saw Anfortas suffering. Kühlewind explains that Parzival did not ask because he identified so deeply with the king's suffering that he could not maintain the necessary distance (objectivity) to be able to ask. The consequences of this fact fell upon the king, who continued to suffer, and upon Parzival, who now had to undertake a long and arduous journey of self-improvement to develop the qualities he still needed, FREEDOM and SELFLESS LOVE—the exact qualities that human beings need to develop (see above). In *An Outline of Esoteric Science* Steiner says: "Wisdom is the precondition of love, and love is wisdom reborn within the Self." Therefore, one can also consider Parzival's omission to be an opportunity for development.

When Parzival arrived at the Grail Castle for the second time, he knew all the facts related to Anfortas' suffering. He also acknowledged the truth in Cundrie's words: "… Your truthful lips are now to address noble, gentle King Anfortas and with their questions banish his agony and heal him […]." (B. XV, 387) Each time a musician plays the same piece of music she nevertheless recreates it, as if she were playing it for the first time. In the same way, Parzival asked the question not as a mere repetition of something he had heard, but as if he were recreating it, as if it were something new and original. However, even though he was not certain that he would cure the king, because Trevrizent had said that the question would have to be asked without the questioner having been prompted to do so, Parzival eventually asked it: This represents an act of freedom. Also, the development of selfless love is indicated by the fact that Parzival had sought the Grail not to satisfy a personal wish, but in order to serve the King of the Grail. During his journey he had not only perfected his soul, he had been able to redeem himself of all his conscious and unconscious guilt.

In this sense, too, he was free, liberated. Having acquired so many qualities during his journey, Parzival could use some surplus to help others. He asked the question under these conditions, and so he was able to heal Anfortas. It could be said that he did so through the power of love, with the power of Christ, as he pleaded for help before the Grail. Another important aspect is the fact that he assumed his guilt for not having ASKED THE QUESTION before, which enabled him to start on the path of self-development; this would not have happened had the question been asked the first time round. On that occasion the question would have been asked simply out of curiosity, and Gurnemanz's advice was precisely to avoid this kind of question.

Until his first visit to the Grail Castle, everything had been quite easy for the youth. He had not yet gone through great suffering, and therefore could not feel compassion. He had to suffer, and quite intensely, for only then could he feel what another suffering person felt. "Com-passion" means to "suffer with" the other. We may conclude that to develop compassion and selfless love one must, of necessity, go through pain.

In German, there are three words with the common root *heil*:

heilen	to heal
heilig	holy
Heiland	understood as "Savior," though its literal meaning is "healer"

The various meanings of the German word *heil* are: whole, wholesome, perfect, intact, untouched, pristine, without injury, pure, safe. The verb *heilen* is derived from it and means to cure, heal, recompose, put in order. During human history, there have always been people who could heal others, nowadays considered performers of miracles. In general they were special people with qualities such as integrity, purity, an "immaculate" state of "near perfection." The Catholic Church canonized personalities with these characteristics, people without sins who led a selfless life dedicated to others, striving to attain the highest possible purity and perfection, as long as at least two cases of miraculous healing could be proved, even after their death. This would be the proof of highest purity.

Perhaps it is fair to say that in Paradise, humanity lived in a condition of immaculate purity. With the "expulsion from Paradise"—estrangement from divine perfection—pain, sickness, imperfection, and death came to plague humanity. Our goal, as already mentioned, is to return to paradisiacal perfection in full consciousness and freedom. If there were (and there surely are) people capable of effecting miraculous cures, they are certainly ahead of their fellow citizens in their personal development. They are more "whole," "pure," and "without injury" not only in terms of physical health, but also and especially in terms of soul health. In the example of Parzival, Wolfram said that the hope of the Grail Community was that he might heal the king. However, his soul was tainted, imperfect and sick. He was not able to heal Anfortas because someone who is sick first needs to see to his own recovery; only then will he have the strength to heal others. In other words, only if one can achieve purity and harmony, remove one's imperfections and become immaculate, will one be able to heal others with the forces of love emanating from within. For example, Rudolf Steiner mentioned that what emanated from Saint Francis as a healing force was his profound morality. He did not preach morality; he simply acted according to it.

In German, Christ is also called *Heiland*, meaning "Savior." His level of purity and perfection, His love, and His compassion allowed Him to not only heal the sick that were presented to Him, but also, through the Mystery of Golgotha, sow the seeds for the healing of all humankind. In fact, Christ came to save humankind from the effects of the Fall, serving as a model, on a macrocosmic scale, for the further development of every human being until the end of earthly evolution.

So the model is there, and it is up to each one to follow it or not. In this sense, Parzival, who achieved his final degree of evolution on a microcosmic scale, became a model of personal development for the present evolutionary stage of the human being. In fact, when we analyze medieval literature it turns out that even before the advent of the fifth post-Atlantean cultural epoch (from the 15th century on), Wolfram described Parzival as the first person who consciously undertook the search for the Grail. He suggested that the young knight had already felt the inner call that nowadays drives humanity to seek values transcending what is merely material.

Now this inner call is nothing other than the path of conscious self-development. To understand this path better, and to find out how to follow it today, we will embark on a brief discussion of the various processes of initiation in the course of human evolution.

In the chapter "The Symbol of the Grail" it was mentioned that initiation is achieved in a state of consciousness different from normal waking consciousness. In several of his works, Rudolf Steiner addressed the issue of initiation or self-development, also called self-education, not only describing the various forms and paths, but also providing concrete exercises which anyone can practice. The latter are based solely on active thinking and can be found in books such as *Theosophy*, *An Outline of Esoteric Science* and *Knowledge of the Higher Worlds: How Is It Attained?*, among others.

In numerous lectures, Steiner mentioned the existence of two opposite initiation paths. One is the OUTER PATH, the way of the macrocosm or the Northern Mysteries, wherein the human being pours him- or herself out into the Universe. This occurs physiologically during sleep, but in a state of unconsciousness; today this path requires one to maintain consciousness during the state of expansion. In the lecture cycle *The Gospel of St. Matthew*, Steiner said on September 7, 1910:

> However, a human being can never absolutely leave for the macrocosm in one direction only. He has to move in all possible directions. The way out there is an expansion, spreading out into the Macrocosm. Then the possibility of having a single viewpoint completely disappears. [...] This means that, first of all, it is necessary to develop some flexibility in observation, acquiring the possibility of looking at all sides.

This is the reason that apparently contradictory statements exist in Steiner's work: He was certainly an initiate, who would address the same subject by contemplating it from the most varied points of view. One must always seek to understand the context in which his statements were made. A statement taken on its own can generate great confusion.

The other path is the INNER PATH, the way of the microcosm or the Mysteries of the South, and it requires one to consciously enter one's own physical and nonphysical corporeality. In this state, as Steiner said on Sept. 7, 1910, the human being is as if "compressed and closed in his or her 'egoity,' intensely concentrated in that point where one does not desire anything other than being a Self."[200] This means, among other things, coming face to face with our wishes and desires, our selfish instincts, everything that is evil in us. Many Christian martyrs and mystics described the experiences they suffered during this path, also called "mystical internalization."

According to the mystics of the Middle Ages, the human being is a fourfold entity. First there is the *physical, external human,* who lives in the world and wants possessions. Then there is the *soul human* who suffers, feels joy and has desires, impulses and sensations, all of which must gradually be sublimated. The third, still more internalized, is the *spiritual human* who gradually gains access to the spiritual world. In the innermost recesses is the *divine human* who has to develop ever further his or her divine spark. Through Christian initiation, God should be sought in the depths of each being, in the sanctuary of the soul.

Rudolf Meyer says that, according to Robert de Boron's description, Joseph of Arimathea, while imprisoned in the tower and totally separated from the world of the senses, could be considered the founder of Christian mysticism. The inner light of his heart kept him out of darkness and made his survival possible.

In pre-Christian times, both paths were clearly separated. The opening to the macrocosm was mainly developed by Aryan and Nordic

---

200 R. Steiner, *The Gospel of St. Matthew,* GA 123.

peoples (the Germanic people and Celts), and the microcosmic path was practiced especially among the Egyptians. These initiations were always carried out by hierophants, the masters who were in control of this risky process, which in some cases could lead to the death of the person being initiated (see chapter "The Symbol of the Grail"). Therefore very strict preparation of the soul was required. As already mentioned, there was a circle of twelve initiated people in the Celtic initiation process, and each one developed a specific soul or spiritual quality which was made available to the whole group. The so-called "temple sleep" of the Egyptians lasted three days and often resembled a state of near-death. As humanity matured, the mystery wisdom of ancient times was later imparted initially in the form of poetic images, and then through philosophical concepts.

In medieval times, the stream from the North, from Ireland (in the West) invaded all of Europe together with migrating people. The Greco-Roman stream from the south brought Eastern wisdom as it conquered Europe, founding cities like Paris, Vienna, Cologne, and so on. This means that during the evolution of humankind the same spiritual stream needs to take on new forms, adapting itself to particular evolutionary stages. For example, the same spiritual stream can be followed from the ancient Persian mysteries through the initiations of Isis in ancient Egypt. These streams underwent a transformation with the advent of Christ, to re-emerge as the Mysteries of the Grail.

Nowadays, a proper initiation process occurs in full waking consciousness without the help of a hierophant, master, or guru. Access to the spiritual world, that is, conscious observation of it, requires preparation: the path of initiation or self-development. Only when the spiritual world considers a person fit to enter will it open; that is, access is given as grace from the spiritual world. Yet even in the modern initiation process there are descriptions of situations similar to near-death experiences.[201] Actually, there are certain steps common to all

---

201 S.O. Prokofieff, *What Is Anthroposophy?*

initiation processes, whether Eastern, Southern, Western or Northern, and the first one is even called "approaching the threshold of death."

Modern Rosicrucian initiation is the path indicated by Rudolf Steiner for contemporary humanity to follow. This path is described in the abovementioned Steiner works and in many others. It is based on fully conscious and active thinking, unlike Christian initiation (chapter 10), in which the predominant element is feeling. Another feature of Rosicrucian initiation is that the person undergoing it feels completely alone. This loneliness is quite a common feeling in present times, even when one is surrounded by other people; in times past this never occurred. Parzival, however, deeply experienced this state of loneliness. During the initiation process described by Rudolf Steiner, after undergoing preparation to strengthen the soul, one reaches a first level of experiences in which one contemplates the suprasensory world in the form of images. This stage is called imaginative consciousness. Then, through other exercises, all images acquired through *imaginative* consciousness have to be erased so as to reach total emptiness in consciousness.

Only then will the spiritual world begin to resound, to speak. This stage is called *inspirational* or *inspirative* consciousness. The ancients called "music of the spheres" what echoed from the spiritual world. At this stage, after a period of voluntary oblivion, one is able to understand the meaning of the imaginations from the previous level. The third level is that of *intuitive* consciousness, in which one lives and interacts with the entities of the spiritual world in mutual permeation.

Meyer explains that the fisherman who appears with some frequency in fairy tales and legends represents certain situations in which the soul begins to walk the path leading to the boundary of the physical world: The fisherman signifies that one is entering the realm of imaginative consciousness. Just before arriving at the Grail Castle, Parzival encountered a fisherman, an image meaning that he was approaching the threshold between the sense-perceptible and the suprasensory world. While he was in the Grail Castle the first time, the young knight just *stared* at what was happening around him (the imaginative level). He could not yet read or decipher the "starry script" which corresponds to the words resounding from the spiritual world (the inspirational level). In the period between his two visits to the Grail Castle, Parzival managed to progress from the path of imaginative consciousness to the inspirational level. Georg Kühlewind points out that, after struggling with Gawain and Gramoflanz, Parzival resigned himself:

> "Since I lack what the happy ones command—I mean Love, who cheers the sad thoughts of many with the aid of her delights—since I have been cut off from my part in this, I do not care what happens to me now." (B. XIV, 364–365)

In a way, Parzival abandoned his goal and handed his fate over to destiny. According to the author, this is another decisive turning point in the life of the knight. It is, in fact, quite common for a person concentrating on the solution of a seemingly insoluble problem to relax out of exhaustion or despair; yet when concentration becomes a "receptive emptiness," the solution is there all of a sudden. When Parzival ceased to tirelessly seek the Grail, it came to him in the form of Cundrie's invitation to become the new King of the Grail. One can relate the above resignation to the act of erasing images obtained through one's imaginative consciousness; shortly thereafter, the spiritual world presents itself in the *resounding* of words (in this case, Cundrie's words).

The fact that the Grail Castle is of such difficult access and only those who are called manage to get to it, shows that it is not an earthly abode, but belongs to the spiritual world. During normal waking consciousness one cannot reach it; only through the development of inspirational consciousness is someone called to enter it.

Parzival, being of the lineage of the Grail, had his path predestined from the beginning. Yet, being a representative of the fifth post-Atlantean epoch—our current period, not the one he lived in—he had to act in full freedom. For humanity to be able to develop free will, the spiritual beings who lead the evolutionary process had to withdraw, so to speak: They could no longer interfere in human decisions. They can still lead a person to favorable situations, but the attitude each person will take in each situation must be out of absolute free will. In this sense, according to Meyer, Parzival represented the hope of the spiritual world. He contemplated the mysteries of the Grail in youth and innocence, but failed to evaluate them with a mature and fully awakened consciousness.

Then he had to go through suffering, along the path marked by destiny, and despite having completely lost the capacity for spiritual contemplation, he remained firm when facing the problems presented to him, always true to his decision. This allowed him to develop the necessary strength to fulfill his mission.

In his lecture of October 16, 1918,[202] Steiner said that anyone truly committed to seeking self-knowledge will discover sooner or later that s/he is unable to reach this goal. The person then feels a sense of impotence, and this experience is very significant and healthy, because it makes the person realize that by means of the body, the way it is constituted nowadays, the soul would be unable to develop and would have to die along with it. On having to endure this intense experience of impotence, there is a change, a new experience: Not to surrender to what can be achieved only through bodily strength, and accepting what the spirit has to offer, makes it possible to overcome this soul death. In other words, one can experience the void of existence in impotence, and to overcome this impotence will allow for the resurrection of the soul in the direction of the spirit. When it occurs, a true relationship with Christ ensues.

Gerard Klockenbring explains that when we recognize our faults we are deeply touched, and when we realize that we cannot fall much further, something very subtle happens: We recognize ourself as we really are, as the spiritual beings see us. This can fill the soul with a

---

[202] R. Steiner, *The Work of the Angels in Man's Astral Body / How Do I Find the Christ?* GA 182.

sensation of inner peace, and one recognizes that these spiritual beings have always been by one's side, helping, and will continue to do so. Christ came to earth when humankind had reached its lowest point, furthest from the spiritual world. We can all experience the presence of Christ close to us when we are at the lowest point in our personal lives.

Walter Johannes Stein draws attention to the fact that at his second arrival at the Grail Castle, Parzival did not adopt an attitude of mere contemplation, as he had the first time; he became *active* and asked the question.[203] To become active, to interact, is what characterizes the third level of the path of self-education, intuitive consciousness. Therefore, it can be assumed that when Parzival cured his uncle and became King of the Grail, he had reached the highest level of initiation.

One must also remember that during Parzival's conversation with Trevrizent, the latter makes him aware of his three major unconscious faults: his mother's death when he left, the death of a relative on his father's side, and the fact of not having asked the question. But rather than reprimanding and punishing him, the hermit gave him profound explanations. Heinrich Teutschmann shows that these "faults" cannot actually be considered common shortcomings, but situations necessary for the path of self-development.[204] In this case, they are "soul wounds" (resulting from acts that hurt others), the counterpart of Anfortas' physical wound (the result of his own desire), and only when these soul wounds are cured can one cure the physical wounds of others.

In his lecture of March 26, 1913, Rudolf Steiner pointed out an important feature of the astral body: the development of selfishness.[205] In this context, he indicates a positive side of selfishness, evident when we care for something that belongs to us and protect it as if it were part of us. When someone assaults a child, the mother feels as if the attack were directed at her and comes to her child's defense. Maternal

---

203 W.J. Stein, *The Ninth Century and the Holy Grail*.
204 H. Teutschmann, *Der Gral. Weisheit und Liebe*.
205 R. Steiner, *The Effects of Spiritual Development*, GA 145.

selfishness transcends the mother alone and expands to encompass the child. Steiner explained that we need to expand universal human interests more and more to achieve healthy development of the astral body. This means that the interests of humankind need to become the interests of each individual. Comparing Anfortas with the young, naïve Parzival, Steiner revealed that in the case of the former, the egotistical forces of his astral body were restricted to his own desires and personal aspirations, which caused the injury to his personality. In contrast, Parzival had not yet developed any interest in the world. He still needed to lift his interest level above his one-sidedly naïve contemplation of the world so he could understand what is common to all people and valid for all humanity. One of the evolutionary goals of the human being is to feel unhappy, hurt, or offended when any part of humanity is injured.

Meyer points out that this initiatory path is also evident in Wagner's opera *Parsifal*.[206] When the young knight accompanies the master of the Grail, leaving the forest and going toward the castle, Wagner suggests a change of scenery while both characters look as if they are walking. Then Parzival says (free translation): "Just a short walk, but it seems to me that I have gone far," to which the master replies: "You see, my son, here time becomes space." (This last phrase is the title of the latest edition of Meyer's book.) The author says that one does not reach the Grail just by wanting to get there; the Grail has to come and meet the chosen one.

It is a blessing to be able to experience this, but obviously one has to take the first steps—to become active, for example, and to develop living thinking, regardless of the sense world, so that the Grail can come to us. This journey corresponds to the overcoming of sensory existence, with its laws relating to time and space. One reaches a soul space where everything that happens sequentially in the sense world now exists simultaneously side by side, so to speak. That is, time acquires

---

206 R. Meyer, *Der Gral und seine Hüter*.

the characteristics of space, and sequences in time will be experienced simultaneously. Then one is entering the suprasensory world.

Therefore the Grail Castle can be considered, in reality, a representation of the spiritual world. On entering it one can observe disparate things and events with images disconnected from earthly reality, as in dreams, and one will be unable to understand them. One must take a long journey, expanding one's consciousness, to enter consciously into that world, understanding what it intends to reveal. However, there is no point in getting there alone without taking someone along. In his abovementioned work *Knowledge of the Higher Worlds: How Is It Attained?*, Rudolf Steiner referred to a spiritual entity called "the great guardian of the threshold"; whoever goes through the gate into the spiritual world[207] will meet him. This entity says the following to the one entering the suprasensory world:

> "Someday, you will be able to unite with my form, but I myself cannot find perfect blessedness as long as there are others who are still unfortunate! As a single liberated individual, you could enter the suprasensory realm immediately, but later you will have to look down at all the sentient beings who have not yet been freed. Your destiny will have been separated from theirs. But you are all interlinked. All of you had to go down to the sensory world in order to seek forces for a higher world. If you were to separate from them, you would abuse the forces which you could only acquire and develop in their community. Had they not descended, neither would you have descended. Without them, you will lack the forces you need for suprasensory existence. These forces which you achieved with them, you must share with them."

In other words, there is a spiritual law that says no one should go unaccompanied into the spiritual world. Those who reach a certain

---

207 This entity was already mentioned in connection with the symbolism of Cundrie (chapter 5).

stage of evolution should turn to those who are not yet at the same level and help them on, otherwise their attitude would be selfish, contrary to the Christ impulse. Wolfram knew about this law; when Cundrie called Parzival to become the new King of the Grail, she told him to take a companion with him, and he chose his brother Feirefiz. According to Stein, Feirefiz, a pagan, represents those who have not yet recognized the spiritual entity Christ.[208] For this reason Feirefiz could not see the Grail, but only its bearer. As soon as he was baptized, he too could see the Grail. Feirefiz is a representative of the destiny of the Eastern people, who will only be able to receive the Christ impulse when they see the bearer of Christianity and join him. But they "must accept baptism," and then they will see Christ himself. This means that in the modern world the Grail must be taken from the West to the East, which is what Feirefiz did. "Feirefiz had letters sent throughout the land of India describing the Christian life, which had not prospered so much till then." (B. XVI, 408)

In his work *Titurel*, Albrecht also reports that the noble knight, Titurel, accompanied by Parzival, took the Grail to India, where they were reunited with Feirefiz and Prester John. Meyer says the magnificence of the Grail is only fully revealed to the soul that accepts Christ, although knowledge of His existence may also date back to pre-Christian times. Meyer quotes Wolfram's mention of Kyot and the book found in Toledo:

> It helped him [Kyot] that he was a baptized Christian—
> otherwise this tale would still be unknown. No infidel art
> would avail us to reveal the nature of the Gral and how one
> came to know its secrets. (B. IX, 232)

It was mentioned before that Parzival's trajectory was dominated by the forces of the head, the nerve-sense system, the forces of thinking and knowledge—to which, however, it is necessary to join the forces

---

208 W.J. Stein, op. cit.

of selfless love. Gawain followed the path of the heart, of feelings and courage. Feirefiz went on a third path, the path of willing. These three paths of initiation are described by Bernd Lampe in his work *Gawain*.

The pagan initiation, the path of the will, had a more ancient, pre-Christian aspect. It focused on the recognition of the Mysteries of the Father, the Creator. With the advent of Christ, the Mysteries of the Son (related to the feelings) began, and from the 9th century onward, according to Rudolf Steiner, humanity had reached the dawn of the Mysteries of the Spirit (related to thinking).

In his lecture of November 4, 1906,[209] Rudolf Steiner discussed the seven steps of the Eastern or Hindu initiation, which could only be accomplished under the strict guidance of a guru on whom the disciple was totally dependent. The first step was to abstain from killing, stealing, lying, and having desires. The candidate should never harm other people. The result of this exercise was to feel content with less and less. In the second step, the disciple should respect the symbols of the cult and perform rituals. The third step was related to correct body posture, and the fourth had to do with the breathing rhythm, which would later restructure the human organism. In the fifth step, the aim was to have mental representations completely disconnected from the outside world. In the sixth step, these representations had to be mastered in such a way that one had no other impressions except for the selected one, which should stay in the mind for a time and then be suppressed, without losing consciousness: This meant to maintain the form of representation, but devoid of content. In the seventh step, the contents of the spiritual world would flow into that form.

These seven steps of Christian initiation were described in the chapter "The Journey of Gawain." In his lecture of March 14, 1906, entitled "Who Are the Rosicrucians?" and in that of November 5, 1906, and many others, Steiner succinctly summed up this Rosicrucian

---

209 R. Steiner, *Reading the Pictures of the Apocalypse: Cosmogony*, GA 94.

initiation.[210] While in the Eastern initiation the disciple totally depended on the guru, and in the Christian initiation the master had to lead the disciple toward the "great guru"—the Christ—in the Rosicrucian initiation the disciple's relationship with the teacher is quite free, based on trust. The teacher is a friend and advisor who does not impose rules or obligations but only gives advice. Besides, this relationship can be interrupted at any time. The practices described are not generic life practices, but the task of those who, of their own volition, decide to follow this path of self-education. This path also consists of seven steps:

The first step is the STUDY "in the Rosicrucian sense," which should not be understood as an acquisition of intellectual erudition. Through it one must acquire absolutely sensible, logical thinking which allows for objective judgment. One should develop "living thinking" as described by Steiner, for example, in his works *Truth and Science* and *The Philosophy of Freedom*. This way of thinking provides thinking with great autonomy and allows for greater security in the perceptions and experiences one will have in the spiritual world, since they are of a completely different nature from the ones in the sensory world.

This way of thinking is a protection against "losing one's footing" when attaining higher levels along the path of self-development. Nowadays the study of spiritual science already accounts for this first step, and anyone can try it. It is not an easy task, and difficulties in the texts should not be attributed to imperfections by translators, because the same difficulties arise in the original texts. Steiner wrote and spoke in the way he did precisely to allow his work to lead the reader or listener to exercise this first step.

In the second step one achieves what Steiner called IMAGINATIVE KNOWLEDGE, in which one develops the ability to recognize that in everything in the world there is something spiritual and eternal. Today,

---

210 Respectively in *Supersensible Knowledge*, GA 55, and *Reading the Pictures of the Apocalypse: Cosmogony*, GA 94.

for example, we can discern a person's state of soul from his or her facial expression—a smile reveals joy, tears reveal suffering. The goal is to be able to "read," from what we can observe in nature, the spiritual aspect it reveals. In a lecture on March 14, 1906, Steiner describes this as happening "when one can see the joy of the spirit of the earth in the plant, when the soil itself becomes the expression of the suffering of the spirit of the earth."[211] This means that one is freed from the dead, sense-bound realm of things observable through the senses, and one tries to understand them as an expression of something hidden within them. Any object is the materialization of a concept, of its spiritual essence, and therefore has a deeper meaning. When one can observe it, this is called imaginative knowledge.

The third step consists of READING THE SECRET WRITING (also known as the "occult script.") This is not just any kind of writing: It is related to the secrets of nature. Many symbols comprise this writing, which are used to designate certain events in the physical and spiritual worlds and allow the interpretation of the corresponding signs as "forms of thinking." As an example, Steiner describes a symbol comprised of two interlocking spirals that do not touch. This represents the passage of something old (the spiral that moves toward the center) to something new (the spiral that comes out of the center).

It also may be seen as characterizing the process of a seed originating from its parent plant and forming a new plant (a phenomenon of the physical world), as well as the passage from the Atlantean age to the post-Atlantean age. The secret writing permits the deciphering of the laws of nature underlying everything and allows one to penetrate deeper into the essence of phenomena. It also provides ways to sort out and understand the manifestations experienced in the second step. This occult writing is not the result of mental speculation, but represents currents flowing through the universe that can be interpreted as thought forms.

---

211 R. Steiner, *Supersensible Knowledge*, GA 55.

The fourth step is called CULTIVATION OF THE RHYTHM OF LIFE or PREPARATION OF THE PHILOSOPHER'S STONE. It constitutes the foundation of spiritual life. Nature as a whole and the entire universe are permeated by rhythmic laws, such as the orbits of the planets and the cycles of plants and animals, though in the latter the laws are internalized. In humans the rhythm has become chaotic because of our free will (for example, electric light has altered our sleep rhythm, which used to follow the course of the sun). Each person must establish his or her own rhythm, which means to create a new universe. One way of doing this is to perform acts that are repeated daily, such as exercises for soul development. There are other specific exercises, described by Steiner in his abovementioned books, for those who want to tread the path of self-development, constituting anthroposophic meditative practice.

On the other hand, rhythm is also related to the breathing process. Today we breathe in oxygen and exhale carbon dioxide (carbon and oxygen), while the plant absorbs carbon dioxide and eliminates oxygen. The survival of the human being depends on the plant kingdom in this process of gas exchange. The plant retains carbon, which after thousands of years can be found as coal deposits. In a very distant future, after having gone through a long process of purification through the abovementioned exercises, the human being will no longer need plants to absorb our exhaled carbon. We will be able to transform carbon in our own organisms, not into coal but into diamonds. This is the alchemy leading to the preparation of the Philosopher's Stone.

The fifth step is UNDERSTANDING THE MICROCOSM, or one's own human nature. It was Paracelsus[212] who said that if one extracted everything that exists in the world, the result would be a human being. In other words, everything that exists in nature is the great archetype of what manifests itself as a copy in the human being. The origin of everything is in the macrocosm. The secret is to delve into one's own

---

212 Philippus Aureolus Theophrastus Bombastus von Hohenheim (1493–1541), physician and alchemist.

body to be able to understand not only the physical world but also the spiritual one, as well as the natural surroundings. This means discovering in oneself something that corresponds to a macrocosmic fact. In this way a relationship is established between the microcosm and the macrocosm.

After acknowledging in oneself what was created from the macrocosm, the human being can recognize within him- or herself, in the sixth step, the laws governing the great world around us. To attain this, a person has to stand "outside oneself" so that one's consciousness encompasses the whole universe. This means to surrender, to INTEGRATE OURSELVES INTO THE WHOLE UNIVERSE, THE MACROCOSM, to seek our own spiritual entity in all beings, to dive into them and receive them lovingly.

The seventh step is reached when the human spirit opens up so we can feel that we are part of all beings, who now reveal their essence to us, no longer in words or concepts, but in the innermost feelings. Knowledge becomes feeling and the essence of the universe acquires a spiritual physiognomy. This corresponds to extreme devotion or BLISS.

The table on the following page summarizes the seven steps of the three types of initiation described.

One of the most important aspects of modern, present-day initiation is to maintain full awareness as one crosses the threshold into the spiritual world. There is no more room for the hermit or the ascetic; even initiates must now be fully inserted into the earthly context, in society.

It is noteworthy that the human being is, in fact, a citizen of two worlds: the sense-perceptible and the suprasensory world. Wolfram describes this in an interesting image when Parzival is called to become the King of the Grail, that is, when he reaches the highest level of initiation. Cundrie tells him that he has twin sons: Lohengrin and Kardeiz. The fact that the former was summoned to become a knight of

Chapter 14

	PAGAN INITIATION	CHRISTIAN INITIATION	ROSICRUCIAN INITIATION
	Mysteries of the *Father* (pre-Christian) *Feirefiz* (willing)	Mysteries of the *Son* (The Mystery of Golgotha till the 9th century) *Gawain* (feeling)	Mysteries of the Holy Spirit (as of the 9th century) *Parsival* (thinking)
1.	Abstention	Washing of the feet	Study (of Spiritual Science/anthroposophy) (rational, waking consciousness)
2.	Compliance with rituals	Flagellation	Acquisition of imaginative knowledge (imaginative consciousness)
3.	Correct body posture	Crowning with thorns	Reading the occult writing (inspirational consciousness)
4.	Correct breathing	Carrying the cross and Crucifixion	Cultivating the rhythm of life, or preparation of the Philosopher's Stone (intuitive consciousness)
5.	Mental representations detached from the outside world	Mystical death and descent into hell	Knowledge of the relationship between microcosm and macrocosm
6.	Control over mental representations	Resurrection	Integration in the macrocosm
7.	Union with the spiritual world	Ascension	Bliss

the Grail and the latter stayed behind to care for his father's kingdoms means, according to Rudolf Meyer, that one part of the human entity develops the ability to live in the spiritual world in full consciousness, while the other dedicates itself vigorously to earthly tasks.

Ancient astrology still recognized the relationship between each person and his or her destiny, in connection with the planetary spheres. The influence of the stars determined everyone's actions and fate. To develop freedom, the human being must first suppress this influence of the celestial bodies and learn how to act out of his or her own Self. Therefore, the "wisdom of the stars" played no part in early Christianity. Only with the Moorish invasions during the Middle Ages did this ancient wisdom come to Europe.

However, it can be said that it is anachronistic: It is something from former times that has lost its purpose in the present stage of human development, when humankind needs to struggle to gain its freedom, which means to become independent of the stars and planets.

Julius Evola (not an anthroposophical writer) says that the path to follow in search of the Grail is a process of initiation.[213] Citing Wolfram, he points out that the Castle was invisible or of difficult access, and that inside there were such splendors as never existed on earth (an allusion to a higher spiritual world), and that the path leading there required much (internal) struggle.

To reach it means one has to be in a state similar to death. In the words of Evola, the elect from all regions are called to the Kingdom of the Grail, and from there knights depart to distant lands on secret missions. They are not allowed to reveal their origin, name, or lineage. There is no connection between the Kingdom of the Grail and any other kingdom on earth. It is inaccessible, inviolable, and cannot be invaded. "One becomes part of the Grail through a birth different from physical birth, through a dignity different from all dignities of the world, which

---

213 J. Evola, *The Mystery of the Grail*.

unites, in an unbroken chain, men who may seem dispersed in the world, in space and time and nations."[214]

At times Wolfram mentions the Holy Trinity. Some considerations follow.

The Mysteries of God the Father are related to forces directed toward the past, that is, they still do not admit freedom. Ewald Koepke states that we owe our intellect, itself something spiritual but in a terminal stage, to the world (in extinction) of God the Father.[215] The Self can mirror itself in this intellect and therefore have self-awareness. Whoever does not find God the Son in his or her soul cannot escape the past, nor acquire freedom of spirit. Freedom of spirit allows the human self to transcend earthly bonds and move from the sensory world to the spiritual world. The union with God the Son allows for new life arising out of death; that is, something eternal rises out of something perishable, for God the Son transformed what was decaying into something arising. According to Meyer, when Parzival doubted God Almighty and disowned Him, he actually disowned God the Father.[216] The God of the Old Testament seems more like a father to the Hebrew people: He punishes people when they disobey and rewards those who follow His commandments. One notes a strong determinism; one cannot speak about freedom here, only obedience or disobedience.

Before encountering Trevrizent, Parzival was looking for a God (individually) faithful to him, like someone who would return the services he had rendered to Him:

> "[T]hen I set it [all suffering] down to the shame of Him who has all succor in His power, since if He is truly prompt to help He does not help me—for all the help they tell of him!"
> (B. IX, 236)

---

214 J. Evola, *The Mystery of the Grail*.
215 E. Koepke, *Rudolf Steiner und das Gralsmysterium*.
216 R. Meyer, *Der Gral und seine Hüter*.

Only from the hermit did Parzival get to know the true meaning of divine faithfulness:

> "[…] that to gain His abundant help mankind should persevere in God's service, Who never wearied of giving His steadfast soul against the soul's being plunged into Hell. Be unswervingly constant toward Him, since God Himself is perfect constancy, condemning all falsity. We should allow Him to reap the benefit of having done so much for us, for His sublime nature took on human shape for our sakes. God is *named* and *is* Truth, He was Falsity's foe from the Beginning." (B. IX, 236)

Trevrizent was speaking of God the Son, who "consented" (an act of freedom) to live in a human body and died on the cross for all humankind (an act of selfless love). This proves His faithfulness, for in this way He joined with human nature and the destiny of humankind. Only with His advent came the possibility of the full development of human individuality and freedom by way of the conscious Self. In his lecture of October 14, 1911, Rudolf Steiner said the following: "We owe it to a divine act of love that we are free beings."[217] And a little later: "Men should not conceive the notion of freedom without the thought of redemption through Christ."

Meyer, however, considers it possible that Anfortas was still quite focused on the forces of the Father: the forces related to matter, the body, and also death. When Jesus Christ, speaking to His disciples, warned them about His approaching death, He said, "I am going to the Father" (John 14:12). The injured Anfortas could not die because he had to contemplate the Grail directly. When Parzival arrived the second time, Anfortas even asked: "If you are Parzival, keep me from seeing the Gral for seven nights and eight days—then all my sorrows will be over." (B. XVI, 394) He could not find the path that leads from the Father to

---

217 R. Steiner, *From Jesus to Christ*, GA 131.

the Son. Parzival, however, did not comply with that request. On the contrary, he asked where the Grail was, and going down on his knees before it three times, in honor of the Holy Trinity, he asked that the suffering king be helped. Then he asked the healing question.

In other words, when Parzival was able to act upon his full knowledge and allied himself with the forces of selfless love—that is, in total freedom—he released his uncle from earthly bonds, adding to the forces of the Father the forces of the Son. The union of both allows for the renewal of nature in the process of dying, and in it, the power of the Holy Spirit manifests itself.

The schism in the Church occurred because of the argument regarding the origin of the Holy Spirit. One group asserted that it came from the Father; the other, that it came from the Son. Now the Holy Spirit comes from the Father, because at the time of Jesus's baptism by John the Baptist, the voice of God the Father was heard saying, "This is my beloved Son, in whom I am well pleased" (Matt. 3:17; Mark 1:11) as the Dove, representing the Holy Spirit, brought the Sun Spirit, Christ, to "deposit" Him into the body of Jesus, which had been prepared to welcome it. In his lecture of September 7, 1910, Steiner makes his own translation of this phrase, going back to the original text of the New Testament: "Thou art my beloved Son, in whom I see myself, in whom I find my own being" (Luke 3:22). He mentions other Gospels which read as follows: "Thou art my beloved Son; today I have begotten you." This supports the argument of Christ's birth in the physical body of Jesus of Nazareth.[218]

After His death, however, it is God the Son who at Pentecost sends the Holy Spirit to His disciples. Therefore, both lines of reasoning are correct. This difference of opinion is related to the different impulses found in the East and the West. As both are present in the legend of the Grail, the Mystery of the Trinity can also be found in it. In fact, in the

---

218 R. Steiner, *The Gospel of St. Matthew*, GA 123, Sept. 9, 1910.

first book written about the Grail, *Estoire del Saint Graal*, quoted here in chapter 2, "Works Relating to the Grail," the central theme is precisely the understanding of the Trinity achieved by the monk at the end of his initiation process.

As mentioned, Rudolf Steiner considered anthroposophy, which he founded, to be the "Science of the Grail," and whoever studies it deeply to be someone in search of the Grail. Ewald Koepke says that to study anthroposophy is to awaken the "nature of Parzival" in oneself.[219] One becomes a "knight of the Grail." This means establishing a more and more encompassing connection with Christ. One turns the human Self into an organ capable of receiving Christ. In our time, however, if the soul passively accepts only what is provided, it will not transcend itself. Today the soul must ask, must rise above itself, and transcend itself. In the chapter "Differences between the Communities of Arthur and the Grail" it was mentioned that, in the Middle Ages, people still had the perception that they would rise to Christ only if they *understood* the figure of the "representative of humanity," i.e., Parzival. Nowadays it is not enough simply to understand this hero. To rise to Christ one must *actively follow* the path of Parzival.

This justifies the main thesis of this book: Parzival is a forerunner of the evolution of the modern human being in his or her development. This may be the reason that this story has been with humanity for over a thousand years.

---

219 E. Koepke, *Rudolf Steiner und das Gralsmysterium*.

Appendices

The Meanings of Some of the Names

"Upon my word, you are Parzival! [...] Your name means 'Pierce-through-the heart."
— Wolfram von Eschenbach, *Parzival* (B. III, 81)

With the exception of Arthur and John, the names of the various characters in Parzival's story sound quite strange. The same applies to the many unfamiliar locations. It is possible that many of the names have meanings; after investigating various sources, and based on my knowledge of German and French, I can clarify at least some of them. At the end of Heinrich Teutschmann's book[220] some of the names are listed, several of which were not even mentioned in the summary of the story. He refers to two scholars, San-Mars and Karl Bartsch. In the list below, when Teutschmann's book is the source, it will be identified with a "T." As it was not possible to establish the relationship between some of the explanations and names, the former will be omitted. Some meanings are the result of my thoughts and those of participants in my courses, for which I am very grateful. I intend to continue my research and will be grateful for any further contributions. The names of the people are in alphabetical order; Parzival was left until the end, as were Munsalvaesche and the Grail.

ANFORTAS: There are two possible meanings for this name. The first would have its origin in the French language, in which *infirme* (pronounced "anfirme") means "ill," which corresponds to this king's health (T.). As was pointed out, Anfortas reached a certain stage of initiation. Yet because he failed, he could not cross the threshold into the spiritual world. In German *Am* means "beside, next to," and *Pforte* is a "gate," which may also mean "threshold." So he is the one who got "to the threshold" without, however, crossing it.

---

220 H. Teutschmann, *Der Gral. Weisheit und Liebe.*

ARTHUR: According to Richard Seddon, this name is of Celtic origin, deriving from *Art-Hu*.[221] *Art* means "to plow," and *Hu* was the Welsh name of the Sun God who was approaching earth, namely Christ. Therefore, its meaning would be "the plowman of Christ," that is, "one who prepares the ground for the coming of Christ." According to Nennius, a 9th-century writer, Arthur means "bear." The constellation of Ursa Major, the Big Bear or Big Dipper, most visible in the Northern Hemisphere, would represent the spiritual forces originating in Northern Europe. Therefore, many relate Arthur to this constellation.

BELAKANE: According to Rudolf Meyer, this name might derive from *Balkis* or *Bilkis* in Arabic.[222] This would be the name of the Queen of Sheba. What both have in common is that they are Moorish queens of breathtaking beauty. Another explanation given by the same author relates Belakane to the pelican, a bird that rips its breast open to feed its young with its own blood. In the Christian tradition, the pelican is related to Christ and His sacrifice for the benefit of others.

CONDWIRAMURS: She is the young queen who, freed from her enemies by Parzival, became his wife, teaching him about love between a man and a woman. In other words, she "leads him toward love." In French, *conduire* means "to drive," and *amour* means "love." Therefore her name corresponds to what she does.

CUNDRIE: She is the messenger of the Grail. *Künder* is the word for "messenger" in German.

FLEGETANIS: In Arabic, *Felek-Thâni* means "second sphere" or "the other sphere."[223] He was the pagan sage who "knew how to read the stars" i.e., "in the other sphere."

---

221 R. Seddon, "The Matter of Britain" in *The Mystery of Arthur at Tintagel*.
222 R. Meyer, *Der Gral und seine Hüter*.
223 P. Ponsoye, *El Islam y el Grial*.

FEIREFIZ: In French, *fée* means "fairy" and *fils*, "son," which would result in "fairy son" (T). Indeed, Gahmuret and Arthur come from the Mazdan lineage. "A fairy, Terdelaschoye, lured him to the land of Feimurgan: Her heart was moored to him." (B. I, 39) This excerpt appears immediately before the birth of Feirefiz. Another explanation is given by A.R. Schmidt Patier, *Parzival*'s translator into Portuguese: *Feirefiz* means "colorful son," reminding one of the black and white spots on his skin.

GURNEMANZ: One bit of advice given by this elderly knight to Parzival was, "Why do you not stop talking of your mother and turn your mind to other things?" (B. III, 95) a little later, Wolfram continued: "Not a word did he say of his mother aloud, though he did so in his heart, as an affectionate man may still do today." (B. III, 97) That is, this noble knight "emancipated" the youth from his mother, as the last two syllables in his name suggest.

HERZELOYDE : In German, the name can be divided into two words: *Herz*, which means "heart," and *Leid*, meaning "suffering." In fact, Parzival's mother was someone who suffered much, and seeing her son depart, "sorrow gave her such a cut that death did not hold off." (B. III, 76)

JESCHUTE: In French, *chute* means "fall"; the wife of the Duke of Orilus was disgraced in the eyes of her husband after Parzival had invaded her tent, stolen her ring, and devoured the meal she had prepared for her husband.

ORGELUSE: In French, *orgueil* means "pride." The Duchess whom Gawain finally married after enduring difficult trials had earlier shown the proud behavior that lived up to her name.

ORILUS: According to several authors, this name also means "proud," a typical attitude of this knight.

REPANSE OF SCHOYE: This is the name of the Queen of the Grail, the sister of Anfortas, Trevrizent, and Herzeloyde. She is the bearer of the Grail, and eventually becomes the wife of Feirefiz. The meaning of her name, also from the French, would be *répandre*, "to spread out," and *joie*, "joy." Most certainly, whoever brings sustenance to the whole community "spreads out joy." According to Wolfram's Portuguese translator, this name means "dawn of happiness."

SIGUNE: This name may also derive from two French terms. *Signe* means "sign" or "indication"; in fact, this damsel is always indicating (or failing to indicate) directions to her cousin. The other possibility is that this name has its origin in *cygne*, "swan." In many fairy tales and other traditions, a white bird establishes the relationship between the earthly and spiritual worlds. The story of the stork that brings children (obviously their spiritual part, not their body) is one of them. Wolfram writes about the white dove which renews the power of the Grail, bringing a wafer from heaven every Good Friday. Writing about Sigune, he said that in order to lead Parzival as she did, she must represent an entity of a spiritual nature. Another striking feature of this damsel is her fidelity to her dead bridegroom. The swan is a monogamous bird: Pairs of swans remain faithful to each other for their whole lives.

TITUREL: The name of the guardian of the Grail comes from *tuteur*, meaning "tutor" or "protector" (T).

UTE PANDRAGUN (UTHER PENDRAGON): He was the father of King Arthur. According to A.R. Schmidt Patier, "Pandragun" or "Pendragun" would refer to a position in society, as in the language of the Bretons *pen* means "head" and *dragon* a "leader," i.e., "supreme leader." The character's name would thus be Ute or Uther, followed by his title.

MUNSALVAESCHE: *Munt* means "mount"; for some authors, *salvaesche* means "wild" (as in "savage"), while for others it means "salvation." Both explanations, "Wild Mount" (inaccessible, surrounded by dense forests) or "Mount of Salvation," make sense.

Many authors have sought the meaning of the word GRAIL: In old French, *greal* or *grasal* designates a container made of wood, clay, or metal.[224] In Portuguese, *gral* refers to a mortar (the container used with a pestle). Some authors derive this term from the Latin word *agradabilis*, similar to "agreeable" or "gratifying," and it certainly is "pleasant" to be in the presence of the Grail, provider of food and life.

Heliandus, a French monk, wrote in a chronicle that *gradalis* or *gradale* was a large, fairly deep bowl made of silver or another precious metal, in which delicious food was served to nobles.[225]

Rudolf Meyer explains that in Latin, *gradale* is something that reveals itself "gradually," in stages.[226] It can be assumed that "gradually" refers to various aspects of the Grail. Koepke says that both the manifestation of the divine-spiritual realm as well as the descent of the Christ being happened gradually.[227] The same goes for the evolutionary process of humanity, which takes place step by step, gradually. In the chapter "The Trajectory of *Parzival*," it was also stated that his development took place gradually; therefore, one can consider it a Grail mystery.

There are several possible explanations for the name PARZIVAL or PARSIFAL. Meyer reports that the prefix "per," which appears in names like Perceval, Peredur and Peronnik—the latter ones being heroes of British literature who are fools to begin with but, after many trials, reach a very high destiny—characterizes people who confront any kind of obstacle. They go forth where others see insurmountable difficulties. Indeed, in French the verb *percer* means "to pierce" or "to break through."

When the hero first met Sigune she told him his name, of which he had been ignorant until then:

---

224 E. Jung and M.-L. von Franz, *The Grail Legend*.
225 Ibid.
226 R. Meyer, *Der Gral und seine Hüter*.
227 E. Koepke, *Rudolf Steiner und das Gralsmysterium*.

"Upon my word, you are Parzival [...]. Your name means 'Pierce-through-the heart.' Great love ploughed just such a furrow through your mother's heart. When he died, your father left sorrow for her portion." (B. III, 81)

Moreover, separating the syllables *Per-ce-val* (French) one can read it as "through this valley," and in fact, the hero went through "this valley" in his journey. Wolfram used the spelling "Parzîval," which was understood as the Germanized form of "Perceval."

According to Gerhard von dem Borne, Parzival's name would encompass a geographical range, from the region where the Persian religion was practiced in the East (a *pársi* was an adept of the ancient Zoroastrians) to the Irish realm in the West, represented by the stone *Fál*.[228] This stone was also called "stone of destiny" or "royal stone" because the coronation of the Scottish kings took place above it. Later it was taken to England, and to this day, the coronation throne used in the coronation ceremonies of British kings and queens sits upon this stone. In other words, the name "Parzival" may join Eastern religion (transformed during humankind's evolution) and Celtic royalty, which actually happened.

The spelling "Parsifal" was adopted by Richard Wagner in his opera of the same name. In the second act Kundry makes the following pun: "I called you a mere fool, 'Fal Parsi,' you pure fool: 'Parsifal.'" Now in Arabic *parseh* means "pure fool"; in the Celtic language, *par* is "boy," *syw* means "to arm," and *fal* is "insufficient"—which would correspond to an "insufficiently armed (or prepared) man." In Persian, *parsi* means "man" and *whal* means "purified by the light." The three meanings correspond to definite stages in the hero's life.

---

228 G.v.d. Borne, *Der Gral in Europa*.

The Crown of Lucifer

Der Sängerkrieg auf der Wartburg[229]

So höre von der Krone Pracht:
Nach Sechzigtausend Engel Wunsch ward sie gemacht,
Die wollten Gott vom Himmelreiche drängen.

Sieh, Luzifer, so ward sie dein!
Wo irgend werthe, weise Meisterpfaffen sei'n,
Die wüssten wohl, dass ich die Wahrheit sänge.

Sankt Michael sah Gottes Zorn um solchen Hochmuths Pralen:
Die Krone brach sein Schwert im Saus
Ihm von dem Haupte: seht, da sprang ein Stein daraus,
Der ward hernach auf Erden Parzivalen.

The Dispute of the Troubadours in Wartburg

Listen, then, what is said about the beauty of the crown:
It was made according to the wish of sixty thousand angels,
Who wanted to expel God from the celestial kingdom.

See, Lucifer, so it became yours!
If somewhere there were wise and valiant prelates,
They would certainly confirm that I am singing the truth.

Saint Michael saw the wrath of God caused by such pride.
At one stroke his sword broke the crown,
Pulling it off his head: See, a stone came loose,
And later, on earth, it became Parzival's.

— Free Translation

Der Singerkriec uf Wartburc.
Gedicht aus dem XIII, Jahrhunderte[230]

(CXV-LXXXIV)"Soll ich die Krone vorbringen? Die ward gewirkt nachsechzig tausend Engel Wahl, die Gott vom Himmel drängen wollten. Sieh, Lucifer, da ward sie dein! Wo noch werthe weise Meisterpfaffen sind, die wohl wissen, dass ich die Wahrheit singe. Michael sah Gottes Zorn über Uebermuthes Dauer, die Krone brach er dem Engel vom Haupte; da sprang ein Stein heraus, den seitdem Parceval erhielt."

The Troubadours' Dispute in Wartburg
13th Century Poem

"Must I present the crown? It was made according to the choice of sixty thousand angels who wanted to expel God from heaven. You see, Lucifer, so it has become yours! If somewhere there were wise and valiant prelates, they would certainly confirm that I am singing the truth. Michael saw the wrath of God caused by such pride, he tore the crown of the head of the angel; and then a stone came loose, which now belongs to Parzival."

---

229   K. Simrock, *Der Wartburgkrieg*, 13th century. From N. Stein von Baditz, *Aus Michaels Wirken.*
230   L. Ettmüller, *Der Singerkriec uf Wartburc: Gedicht aus dem XIII. Jahrhunderte.*

General Bibliography*

Adams, G. *Das Rosenkreuzertum als Mysterium der Trinität*. 2. ed. Stuttgart: Freies Geistesleben 1994.

Ashe, G. *The Landscape of King Arthur*. London: Grange Books, 1987.

Borne, G.v.d. *Der Gral in Europa*. Stuttgart: Urachhaus 1976.

Boron, Robert: see Robert de Boron.

Bos, L. "Os Templários." Handout. São Paulo: Anthroposophical Society in Brazil.

Böttcher, C. *Non nobis, domine, non nobis*. Die Christengemeinschaft, 10, October 2007.

Bumke, J. *Wolfram von Eschenbach*. 4. ed. Stuttgart: J.B. Metzlersche Verlagsbuchhandlung, 1976.

Burdach, K. *Der Gral*. Stuttgart: W. Kohlhammer, 1974.

Charpentier, L. *Les mystères de la Cathédrale de Chartres*. Paris: Robert Laffont, 1966.

Chrétien de Troyes. *Le Roman de Perceval ou Le Conte du Graal*. 2. ed. Paris: Triades, 1969.

———. *Das Buch vom Gral*. 2. ed. Stuttgart: Freies Geisteleben 1980.

Eschborn, M. *Karlstein, das Rätsel um die Burg Karls IV*. Stuttgart: Urachhaus, 1971.

Eschenbach, Wolfram von: see Wolfram von Eschenbach.

Ettmüller, L. *Der Singerkriec uf Wartburc: Gedichte aus dem XIII. Jahrhunderte*. Ilmenau: Fr. B. Voigt, 1830.

Evola, J. *The Mystery of the Grail*. Inner Traditions, 1996.

Forward, W. and A. Wolpert (eds.). "The Quest for the Grail." *The Golden Blade*, 47. Edinburgh: Floris Books, 1994.

Ginsburg, C.D. *The Essenes: Their History and Doctrines*. Andesite Press, 2015.

---

*Possible English versions of any of these books listed in Spanish and German can be researched on www.rudolfsteinerweb.com or on www.rsarchive.org

Gleich, S. von. "Gondi-Shapur." *Ampliação da arte médica.* São Paulo: Brazilian Association of Anthroposophical Medicine. Caderno especial No. 1, October 1992.

Greiner, W. *Grals-Geheimnisse.* Dornach: Philosophisch-Anthroposophischer Verlag, 1983.

The Holy Bible, King James Version.

Hutchins, E. *Parzival, an Introduction.* London: Temple Lodge, 1979.

James, J. *The Master Masons of Chartres.* New York / Chartres: West Grinstead Publishing, 1985.

Jung, E. and M.-L. von Franz. *The Grail Legend.* Princeton University Press, 1998.

Klockenbring, G. *El Santo Grial y el hombre moderno.* Notes from a cycle of lectures held in Madrid, Spain, from March 26 to 30, 1983.

Klug, S.U. *Catedral de Chartres, A geometria sagrada do Cosmos.* São Paulo: Madras, 2002.

Koepke, E. *Rudolf Steiner und das Gralsmysterium.* Stuttgart: Freies Geistesleben, 2005.

Kollert, G. *Apocalipse português.* São Paulo: Editions on Religion and Culture, 1993.

Kovacs, C. *Parzival and the Search for the Grail.* Waldorf Education Resources. Edinburgh: Floris Books, 2002.

Krück von Poturzyn, M.J. *Der Prozess gegen die Templer.* Stuttgart: Freies Geistesleben, 1963.

Kügelgen, E. von. Notes (by S. Setzer) on a lecture of Sept. 26, 1998, in Dornach, Switzerland.

Kühlewind, G. *Der Gral oder Was die Liebe vermag.* Ostfildern, Stuttgart: Tertium 1997.

Kutzli, R. *Die Bogumilen.* Stuttgart: Urachhaus, 1977.

Lampe, B. *Graalssuche und Schicksalserkenntnis.* Vol. 1: *Parzival.* Dürnau: Verlag der Kooperative Dürnau, 1987.

———. *Graalssuche und Schicksalserkenntnis.* Vol. 2: *Gawain.* 2. ed. Dürnau:Verlag der Kooperative Dürnau, 1988.

———. *Graalssuche und Schicksalserkenntnis.* Vol. 3: *Anfortas.* Dürnau: Verlag der Kooperative Dürnau, 1990.

Lanz, R. *A Pedagogia Waldorf*. 8. ed. São Paulo: Antroposófica, 2003.

———. *Noções Básicas de Antroposofia*. 7. ed. São Paulo: Antroposófica, 2005.

———. *Passeio através da História na luz da Antroposofia*. 3. ed. São Paulo: Antroposófica, 2004.

Laperrousaz, E.-M. *Os manuscritos do Mar Morto*. São Paulo: Cultrix 1990.

Macedo, J.R. *Viver nas cidades medievais*. São Paulo: Moderna, 1999.

Macdonald, F. *O cotidiano europeu na Idade Média* [Everyday Life in the Middle Ages].12. ed. São Paulo: Melhoramentos, 2003.

———. *How Would You Survive in the Middle Ages?* Scholastic, 1997.

Malory, T. *Le Morte d'Arthur*. Digireads.com Publishing, 2017.

Matthews, J. *At the Table of the Grail*. Penguin Books, 1987.

Megale, H. (ed.). *A Demanda do Santo Graal*: 13th-century manuscript. São Paulo: T.A. Queiroz, University of São Paulo, 1988.

Meyer, R. *Der Gral und seine Hüter*. Stuttgart: Urachhaus, 1956. (As of 1980, the title is *Zum Raum wird hier die Zeit: Die Gralsgeschichte* [Time Becomes Space: The Story of the Grail]).

Papasov, K. *Christen oder Ketzer–Die Bogomilen*. Stuttgart: Ogham, 1983.

Pastoureau, M. *No tempo dos cavaleiros da Távola Redonda*. São Paulo: Companhia das Letras, 1989.

Ponsoye, P. *El Islam y el Grial*. Barcelona: Ediciones de la Tradición Unanime, 1984.

Poturzyn, M.J.K. von. *Der Prozess gegen die Templer*. Stuttgart: Ogham, 1982

Prokofieff, S.O. *O que é Antroposofia?* [What Is Anthroposophy?]. São Paulo: João de Barro, 2006.

Quadros, A. *Portugal: Razão e mistério*. Volume I. 2. ed. Lisboa: Guimarães Editores, 1988.

Reimann, H. *Manichäismus—Das Christentum der Freiheit*. 2. ed. Dornach: Rudolf Geering-Verlag, 1980.

Robert de Boron. *The Story of the Holy Grail*. 3. ed. Stuttgart: Ogham, 1979.

———. *Merlin*. 2. ed. Rio de Janeiro: Imago, 1993.

Schüpbach, W. *Der Arabismus, seine historischen und spirituellen Hintergründe und sein Fortwirken in der Gegenwart.* Freiburg i. Br.: Die Kommenden, 1970.

Seddon, R. *The Mystery of Arthur at Tintagel.* London: Rudolf Steiner Press, 1990.

———. "The Matter of Britain." *The Golden Blade, 47: The Quest for the Grail.* Edinburgh: Floris Books, 1994.

Simrock, K. *Der Wartburgkrieg.* Stuttgart / Augsburg: J.G. Cotta'scher Verlag, 1858.

Sioen, G., Gougaud, H. *Vivre le Pays Cathare.* Paris: Mengès, 1992.

Stein von Baditz, N. *Aus Michaels Wirken.* Stuttgart: J. Ch Mellinger, 1959.

Stein, W.J. *The Death of Merlin: Arthurian Myth and Alchemy.* Edinburgh: Floris Books, 1990.

———. *The Ninth Century and the Holy Grail.* London: Temple Lodge Publishing, 2001.

Steiner, R.: see "Works by Rudolf Steiner."

Teichmann, F. Notes (by S. Setzer) of three lectures held in Dornach, Switzerland, on September 16, 17, and 18, 1999.

———. *Der Gral im Osten.* Stuttgart: Freies Geisteleben, 1986.

———. "The Polarity of Parzival and Gawain in Eschenbach's *Parzival*." *The Golden Blade, 47: The Quest for the Grail.* Edinburgh: Floris Books, 1994.

Teutschmann, H. *Der Gral. Weisheit und Liebe.* Dornach: Philosophisch-Anthroposophischer Verlag am Goetheanum 1984.

Vanderkam, J.C. *The Dead Sea Scrolls Today.* William B. Eerdmans, 1994.

Veltman, W.F. *Tempel und Gral. Die Mysterien des Templerordens und des Heiligen Grals. Die Bedeutung dieser Impulse für die Gegenwart.* Frankfurt Main: INFO3-Verlag, 1993.

Vermes, G. *Os Manuscritos do Mar Morto.* São Paulo: Mercuryo,1991.

Welburn, A. *The Beginnings of Christianity: Essene Mystery, Gnostic Revelation and the Christian Vision.* Stuttgart: Freies Geistesleben, 1992.

Weymann, E. *Zepter und Stern. Dier Erwartung von Zwei Messiasgestalten in den Schriftrollen von Qumran.* Stuttgart: Urachhaus, 1993.

Wilson, E. *The Scrolls from the Dead Sea*. Oxford University Press, 1955.

Winkler, F.E. "The Mythology in Richard Wagner's *Parsifal*." *Proceedings of the Myrin Institute*, 21, Winter 1968–1969, Garden City, NY: The Myrin Institute for Adult Education.

Wolfram von Eschenbach: *Parzival*. 3. ed. São Paulo: Antroposófica, 2006.

_____. *Parzival*. Stuttgart: Philipp Reclam Jun. 1989.

Works by Rudolf Steiner

GA = *Gesamtausgabe*, German acronym for "complete works."
CW = Complete Works in English
For more information on any of these, consult rsarchive.org

Agriculture Course: The Birth of the Biodynamic Method (CW 327). Rudolf Steiner Press, 2004.

The Apocalypse of St. John: Lectures on the Book of Revelations (CW 104). SteinerBooks, 2021.

Christ and the Spiritual World and the Search for the Holy Grail (CW 149). Rudolf Steiner Press, 2008.

Christianity as Mystical Fact (CW 8). SteinerBooks, 1997.

The East in the Light of the West: The Children of Lucifer and the Brothers of Christ (CW 113). Rudolf Steiner Press, 2018.

The Effects of Spiritual Development (CW 145). Rudolf Steiner Press, 1978.

Esoteric Christianity and the Mission of Christian Rosenkreuz (CW 130). Rudolf Steiner Press, 2001.

An Esoteric Cosmology: Evolution, Christ and Modern Spirituality (CW 94). SteinerBooks, 2008.

The Fifth Gospel: From the Akashic Record (CW 148). Rudolf Steiner Press, 1985.

From Jesus to Christ (CW 131). Rudolf Steiner Press, 2005.

The Gospel of John (CW 103). SteinerBooks, 1984.

The Gospel of St. Luke (CW 114). Rudolf Steiner Press, 1991.

The Gospel of St. Mark (CW 139). SteinerBooks, 1991.

The Gospel of St. Matthew (CW 123). Rudolf Steiner Press, 1990.

How Do I Find the Christ? (CW 182). SteinerBooks.

The Human Heart (GA 212). Mercury Press, 1985.

Intuitive Thinking as a Spiritual Path [*A Philosophy of Freedom*] (CW 4). SteinerBooks, 1995.

Karmic Relationships 4 (CW 238), 2017; and *Karmic Relationships* 8 (CW 240), 2015. SteinerBooks.

Knowledge of the Higher Worlds: How Is It Attained? (CW 10). SteinerBooks, 1994.

The Lord's Prayer: An Esoteric Study (GA 96). See rsarchive.org

Love and Its Meaning in the World (GA 143). SteinerBooks, 1998.

Materialism and the Task of Anthroposophy (CW 204). SteinerBooks, 1987.

Michael's Mission: Revealing the Essential Secrets of Human Nature (CW 194). SteinerBooks, 2016.

The Mysteries of the East and of Christianity (CW 144). Forest Row, UK: Rudolf Steiner Press, 1972.

The Mystery of the Trinity: Mission of the Spirit (CW 214). SteinerBooks, 1991.

Mystery of the Universe: The Human Being, Image of Creation (CW 201). SteinerBooks. 2001

Mystics at the Dawn of the Modern Age (CW 7). SteinerBooks, 2018.

Occult Science: An Outline (CW 13). SteinerBooks, 1997.

Old and New Methods of Initiation (CW 210). London: Steiner, 1991.

The Philosophy of Freedom (CW 4). SteinerBooks, 2011.

The Philosophy of Thomas Aquinas (CW 74). Kessinger Publishing, 2008.

The Principle of Spiritual Economy in Connection with Questions of Reincarnation (CW 109). SteinerBooks, 1986.

The Riddle of Humanity (CW 170). See rsarchive.org.

The Riddles of the World and Anthroposophy (CW 54). See rsarchive.org.

Rosicrucianism Renewed: The Unity of Art, Science & Religion (CW 284), lecture: "The Apocalyptic Seals." SteinerBooks, 2006.

The Spiritual Guidance of the Individual and Humanity (CW 15). SteinerBooks, 1992.

The Spiritual Hierarchies and the Physical World: Zodiac, Planets & Cosmos (CW 110). SteinerBooks, 1970.

Spiritual-Scientific Anthropology/ Knowledge of Man (CW 107). See rsarchive.org

Supersensible Knowledge (CW 55). SteinerBooks, 1988.

The Temple Legend: Freemasonry and Related Occult Movements (CW 93). SteinerBooks, 2000.

Theosophy (CW 9). SteinerBooks, 1994.

Bibliography for Selected Topics
(See complete information in the General Bibliography)

THE MIDDLE AGES

Macdonald, F. *O cotidiano europeu na Idade Média*. [Everyday Life in the Middle Ages]

_____. *How Would You Survive in the Middle Ages?*

Macedo, J.R. *Viver nas cidades medievais*.

Pastoureau, M. *No tempo dos cavaleiros da Távola Redonda*.

CHRISTOLOGY (Only works by Rudolf Steiner)

The Apocalypse of St. John.

Christianity as Mystical Fact.

The Fifth Gospel.

From Jesus to Christ.

The Gospel of John.

The Gospel of St. Luke.

The Gospel of St. Mark.

The Gospel of St. Matthew.

THE ESSENES

Ginsburg, C.D. *The Essenes. Their History and Doctrines.*

Laperrousaz, E.-M. *Os manuscritos do Mar Morto.*

Vanderkam, J.C. *The Dead Sea Scrolls Today.*

Vermes, G. *Os manuscritos do Mar Morto.*

Welburn, A. *The Beginnings of Christianity: Essene Mystery, Gnostic Revelation and the Christian Vision.*

Weymann, E. *Zepter und Stern. Die Erwartung von zwei Messiasgestalten in den Schriftrollen von Qumran.*

Wilson, E. *The Scrolls from the Dead Sea.*

THE ORDER OF THE KNIGHTS TEMPLAR AND THE ORDER OF CHRIST

Bos, L. "Os Templários."

Böttcher, C. *Non nobis, domine, non nobis.*

Krück Von Poturzyn, M.J. *Der Prozess gegen die Templer.*

Kügelgen, E. von. Notes (by S. Setzer)

Quadros, A. *Portugal: Razão e mistério*, Volume I.

Veltman, W.F. *Tempel und Gral. Die Mysterien des Templerordens und des Heiligen Grals. Die Bedeutung dieser Impulse für die Gegenwart.*

FREEMASONRY

Charpentier, L. *Les mystères de la Cathédrale de Chartres.*

James, J. *The Master Masons of Chartres.*

Klug, S.U. *Catedral de Chartres, A geometria sagrada do Cosmos.*

THE GRAIL TEMPLE

Borne, G.v.d. *Der Gral in Europa.*

Eschborn, M. *Karlstein, das Rätsel um die Burg Karls IV.*

Matthews, J. *At the Table of the Holy Grail.*

Quadros, A. *Portugal: Razão e mistério,* Volume I.

Sioen, G. and Gougaud, H. *Vivre le Pays Cathare.*

Teichmann, F. *Der Gral im Osten.*

Index of Key Words

A
Adam 130, 271, 288
Ahriman 264
Ahura Mazdao 147, 264
Alanus 199
Albrecht von Scharfenberg 33, 120, 203, 213-214, 253, 262, 264-266, 288, 308
Al-Mansur 146
Al-Rashid, Harun 136, 146
Andreae, Johann Valentin 266
Anfortas 29, 57, 72-74, 85, 94-96, 99-101, 108, 111, 113-115, 118, 126-124, 127, 131-132, 145, 153, 155-158, 168-169, 173, 177, 193, 198, 202, 245, 278-280, 285-289, 295-296, 298, 305-306, 317, 322, 325
Angel
    of Darkness 225
    of Truth 225
angels
    fallen 207-209, 271, 288
    faithful to God 209
    neutral 131, 209
    rebellion of 209, 271, 288
anthroposophy 9, 219, 270, 314, 319
Antikonie 67, 173, 179, 185-186
Arabism 10, 139, 144-147, 212, 246
Arnive 81-82, 86-88, 90, 157, 169
Arthur – *see* King Arthur
Arthurian legends 29, 37-38, 139-140
Arthur's knights – *see* knights
Arthur's court – *see* Court of Arthur
Ascalun 63-64, 67-68, 177, 179, 186, 290
Atlantis 35, 204

B
Babylon 32, 35, 139-140
Baghdad 43-44, 98, 121, 134, 136, 146-147
Bahram I 230
Baldwin III 38
Balkan Peninsula 238-240
Basilius Valentinus 30, 220
Bearoche 64-66, 134, 171, 178, 186, 231
Beauty and the Beast 231
Belakane 43, 97, 144, 147, 323

Benedict of Nursia 233
Bernard of Clairvaux 246
boatman 78-83, 85-86, 166-168, 180-181
Bogomils 238-239, 240
bonshommes (good men) 198, 241
Borne, Gerhard von dem 33, 147, 199, 327
Brabant 29, 96, 101
Brittany 134, 142, 157
Brobarz 51, 93-94
Bron 196, 198-199, 242
Bumke, Joachim 40
Burdach, Konrad 236

C
Cain 71, 120, 256, 259
Cathars 198, 239-245, 265
cathedral 150, 190, 259-260, 263-264
    Gothic 189-190, 258-259
Celts (Celtic) 140-144, 162-163, 199, 204, 206, 217, 301, 323, 327 – *see also* culture, Celtic; initiation, Celtic; *and* mystery, Celtic
    sacred treasures 144, 222
Chaldea 139, 142
Charlemagne 21-22, 136-137, 146
Charles IV 266
chivalry 8, 14, 22, 26, 29-30, 45, 50, 98, 163, 217, 277
    code of honor 16,19, 26, 98, 106-107
    decadence 26
    virtues 16, 160, 202
Chrétien de Troyes 27, 30-33, 37-39, 98, 116, 175, 194, 198, 202-203, 212-214, 242, 245
Christ 31-32, 38-39, 130, 133, 138, 140-142, 147, 150, 156, 158-159, 162, 164, 188-192, 195-199, 203, 205-208, 210, 213-215, 218, 220-222, 226, 232, 239-240, 243-244, 257-258, 263, 273-274, 281, 297-298, 305
    Community of 198
    cosmic 143, 188, 207, 218, 254, 261
    disciples of 158, 226, 263, 317
    encounter 133
    impulse 295, 308

CHRIST *continued*
  Order of 245, 251-252
  Passion of 184
  Sun Spirit/sun being 135-136, 215-216, 286, 318, 323
  vision 248
Christian(s) 28, 31, 135-136, 144, 162-163, 188, 190, 196, 223, 226, 232, 234, 241, 248
  army 43
  burial 121
  Europe 136
  festivals 19, 158
  initiation – *see* initiation, Christian
  Irish 234
  life 135, 308
  martyrs 300
  mysteries – *see* mystery(ies), Christian
  persecution 233
  precepts 158
  primitive 199
  rituals 144
  Spain 236
  virtues 144
Christianity 96, 101, 138-139, 143-144, 147, 158, 162-163, 189, 199, 210-212, 217, 223-224, 227, 232, 234-236, 238, 241-242, 245, 247, 253, 315
  esoteric 10, 31, 138, 143-144, 162, 235, 243, 251-252, 265-270
  evolution of 210-213
Chrysostom, John 188-189, 191
Church, Catholic (Roman) – *see* Roman Catholic Church
Cidegast 84, 91
Clamide 52-53, 63, 66, 107-108, 111, 115, 285
clergy 15-16, 18, 21-24, 146, 234-236
Clinschor 29, 37, 83, 85-87, 159, 181, 183, 196, 230, 232
Community of Christ 198
Community of the Grail 10, 112, 157-163, 169-170, 214, 223, 241, 254, 261, 281, 298
Condwiramurs 52-54, 60, 63-64, 91, 93-95, 99, 102, 107, 111, 119-120, 124, 171-173, 278-279, 280, 284, 286-287, 323
Constantine 232
Constructions, megalithic 140

Council
  of Constantinople 128, 138, 236-237
  of Troyes 247
  of Vienne 251
Court of Arthur 10, 26, 28-30, 37, 47, 50, 53-54, 58-59, 110, 117, 127, 161-164
Crusade(s), Crusaders 137, 188
  First 188
  Second 38
culture
  Arabic 139
  Babylonian-Egyptian-Chaldean 32, 35, 140, 244, 259-260
  Celtic 10, 139-141, 144, 157-158, 162-163, 217
  Christian 139, 162, 206
  Egyptian 141
  Germanic 14, 140, 149
  Greco-Roman 35, 139, 301
  Greek (Hellenism) 36, 141-142, 144-145, 148-149, 258-259
  India 35, 204
Cundrie 36, 61-63, 68-69, 77, 90, 93-94, 99, 103, 111, 114-116, 119, 123-128, 134, 138, 145-146, 155-156, 161, 169, 171-173, 180, 214, 230, 278-279-280, 282, 285-286, 290, 295-296, 303, 308, 313, 323
Cunneware 49, 53-54, 58-59, 61, 106-107, 110-111, 115, 154, 284-286
Cusano, Nicholas 286

D

dangerous seat 149
Dante Alighieri 40, 236
Dark Ages 136, 138
Darkness, Prince of 225, 242
David, star of 148
Dead Sea Scrolls 224, 226, 269

E

Egypt(ian) 33, 35, 139-142, 204-205, 214, 225, 230, 252-253, 260, 301
electi 229
Enchanted Castle – *see* Schastel Marveile
Essenes 10, 224-226, 269
Ethiopia 252-253
Evola, Julius 31, 135, 138-139, 144, 151, 221, 248, 315

F

Feirefiz 43, 63, 91-97, 100-102, 111, 114-115, 123, 134-135, 144-145, 147, 172, 252, 279, 282, 286, 290-291, 308-309, 314, 324-325
Fisher King 62, 116, 180, 194, 198, 203
Flavius Josephus 224
Flegetanis 32, 202, 215, 244, 265, 323
Franz, Marie Louise von 38
Freemasonry 254-261
   symbols of 259-260
Frimurtel 73, 202, 245

G

Gahmuret d'Anjou 43-45, 48, 63, 74, 94-95, 100-101, 106, 118, 124-125, 127, 136, 140, 149, 151-152, 185, 334
Galahad 30, 38, 149-150
Gawain 8, 10, 37, 60-61, 63-68, 75-90, 92, 97, 110-111, 113, 118, 144, 157, 159, 161-162, 165-186, 230-232, 248, 278, 289-292, 303, 309, 314, 324
Glastonbury 32, 199
gnosis 138, 227
Godfrey of Saint-Omer 246
God the Father 130, 316-318
God the Son 130, 316-318
Gondi-Shapur 145-146
Good Friday 31, 70, 72, 112, 128-133, 200, 203, 214, 237, 243, 325
good men (*bonshommes*) 198, 241
Grail
   castle 37, 72, 75, 94-96, 99-100, 108, 110-112, 114, 116, 118-119, 132-133, 148, 156-157, 159-160, 166-167, 169-170, 172-173, 177, 180, 200, 248, 265, 278-282, 285-287, 289, 293-294, 296-297, 302-303, 305-307
   horse 69, 112-113, 132, 172, 178, 180, 286
   guardian of 73, 199, 203, 242, 254, 265, 325
   King – *see* King of the Grail
   knights – *see* knights, Grail
   lance *or* spear 10, 37
   legend 139-140, 318
   messenger of 36, 68-70, 111, 119, 124, 127, 145, 155, 169, 285, 323

GRAIL continued
   mystery/Mysteries of 72, 215, 244, 280, 287, 301, 304, 326
   path – *see* initiation
   search/quest for 26, 28-31, 68, 71-72, 113, 118, 137, 179, 235, 290, 299, 315, 319
   sword 10, 57, 108, 118, 153, 156, 168
   temple of 34, 37, 203, 262-266
Gramoflanz 83-91, 113, 174, 182-183, 186, 289-290, 292, 303
Grand Master 246, 248, 251
Greiner, Wolfgang 158, 163
Guinevere 48, 88, 143
Gurnemanz 50-53, 55, 98-99, 102, 107-108, 117, 168, 278-280, 284, 286-287, 295, 297

H

Hellenism – *see* culture, Greek
Henry the Navigator 251
heresy/heretical movements/sects 10, 28, 33, 230, 238-239, 243-245, 266
Herzeloyde 44-45, 47, 63, 73, 93, 98, 100, 103-104, 113, 117, 120-121, 123, 132, 136, 155, 159-160, 171, 242, 279-280, 285, 324
Hiram Abiff 255-257
Holy Trinity 131, 209, 237-238, 316, 318
Hugues de Payens 246
Hutchins, Eileen 40, 171

I

Indies 203
   African India (Ethiopia) 252-253
initiation 28, 177, 181, 198, 299, 302, 305, 313, 319, 322
   ancient: symbol of the fish 197, 210, 281
   Celtic 142, 158, 162-163, 199, 301
   Christian 31, 162-163, 176, 184-185, 248, 281, 293, 300, 302, 309-310
   Eastern 138, 141, 162, 310
   Egyptian 301
   Hindu 309
   Knights Templar 247-248, 250
   Masonic 260
   modern 269, 301, 313

INITIATION *continued*
  pagan (will) 309
  pre-Christian 281, 293
  Rosicrucian 267-269, 302, 309-310
  Temple sleep 301
innocence 25, 46, 58, 64, 70-71, 128, 177, 186, 275, 277, 280, 282, 284, 286, 304
Inquisition 241, 245
Islam 136, 145-146, 148, 239, 246, 252
Ither de Gaheviess 48-50, 73, 79, 91, 98, 100, 105-106, 113-115, 132, 234-286
Itonje 84, 86, 90-91, 169, 174, 292
Iwanet 49-50

J

Jacques de Molay 251
Jerusalem 38, 137-138, 195, 202, 224, 241, 246, 256
  Temple of 224, 254, 257, 261, 265
Jeschute 47, 58, 70-71, 98, 105, 110, 115-116, 121, 128, 173-174, 284-286
John II of Portugal 252
Jonah 197
Joseph of Arimathea 38, 195, 198-199, 208, 211, 214, 226, 241, 281, 300
Jung, Emma 38

K

Kahenis 69-70, 112, 285
Kardeiz 93, 95, 124, 313
Karlstein Castle 266
karma 105, 278
Kai 49, 106, 110-111, 115
King Arthur 29, 44, 46, 48, 59, 62, 64, 84, 88, 90, 92-93, 134-135, 144, 149, 157-159, 164, 199, 325
King of the Grail 29-30, 72-74, 94-95, 101, 113-115, 118-120, 124, 131, 155, 166, 193, 198, 203, 214, 253, 279-280, 282, 285, 288-289, 296, 303, 305, 308, 313
Kingrimursel 63-65, 67, 185-186
Kingrun 52-53, 66, 107, 115, 186
Klingsor 29, 36-37 – *see also* Clinschor
Klockenbring, Gerard 129-130, 209, 284, 304
knights
  Arthur's 22, 28-30, 50, 59, 160, 278, 280
  becoming a knight 19-20, 46, 49, 58, 73, 111, 202, 278, 313

KNIGHTS *continued*
  equipment 20-21, 106, 160, 247
  Grail 69, 96, 101, 112-113, 118, 131, 159-160, 163, 172, 178, 278-280, 285, 314-315, 319
  of the Round Table 60, 144, 157, 161, 266, 278
  of the sword 156, 160
  of the word 156, 160
  Templar – *see* Order
  virtues 16, 160
Koepke, Ewald 232, 283, 316, 319, 326
Kollert, Günter 251-252
Kovacs, Charles 135, 149, 231
Kühlewind, Georg 204, 254, 293, 295-296, 303
Kundry – *see* Cundrie
Kyot 28, 32-33, 39, 173, 215, 244-245, 308

L

Lähelin 47-48, 73, 121, 131, 178
Lampe, Bernd 97, 173, 176-177, 185, 309
lance 14, 19, 44, 50, 59-60, 62, 69, 71, 128, 151, 160, 188-193
Lanz, Rudolf 8
Lapsit Exilis 72, 200, 209
Last Supper 32, 34, 195-196, 208, 214, 281
Liaze 51
Lischoys Gwellius 75, 78-79, 166, 180, 186
Lit Marveile 79-80, 168, 181
Lohengrin 29, 95-96, 101, 117-118, 124, 160, 313
Longinus – *see* Saint Longinus
Lucifer 129, 131, 201, 207-209, 288, 328-329
Luther, Martin 236
Lyppaut 64-66, 171, 177, 231

M

macrocosm(ic) 39, 147, 181, 189, 244, 263, 269, 298, 299-300, 312-314
Malcreatiure 77-78, 145, 180
Malory, Thomas 30, 217
Mani (Manes) 235
Manichaeism, Manichaens 33, 227-233, 235, 238
manna 194, 204-205, 221
Manu (Noah) 204-205
Marco Polo 230

Masons – *see* Freemasonry
Mazdaism – *see* Zoroastrianism
Melianz 64, 66, 171, 177
Messiah 10, 224-226
Meyer, Rudolf 25, 34, 42, 112, 151, 169, 179, 183, 192-193, 196, 207, 212, 242, 245, 293, 300, 302, 304, 306, 308, 315, 316-317, 323, 326
microcosm(ic) 39, 147, 158, 181, 207, 263, 269, 298, 300-301, 312-314
Middle Ages 14-27
  clothing 17-18, 20, 134
  education of children 19, 22, 275
  emblems 21
  feudal pyramid 15
  food 18
  medieval castle/fortress 16, 18
  society 15
  time measurement 23-24
Montségur 241, 265
Mozarabic liturgy 236
Munsalvaesche 57, 69, 74, 94-96, 118, 134, 157, 166, 168, 262-265, 322, 325
mystery(ies)
  ancient/antiquity 38, 140, 206, 217, 259, 268, 294
    Egyptian 145
    of the Phoenix 206-207, 256
  Celtic 139-141, 144
  centers 142, 206, 208, 227
  Christian 140
  Eastern 162, 267
  gnostic 245
  Northern 217, 299
  of the Ascension 186, 314
  of Christ 38, 140, 142, 263, 309
  of Death and Resurrection 147, 199, 244, 256, 314
  of the Earth 256
  of Golgotha 142, 206, 244, 248, 272, 314
  of the Grail 10, 72, 215, 244, 280, 287, 304, 307, 325-326
  of the Trinity 31, 237, 318
    of the Father 309, 314, 316
    of the Holy Spirit 309, 314
    of the Son 309, 314
  Persian 301
  Rosicrucian 268
  schools 267
  Southern 300

mythology
  Flood, the 204
  German(ic) 149, 151
  Greek 275
  operas (other than *Parsifal*) 118
  Norse/Nordic 150, 275
  Western 112

N

Negus of Abyssinia 253
New Testament 24, 151, 240, 318
Nogaret 250
number forty 63, 195, 204-205

O

Obie 64-66, 173, 177
Obilot 64-66, 178, 185-186
Old Testament 197, 204, 221, 255, 275, 316
Order
  Benedictines 23, 220, 233
  Dominican 241
  Franciscan 240
  of Christ 245, 251-252
  of the Knights Templar 163, 245-254
  of Santiago 217
Orgeluse de Logroys 75-78, 82-86, 88-90, 173-175-4, 180-183, 186, 232, 287, 324
Orilus de Lalande 47-48, 58, 68, 70, 99, 105, 110, 115, 117, 119, 121, 159, 172, 174, 178, 180, 285, 324

P

Paradise 14, 204, 206, 271-272, 275, 298
  of Light 229
  fall from 272, 275, 298
pardon 74, 114
Parsifal, opera 34, 36-37, 118, 193, 306, 327
Parzival
  childhood 98, 102, 104
  crisis 99, 102
  destiny 102, 103
  development 30, 104, 115, 117, 119-120, 126, 155, 171-172, 279-282, 286-287, 296-297, 305, 326
  initiation 10, 305, 308, 313
  learning 98-100, 102, 107-108, 110
  purification 100-102, 114, 127, 282-283
  realization 100-102

PARZIVAL *continued*
  representative of humanity 164, 319
  training 51
  youth 50-51, 98, 102, 304
Pelrapeire 52-53, 107, 134, 295
Pentecost 163, 252, 329
Perceval 30-32, 38-39, 116, 194, 287,
    326-327
perfecti 240
perfection 55, 100-101, 171, 200, 278,
    284-286
  conscious 101-102, 167
  unconscious 98, 101-102
Pero de Covilhã 252-253
Persia 35, 136, 145-147, 227, 230, 264, 327
Philip of Flanders 27, 31, 33, 38
Philip the Fair 250-251
Philo of Alexandria 224
Philosopher's Stone 218-221, 269, 312, 314
Phoenicia 214, 217, 265
phoenix 70, 201, 204, 206-207, 256
Pliny 224
Ponsoye, Pierre 221, 245
Pope 135, 223, 234, 236, 251
  Clement V 251
  Innocent III 241
  John XXIII 269
  Pius V 269
Portugal 251-253, 265
post-Atlantean age 35, 143, 213, 322
post-Atlantean cultural epochs
  India (first) 35
  Persia (second) 35
  Babylonian-Egyptian-Caledonian
    (third) 35-36, 139, 144, 258
  Greco-Roman (fourth) 144, 149, 268,
    301, 311
  present day (fifth) 35, 139, 283, 299, 303
pre-Christian era 10, 32, 142-143, 162, 191,
    206, 214, 256, 300, 308-309
Prester John 96, 101, 134-136, 203, 214,
    252-254, 265, 308
Provence 32, 188, 215, 239-240, 244-245

Q

Quadros, António 256, 275
Queen of Sheba 208, 256-257, 323

question(s) 56-57, 63, 79, 96, 108, 115, 117,
    133, 153, 156, 168, 181, 203, 213-214,
    225, 229, 231-232, 235, 238, 250, 281,
    283, 292-294, 297, 305
  right (healing) 57, 74, 94, 99, 108, 111,
    114, 118, 123-124, 132, 168, 293,
    295-297, 318
  unnecessary 51-52, 55, 108, 168, 296

R

Red Knight 49-50, 59-61, 63, 66, 69,
    105-106, 172, 179, 183
Repanse of Schoye 73, 95-96, 101, 134-135,
    147, 169, 252
resurrection 31, 185-186, 199, 204, 206,
    256, 304
Robert de Boron 29, 31-34, 150, 195-196,
    203, 211, 13-214, 241, 243, 281, 288,
    300
Roman Catholic Church 144, 224, 232-238,
    240, 297
Roman Empire 14, 229, 232
Rosenkreuz, Christian 256, 266-269
Rosicrucian fraternity/movement 219, 234,
    245, 256, 266-269, 302, 309-310, 314
Round Table 28, 48-49, 59-64, 90, 92-93,
    99, 106, 111, 114, 123, 134-135,
    141-144, 149, 157-158, 160-161,
    163-164, 176, 266, 278-279, 285-286

S

Saint-Exupéry, Antoine de 109
Saint Augustine 232-233
Saint Columba 239
Saint Francis of Assisi 240, 298
Saint Gallus 234
Saint George 190
Saint Longinus 189
Saint Michael (Archangel) 190-191, 328
Saint Paul 152, 247, 267
Salvaterre 265
Sandkühler, Konrad 198
Schanpfanzun 67
Schastel Marveile 37, 63, 79-80, 84-88, 92,
    159, 166-168, 172-173, 179-183, 186
Schionatulander 34, 95, 119-122, 203
science of the Grail (anthroposophy) 9,
    219, 270, 319

scientific thinking 35, 145, 275
Seddon, Richard 37-38, 134, 139-140, 323
Segramors 60
Shapur I 149, 238
Shapur II 149
Sicily 89, 178
Siegfried (Sigurd) 150-151
Sigmund 150
Sigune 34, 48, 57, 68-69, 73, 95, 99, 103, 116-122, 128, 153-155, 159-160, 169, 171, 173-174, 180, 203, 242, 279, 284-286, 295, 325, 327
solitude 68, 111, 281, 285-286, 292
Solomon 208, 244, 247, 254-257, 264-265
    lineage 244
    prison of 264
    Temple of 196, 247 – *see also* Temple of Jerusalem
    throne of 264
spiritual world 7, 35, 113, 122, 126-128, 140, 162, 179, 181, 185, 190-191, 193, 197, 205, 207, 212-213, 235, 237, 241, 248, 254, 261, 268, 272-274, 277, 279, 282, 287-288, 294, 300-307, 309-311, 313-316, 322, 325
starry script 215, 303
star wisdom 143, 208, 244
Stein, Walter Johannes 30, 38, 116, 137, 154, 159, 178, 181, 193, 209, 218, 263, 305
Steiner, Rudolf 7-8, 25, 34-39, 104-105, 109, 115-116, 120, 125-126, 128-130, 133, 135, 137, 139-143, 154-155, 164, 174, 181, 184, 199, 204-206, 208, 210-212, 215-216, 218-220, 226-227, 256, 258-259, 263, 267, 269-270, 273-275, 277-278, 281-282, 286-290, 294-296, 298-300, 302, 304-307, 309-312, 317-319
stone of destiny (royal stone) 144, 272, 327
suprasensory world 138, 163, 167, 197, 201, 213, 262, 271, 273, 295, 302, 307, 313
sword of the Spirit 152, 156, 162, 247
synagogue 190-191
systems
    metabolic-limb 174-175, 291
    nerve-sense 174-175, 290, 308
    rhythmic 174-175, 181, 291

T

Takht-i-Suleiman (Throne of Solomon) 264
Teichmann, Frank 165, 287
Templars: *see* Order of the Knights Templar
    spiritual armor 249
    treasures 250
Temple of Jerusalem 254, 261, 265 – *see also* Solomon, Temple of
Temple Legend 256, 259, 263
Terre Marveile 79, 84-85, 166, 181
Teutschmann, Heinrich 202, 210-211, 213, 281, 288, 305, 322
therapeutae 225
Tintagel 143
Titurel 26, 33-34, 37, 120, 133, 201-203, 213-214, 243, 253, 262, 308, 325
Toledo 32, 134, 173, 236, 244, 308
Tomar 265
Trevrizent 57, 70-75, 99-100, 102-103, 113-115, 128-133, 135-136, 159-160, 169-172, 200, 209, 223, 230, 238, 242, 244, 263, 279-280, 282, 285-288, 295-296, 305, 316-317, 324
troubadours 22, 26, 28, 237
Tubal-Cain 256-257

U

Utepandragun (Uther Pendragon) 155, 335

V

Vasco da Gama 253
Veltman, W.F. 22, 141, 206, 214, 217, 247-248, 257
Vergulacht 67, 75, 173, 179, 185-186, 290
virtues 155
    Christian 144
    knight 16, 160
    Titurel 202

W

Wagner, Richard 34, 36-37, 118, 193, 306, 327
Waldo, Peter 239-240
Waldorf education, schools 7-8, 11, 104, 116, 137, 192, 275
Wartburg 41, 328-329
widow's son 255

Wild Crossing 84
Winkler, Franz E. 37
Wolfram von Eschenbach 7-8, 27, 29-30,
    32-34, 36-43, 56, 61, 97, 116, 118,
    121-124, 126, 128, 132, 134, 136-139,
    145, 146-147, 154-155, 161-167, 170,
    172, 177, 179, 181, 186, 193, 200-204,
    206-207, 213, 217, 221, 230-231,
    236-241, 243-245, 248, 253, 265, 281,
    283-284, 298-299, 308, 313, 315-316,
    324-325, 327
Word (Logos) 210
    Cosmic, Divine, Spiritual 209, 156
    of God 152, 156

wound
    incurable 29, 295
    of humanity 306
    of Jesus 187, 195
    of the soul 305

Z

Zarathustra 147, 230, 264 – *see also*
    Zoroastrianism
Zindan-i-Suleiman (Solomon's Prison) 264
Zoroastrian(ism) 146-147, 230, 327

Made in the USA
Middletown, DE
11 June 2024